T0323011

A Practical Guide to the 2016 ISDA® Credit Support Annexes For Variation Margin under English and New York Law

A Practical Guide to the
2016 ISDA® Credit Support Annexes
For Variation Margin
under English and New York Law

Paul C. Harding and Abigail J. Harding

HARRIMAN HOUSE

HARRIMAN HOUSE LTD

18 College Street

Petersfield

Hampshire

GU31 4AD

GREAT BRITAIN

Tel: +44 (0)1730 233870

Email: enquiries@harriman-house.com

Website: www.harriman-house.com

First published in Great Britain in 2018

Copyright © Paul C. Harding and Abigail J. Harding

Hardback ISBN: 978-0-85719-675-0

eBook ISBN: 978-0-85719-676-7

British Library Cataloguing in Publication Data

A CIP catalogue record for this book can be obtained from the British Library.

Contents

Authors' Foreword

In this book the terms collateral or margin mean financial security for OTC derivatives risk exposure.

Such financial security normally takes the form of cash in US dollars, the Euro, Sterling and Japanese Yen or highly rated government securities of Belgium, Canada, France, Germany, Japan, the Netherlands, the United Kingdom and the USA.

Collateral is taken, returned and managed by each party's collateral management unit.

Because OTC derivatives and particularly credit default swaps were identified by some market commentators or critics as one of the causes of the global financial crisis of 2007-2009, the G20 Pittsburgh summit in September 2009 committed to a global reform of the OTC derivatives market. This included a higher capital requirement for contracts not cleared through central clearing counterparties ("CCPs") (i.e. clearing houses). This meant it would be more expensive to trade certain OTC derivatives and because they were uncleared, their margin requirements would be higher.

The US Wall Street Reform and Consumer Protection Act (commonly called the Dodd-Frank Act) signed by President Obama in July 2010, the EU's European Market Infrastructure Regulation ("EMIR") which came into force in August 2012 and the work of regulators in North America, Europe and Asia have created a robust if incomplete infrastructure to regulate OTC derivatives and related uncleared margin.

Variation margin relates to collateral used to cover mark to market risk exposure and initial margin is an additional amount related to the risk profile of a counterparty.

In April 2016 ISDA published two new Credit Support Annexes under English law and New York law to cover Variation Margin requirements under the new regulations for uncleared margin.

These documents are the focus of this book which is divided into the following 4 chapters:

Chapter 1 provides extensive coverage of the global financial crisis of 2007-2009 and onwards and a detailed description of OTC derivatives and uncleared margin regulation in the USA and the European Union. It also has sections on the important but vexed subjects of extraterritoriality and substituted compliance.

Chapter 2 is a clause by clause commentary on the 2016 ISDA Credit Support Annex For Variation Margin (VM) under English law. The text of each individual provision of the Annex appears above our commentary which aims to explain it in clear English in each case.

Chapter 3 is a clause by clause analysis of the 2016 ISDA Credit Support Annex For Variation Margin (VM) under New York law which is presented in the same way as in Chapter 2.

Chapter 4 covers the latest developments in regulation and the collateral market and other significant issues and features in the OTC derivatives market.

The book concludes with the following three Appendices which aim to provide useful information in one place.

They are:

Appendix 1. A timeline showing the full implementation dates under EMIR of Initial Margin and Variation Margin under existing uncleared margin regulation.

Appendix 2. A facsimile of the 2016 ISDA Credit Support Annex For Variation Margin (VM) under English law (reproduced with the permission of the International Swaps and Derivatives Association, Inc.).

Appendix 3. A facsimile of the 2016 ISDA Credit Support Annex For Variation Margin (VM) under New York law (reproduced with the permission of the International Swaps and Derivatives Association, Inc.).

One of the other goals of the 2009 G20 Pittsburgh summit was for all standardised OTC derivative contracts to be traded on exchanges or electronic trading platforms and cleared through CCPs by the end of 2012.

Well the 2012 timeframe was not met because this took much longer than anticipated. However, good progress has now been made. At the end of June 2017 the Bank for International Settlements reported that 77% of OTC interest rate derivative contracts and 51% of credit default swap contracts at that time were cleared through CCPs.

However, much as usual still needs to be done and the uncleared margin regulatory timetable for Initial Margin continues to run until 1ˢᵗ September 2020. Indeed it will continue beyond this date on an ad hoc basis for substantial new entrants to the OTC derivatives markets for both Initial Margin and Variation Margin.

Any opinion expressed in this book are those of the authors themselves and do not necessarily reflect those of their employers.

To the best of the authors' knowledge and belief, the information in this book was up to date as at 5th January 2018.

We hope you both enjoy this book and find it useful.

Paul C. Harding
Abigail J. Harding
January 2018

About the Authors

Paul C. Harding is a graduate of the University of London and has been involved with OTC derivatives documentation since 1990. He was a well-known negotiator in the City of London and in 1997 he founded Derivatives Documentation Limited, a derivatives consultancy and project management company, based in the City of London which provides negotiation, recruitment and training services in OTC derivatives documentation (website: www.derivsdocu.com). Its clients include many of the world's leading banks.

Since 2001 Paul has authored or co-authored books on *Mastering the ISDA® Master Agreement, Mastering the ISDA® Collateral Documents, Mastering Securities Lending Documentation* all published by Pearson Education; *A Practical Guide to the 2003 ISDA Credit Derivatives Definitions* published by Euromoney Books; and three editions of *A Practical Guide to Using Repo Master Agreements* published by Euromoney Books (editions 1 and 2) and Harriman House (edition 3).

Abigail J. Harding is a graduate of the University of East Anglia and has been involved with OTC derivatives since 2005. She initially worked in credit derivatives back office and middle office roles with Morgan Stanley in London for three years. Since joining Derivatives Documentation Limited in 2008 (she is now Managing Director) she has worked on a number of in-house and outsourced assignments relating to ISDA, CSA and GMRA negotiations. For the past two years her main focus has been on variation margin and initial margin collateral documentation.

Acknowledgements

Paul Harding

First and foremost I should like to thank my wife, Sheila, for her support, patience and flexibility during the writing of this book.

Secondly, I should like to thank my daughter and co-writer, Abigail, for all her excellent input and practical experience of the 2016 ISDA® Credit Support Annexes For Variation Margin under English and New York Law. Her work on this book and punctual meeting of deadlines has been invaluable.

Abigail Harding

I should like to thank my father and co-writer, Paul, for his superb input and focus in the preparation of this book. His extensive knowledge of OTC derivatives documentation, background research and experience as an author has been outstanding.

Both authors

Both of us would like to thank Simon Leifer for his excellent and detailed review of Chapter 1 of this book. Simon is currently General Counsel for a private investment management office. Paul Harding first worked with Simon in 1997 when Simon was co-head of the trading and derivatives legal team at Dresdner Kleinwort Benson. Over the years Simon has also expertly reviewed the legal chapters in the three editions of *Mastering the ISDA® Master Agreements* and the two editions of *Mastering the ISDA® Collateral Documents* which Paul co-wrote with Professor Christian A. Johnson.

Both authors also thank the International Swaps and Derivatives Association, Inc. for their permission to reproduce the 2016 ISDA® Credit Support Annexes For Variation Margin under English Law and New York Law both in the book text and in the Appendices.

We should also like to thank the editorial staff at Harriman House Limited, the publishers of this book for all their excellent editing and support along the way.

Chapter 1

The new regulatory scene for OTC derivatives and collateral

Causes of the global financial crisis 2007-2009

It has been traditional when a recession or financial crisis hits a country to blame it on banks making bad property loans.

The causes of the 2007-2009 global financial crisis were, of course, more widespread but "bad property financing" did have a role to play as we shall see shortly. It should also be pointed out that the financial crisis was not just confined to 2007-2009. There is evidence that it continued after 2009 with the Eurozone sovereign debt crisis and some still seeing vestiges of it today in those European countries whose GDP is still below 2008 levels.

A list of the causes of the global financial crisis and the worst recession in 80 years would include the following:

- Bad property lending as mentioned above.
- Years of low inflation and stable growth before the crisis which created complacency and excessive risk taking by banks.
- A savings glut in Asia leading to low interest rates which caused huge amounts of Asian money being invested in US Treasury securities on which the interest yield also fell.
- Cheap financing causing banks and investors to take on greater risks in order to increase returns which in turn led to a huge increase in debt.
- Banks inflating their balance sheets but not increasing their capital reserves for losses. Under Basel II Rules big banks could calculate their own capital coverage if they had the systems to do so. This led to over favourable evaluation of asset quality in many cases.
- Regulators being too lax in their oversight of banks particularly in relation to the use of leverage.

There is much useful literature on the global financial crisis and the above points are an outline summary only and others might well want to add further bullet points in apportioning responsibility between banks and regulators. However, although this is not the focus of this book, it is useful to describe a little further how the crisis developed in the USA and Europe.

The crisis in the USA

The two prime causes of the crisis in the USA were deregulation and sub-prime mortgage securitisation.

Deregulation

In 1999, the Gramm-Leach-Bliley Act (also known as the Financial Services Modernization Act of 1999) repealed part of the Glass-Steagall Act of 1933 which had separated US investment and commercial banking activities. In the years before 1933, overzealous commercial bank lending for stock market investment was deemed the main cause of the financial crash then and it was considered that commercial banks had taken too much risk with depositors' money.

The repeal of the Glass-Steagall Act allowed banks to use deposits to invest in derivatives (often with hedge funds) and enabled them to take hugely leveraged positions. Then in 2000 while attention was focused elsewhere on the court battle over the US presidential election, the Commodity Futures Modernization Act came into being. This Act clarified and effectively exempted OTC derivatives from regulation by the Commodity Futures Trading Commission. It also contained an exemption for energy derivatives trading which became known as the "Enron loophole".

Big banks had the resources to become sophisticated in the use of complex derivatives. The banks which sold the most complicated financial products made the most money. That enabled them to buy out smaller, safer banks. By 2008, many of these major banks had become too big to fail and too interconnected. Ironically despite numerous regulatory safeguards since the crisis, some of these banks have grown even bigger through mergers and acquisitions of smaller banks.

Securitisation of mortgages

Securitisation is a process in which certain types of assets are pooled so that they can be repackaged into interest-bearing securities. The interest and principal payments from the assets concerned are passed through to the purchasers of the securities.

With mortgages a bank would lend money to house buyers and then pool them under a mortgage backed security often with tranches of different risk which made them difficult to value. These pooled securities were often called Collateralised Debt Obligations ("CDOs"). The bank then sold the CDOs to investors who were often other banks, municipalities, hedge funds, mutual funds and pension funds.

Investors tended to buy the less risky tranches because they trusted Triple A ratings often given to them by major ratings agencies like Moody's Investors Service, Inc. ("Moody's") and Standard & Poor's Financial Services LLC ("S&P"). This turned out to be a mistake because the banks paid these agencies to assign the ratings to the CDOs and so there was a conflict of interest and the agencies were often over optimistic about the quality of the CDOs.

Since a bank sold the mortgage(s), it could make new loans with the money it received. It still collected the mortgage payments of principal and interest and sent them to their investors. While the mortgages were basically risk-free for the bank, it was the CDO investors who took all of the default risk unless they entered into credit default swaps which were sold by banks and insurance companies like American International Group, Inc. ("AIG"). These investors considered the combination of a highly rated CDO and a credit default swap from a solid, reputable insurance company like AIG to be a safe investment.

A CDO combined with a credit default swap was a very profitable transaction for their providers. As the demand for these derivatives grew, so did the banks' demand for more and more mortgages to back the CDOs. To meet this demand, banks and mortgage brokers offered home loans to just about anyone. Banks offered interest only sub-prime mortgages often at 100% loan to value because they made much more money from the credit default swaps than from the mortgages themselves.

Bear Stearns and Lehman Brothers were major investors in these products and both failed in 2008.

The Fed raised borrowing rates

Banks were hard hit by a recession in the USA in 2001.

In that year many homeowners who could not afford conventional mortgages found that they were eligible for sub-prime interest only loans. As a result, the percentage of sub-prime mortgages doubled, from 10% to 20% of all mortgages between 2001 and 2006. By 2007, it had grown into a USD 1.3 trillion industry. The creation of mortgage-backed securities and CDOs in the secondary market ended the 2001 recession.

However, it also created an asset bubble in real estate in 2005. The demand for mortgages drove up demand for housing, which housebuilders tried to meet. With such cheap loans, many people also bought homes as investments to sell as prices kept rising.

In late 2004 the Federal Reserve Bank started to increase interest rates which rose from 2.25% to 5.25% by mid 2006. Homeowners were hit by payments they could not afford. The Fed's rate increases could not have come at a worse time for these new homeowners.

The housing market bubble burst. That created a banking crisis in 2007 when a loss of confidence by US investors in the value of sub-prime mortgages caused a liquidity crisis. CDOs became hard to value and some banks considered them worthless despite their high credit ratings. They became suspect assets which were hard to sell and impossible to use as collateral for short term loans vital for bank funding. Fire sales took place which reduced banks' capital ratios and accounting rules insisted that these assets be valued at their market value incurring losses which might never actually have been realised. Nonetheless, this reduced banks' creditworthiness in the eyes of their counterparties (usually other banks) and also led to them experiencing a lending freeze / liquidity crisis.

House prices in the United States fell by an average of 31.8%, more than in the Great Depression of the 1930s. This left many homeowners who had taken out sub-prime loans unable to meet their mortgage repayments. As the value of homes plummeted, the borrowers found themselves with negative equity. With a large number of borrowers defaulting on loans, banks were faced with a situation where the repossessed houses and land were worth less in the current market than the bank had lent originally. The banks had a liquidity crisis on their hands here too, and the giving and obtaining of home loans became increasingly difficult in the fallout from the sub-prime lending bubble. This whole scenario was commonly referred to as the credit crunch.

The key mistake the banks made was to assume that property prices would rise and fall independently of each other in different US cities. However, they did not because starting in 2006 the USA had a nationwide house price slump.

When the credit default swaps were triggered, the amounts involved were so large that AIG did not have enough funds to honour payments under them. AIG itself had to be rescued by the US Federal Reserve Bank which ultimately had to pump USD 150 billion into the stricken insurance giant.

The US Federal Reserve Bank injected a large amount of capital into the financial markets through its Term Auction Facility. By September 2008, the crisis had worsened. The US Treasury Department was authorised to spend up to USD 150 billion to subsidise and eventually take over Freddie Mac and Fannie Mae.

Freddie Mac is another name for the Federal Home Loan Mortgage Corporation and Fannie Mae is another name for the Federal National Mortgage Association. Both were formed to stabilise the US residential mortgage market. Their jobs are to purchase and guarantee home loans from lenders so lenders can replenish their supply of capital funds and make more mortgage loans to borrowers.

During the global financial crisis in 2008, Freddie Mac and Fannie Mae guaranteed over USD 5 trillion in mortgage debt (about 90% of US residential mortgages at the time). The share prices of both companies tumbled and investors feared a collapse due to escalating foreclosure rates and plummeting house prices. The fear was that both entities lacked the capital to absorb the predicted losses. In September 2008, Freddie Mac and Fannie Mae were both placed under the conservatorship of the Federal Housing Finance Agency which brought them under direct government control.

Today the role of Freddie Mac and Fannie Mae has not changed very much. Both of them still guarantee and purchase loans from mortgage lenders and they have taken steps to improve their financial condition as well as build a profitable business under government control.

The *Times* newspaper reported that during the crisis the US government advanced USD 187.5 billion to the two companies and recovered USD 270.9 billion, an excess of USD 83.4 billion.

The Insolvency of Lehman Brothers

With the insolvency of Lehman Brothers on 15th September 2008 stock markets around the world crashed and became highly volatile. Many commentators considered that the biggest error made by regulators was to let Lehman Brothers go into insolvency because this multiplied panic in the market and created widespread distrust among counterparties so no one would lend. Huge taxpayer financed bail-outs became necessary to shore up the financial services industry. Ironically this resulted in more government intervention rather than less because regulators had to rescue more companies in the fallout.

On 19th September 2008, the crisis created a run on traditionally very safe US money market funds – the normal home for businesses' surplus cash at the end of each business day. Banks use those funds to make short-term loans. Throughout that day, businesses moved a record USD 140 billion out of their money market accounts into even safer US Treasury bonds. If money market funds became insolvent, business activities and the US economy faced great danger.

Henry Paulson, the US Treasury Secretary and Ben Bernanke, the Federal Reserve Bank Chairman submitted a USD 700 billion bailout package called the Troubled Asset Relief Program ("TARP") to the US Congress. Their fast response reassured businesses to keep their money in the money market accounts.

Republicans blocked the bill for two weeks because they did not want to bail out banks. They did not approve the bill until global stock markets almost collapsed.

TARP was designed to buy toxic bank assets and equity investments from banks to strengthen the financial sector. In December 2014 the TARP was wound up. USD 426.4 billion had been invested and USD 441.7 billion received back from sales – a USD 15.3 billion profit.

What else did the US government do?

In November 2008 the US Federal Reserve Bank ("Fed") started providing financial support to the market through quantitative easing.

Quantitative easing ("QE") is a monetary policy in which a central bank creates new electronic money in order to buy government bonds or other financial assets (e.g. corporate bonds) to stimulate an economy (i.e. to increase private-sector spending and return inflation to its target).

By June 2010 the Fed held USD 1.75 trillion of bank debt, mortgage-backed securities, and Treasury notes. This first stage of quantitative easing became known as QE1.

In November 2010, the Fed announced a second round of quantitative easing by buying USD 600 billion of Treasury securities by the end of the second quarter of 2011. This became known as QE2 in the market.

A third round of quantitative easing, QE3, was announced in September 2012 when the Fed decided to launch a new USD 40 billion per month, open-ended bond purchasing program of agency mortgage-backed securities. This limit was later increased to USD 85 billion per month. Because of its open-ended nature, QE3 earned the popular nickname of "QE-Infinity".

Because of continuing improvement in the US economy QE purchases were halted at USD 4.5 trillion of assets in late October 2014.

On 20th September 2017 the Fed confirmed that it would unwind its portfolio of Treasury bonds and mortgage-backed securities. This would start slowly at USD 10 billion per month for the first three months and then gradually increases by a further USD 10 billion per quarter until it reaches a monthly maximum of USD 50 billion (i.e. USD 30 billion per month of Treasury Bonds and USD 20 billion per month of mortgage-backed securities). Even if the Fed reaches its redemption targets it is estimated that it will take eight years to offload all of its 21% market share of mortgage-backed securities. With Treasury bonds their redemption depends upon their actual maturity dates and not monthly instalments. The scope of the whole exercise also depends upon the size of balance sheet the Fed ultimately wants to achieve.

Overhaul of US financial services legislation

Following the crisis, the US government decided to overhaul US financial services legislation. In July 2010 President Obama signed the 2300 page *Wall Street Reform and Consumer Protection Act* commonly called the Dodd-Frank Act.

The Act is US federal law and places regulation of the US financial industry in the hands of various US government agencies in order to reduce risk and enforce transparency and accountability from market players.

The Act required 390 different rules to be written by 20 different US regulatory agencies. This has proved immensely complex and some rules have still not been completed at the time of writing (January 2018).

As indicated above, it left many of the measures up to federal regulatory agencies (most of whom existed at the time of the crisis) to sort out the details and they are still working on this seven years later.

The main aims of the Dodd-Frank Act are:

- To subject banks to more stringent regulation to avoid future taxpayer bail-outs.
- To make OTC derivatives market more transparent by having most of them traded on exchange platforms and cleared by clearing houses.

- To bar banks through the Volcker Rule from speculative trading for themselves (i.e. proprietary trading) rather than trading on behalf of their clients.
- To require accurate, regular information on trades transacted to be transmitted to regulators so risk can be better assessed.
- To establish the Consumer Financial Protection Bureau to protect consumers from risky practices by US banks which could harm such consumers.
- To create a regulatory structure to oversee credit ratings agencies.
- The creation of a "resolution regime" for the orderly winding-up of failed financial institutions.

The Dodd-Frank Act was initially unpopular with the OTC derivatives community but as so many of its provisions have come into force for OTC derivatives it now has fewer opponents.

Originally the Trump administration proposed to repeal it. On 20th March 2017 President Trump ordered a 120 day review by the US Treasury Department of all US financial services regulation. In June 2017 a 150 page report was published recommending 100 changes to US financial rules. On 8th June 2017 a bill was passed in the House of Representatives but is unlikely to be supported by the Senate. Some commentators consider that the Dodd-Frank Act will survive with minor tweaks by regulators.

The European credit crisis

On 9th August 2007 BNP Paribas froze three hedge funds controlled by it which had heavily invested in US sub-prime mortgages and barred investors from redeeming cash from these funds. It announced that it could not calculate net asset values for these funds because as its statement said: "The complete evaporation of liquidity in certain segments of the U.S. securitisation market has made it impossible to value certain assets fairly, regardless of their quality or credit rating."

The funds had lost over EUR 400 million in value in just a few weeks before this date.

Traditionally this is viewed as the start of the European financial crisis and kickstarted the European Central Bank ("ECB") into pumping about EUR 95 billion of liquidity into the Eurozone market.

Before this the ECB had done little to restrain credit growth because it erroneously considered that an individual country's current account balances did not matter in a monetary union. Some commentators considered that this perceived indifference let many European banks pile into sub-prime CDOs financed by heavy borrowing from money market funds.

Many of the major European banks also held huge quantities of their own governments' debt in this period.

At the time there was also a reluctance to face up to the real creditworthiness of loan books particularly in Italy where non-performing loans abounded.

Moreover, some have criticised bank stress tests in Europe as undemanding and others still regard European banks as undercapitalised compared to their US counterparts.

However, it was the European debt crisis which was the most significant event.

The European sovereign debt crisis began at the end of 2009, when Greece, Spain, Ireland, Portugal and Cyprus were unable to repay or refinance their government debt.

Some of the underlying causes of the sovereign debt crisis include the global financial crisis as well as the property market crisis and asset bubbles in several countries. In 2009 Greece revealed that its previous government had grossly under reported its budget deficit – a violation of EU policy which caused fears of a euro collapse through financial contagion.

The European sovereign debt crisis was subdued by financial guarantees from European countries, and by support measures from the International Monetary Fund and the ECB.

In 2010, two temporary rescue programmes were set up by the ECB - the European Financial Stabilisation Mechanism ("EFSM") and the European Financial Stability Facility ("EFSF"). These facilities provided funds to Greece, Ireland, and Portugal in 2010 and 2011.

In 2012 the European Stability Mechanism ("ESM"), with a lending capacity of EUR 500 billion, was established to replace the EFSM and EFSF programmes. The ESM was intended as a permanent firewall for the Eurozone to safeguard and provide instant access to financial assistance programmes for member states in financial difficulty. Spain and Cyprus drew funds from the ESM programme in 2012 and 2013 to recapitalise their financial sectors.

On 9th March 2015 the ECB started its economic stimulus programme which aimed to stave off deflation and reinvigorate the EU economy. Purchases of government bonds were EUR 60 billion per month.

On 26th October 2017 the ECB announced that purchases would continue at EUR 60 billion per month until the end of December 2017 and then proceed at a monthly rate of EUR 30 billion until the end of 2018. However, the programme could continue beyond that date until the ECB sees inflation being sustained in line with its targets. If this does not happen or if the situation deteriorates, the ECB is ready to increase the programme in terms of size or duration.

Ratings agencies downgraded the debt of several Eurozone countries, with Greek debt at one point being moved to junk status. As part of the loan agreements, countries receiving bail out funds were required to accept austerity measures designed to slow down the growth of public sector debt.

Of the five countries bailed out, Ireland exited the bailout programme in December 2013 and Portugal exited in May 2014. All the others except Greece are progressing.

European banks were heavily invested in their own governments' bonds which they regarded as risk-free and which allowed them to economise on equity. When these bonds fell in value when downgraded and because of the lessons learned from the global financial crisis, it was recognised that European financial regulation needed to be overhauled. As a result, the European Securities and Markets Authority ("ESMA") was set up in Paris in 2011 with the following three objectives:

- To promote investor protection for consumers.
- To promote orderly financial markets by focusing on integrity, transparency, efficiency and proper functioning through a robust market infrastructure.
- To promote financial stability through strengthening the financial system so it can withstand shocks and to encourage economic growth.

ESMA is also responsible for co-ordinating measures taken by national securities supervisors and for adopting emergency measures in a crisis.

It has been called "an EU-wide financial services watch dog".

It is responsible for implementing the European Market Infrastructure Regulation ("EMIR"). EMIR is a body of European legislation for the regulation of OTC derivatives. It came into force on 16th August 2012. We shall be examining its requirements later in this chapter.

The UK banking crisis

One of the authors of this book, Paul Harding, has lived through a number of UK banking crises during his career. All have been typified by banks taking too much risk with poor commercial property lending, corporate loans with light covenants or none at all or overgenerous loan to value ratios on residential mortgage lending. In this instance there was also a considerable mismatch between the decreasing value of bank assets and an accelerating increase in their liabilities.

In September 2007 Northern Rock Bank approached the Bank of England for a loan to replace the short term money market funding which covered 40% of its mortgage book. It was the first British bank run in 150 years with long lines of people queuing to draw out their money from its branches. Northern Rock was nationalised in February 2008 after two failed bids for it. It was bought by Virgin Money in 2012.

Until September 2007 25% of the UK mortgage market was funded by mortgage backed securities. Subsequent problems with some of these loans and the deepening banking crisis due to market liquidity drying up caused banks to doubt the viability of their bank counterparties and involved further interventions by the Bank of England on behalf of the UK taxpayer. In 2008 these covered The Royal Bank of Scotland ("RBS") (then the world's largest bank in terms of assets), Lloyds, HBOS, Bradford & Bingley, Alliance & Leicester and Dunfermline Building Society.

RBS was bailed out with GBP 45 billion of taxpayers' money with the government taking a 79% stake in it which it still has at the time of writing (January 2018). By February 2017 it had racked up GBP 58 billion of losses since the bail out.

In October 2008 the UK government persuaded Lloyds TSB to take over and rescue HBOS. The acquisition was completed in early 2009 but HBOS's losses were found to be GBP 10 billion and Lloyds needed help. The UK government injected GBP 20.3 billion and took a 43.4% stake in Lloyds Banking Group. In April 2017 the UK government recouped all of its investment in Lloyds Banking Group.

Bradford & Bingley was initially nationalised in 2008 and the branch network was then sold to Abbey National (part of Santander UK) and was later rebranded as Santander.

Alliance & Leicester was acquired by Santander in October 2008 and rebranded in 2011.

In March 2009 Nationwide Building Society bought the healthy parts of the stricken Dunfermline Building Society.

As the banking crisis deepened the Bank of England started its programme of quantitative easing, buying gilts from other financial institutions and a much smaller amount of high quality corporate debt to stimulate the economy. Between March and November 2009 the Bank of England's Monetary Policy Committee increased the QE limit to GBP 200 billion. By July 2012 this had increased to GBP 375 billion and in August 2016 the Bank of England said it would buy an additional GBP 60 billion of UK government bonds and GBP 10 billion of corporate bonds, to address uncertainty over Brexit and worries about economic growth.

2009 G20 Pittsburgh Summit

In September 2009 G20 members met in Pittsburgh to discuss the state of the financial markets. One of the outcomes of this summit was a commitment to reform the global OTC derivatives market in order to reduce systemic risk. A simple statement was made:

> "All standardized OTC derivative contracts should be traded on exchanges or electronic trading platforms, where appropriate, and cleared through central counterparties by end-2012 at the latest. OTC derivative contracts should be reported to trade repositories. Non-centrally cleared contracts should be subject to higher capital requirements."

This statement has led to the drafting of thousands of pages of regulation which in many cases is still in the process of being implemented. The "end-2012" commitment proved to be too ambitious but did help national governments to focus on the need to implement change as quickly as possible.

BCBS and IOSCO Margin requirements for non-centrally cleared derivatives

On the back of the G20 Pittsburgh commitment that "Non-centrally cleared contracts should be subject to higher capital requirements", the Working Group on Margining Requirements ("WGMR") was formed in 2011 to develop a consistent global standard for margin requirements for uncleared OTC derivative transactions. This ultimately led to the publication of the *Margin requirements for non-centrally cleared derivatives* final policy framework in March 2015 by the Basel Committee on Banking Supervision ("BCBS") and the International Organization of Securities Commissions ("IOSCO"). Regulators in various jurisdictions have since set about creating their own rules based on these global recommendations.

The objective of the WGMR initiative was to reduce systemic risk and promote central clearing. Since only standardised OTC derivatives are suitable for central clearing, the intention was to standardise terms in collateral agreements and introduce consistent methodologies for calculating initial and variation margin so as to make it easier for uncleared OTC derivatives to transition to clearing houses in the future and create a more liquid market. However, not all transactions are suitable for clearing and some trades (e.g. structured ones) will always remain uncleared and will be required to be collateralised separately.

The BCBS/IOSCO policy framework for uncleared OTC derivatives addresses the following eight key requirements and principles which are summarised as follows:

1. Appropriate margining practices should be in place for all derivative transactions that are not cleared by central clearing counterparties ("CCPs").
2. All financial firms and systemically important non-financial entities ("covered entities") must exchange Initial Margin ("IM") and Variation Margin ("VM") as appropriate to cover risk exposure.
3. The methodologies for calculating IM and VM should (i) be consistent across covered entities; and (ii) ensure that all counterparty risk exposures are covered with a high degree of confidence.
4. Assets collected as margin should be highly liquid and should be able to hold their value in a time of financial stress or counterparty default.
5. Gross IM should be exchanged by both parties and held in such a way as to ensure that (i) the margin collected is immediately available to the collecting

party in the event of the counterparty's default and (ii) the collected margin must be subject to arrangements that fully protect the posting party if the collecting party becomes bankrupt.

6. Transactions between a firm and its affiliates should be subject to appropriate regulation in a manner consistent with each jurisdiction's legal and regulatory framework.

7. Regulatory regimes should interact consistently and avoid any duplication in standards in taking margin for OTC derivatives internationally.

8. Margin requirements should be phased in over an appropriate period of time to ensure that the transition costs associated with the new framework can be appropriately managed. Regulators should undertake a coordinated review of the margin standards once the requirements are in place and functioning to assess the overall efficacy of the standards and to ensure harmonisation across national jurisdictions as well as across related initiatives of other regulators.

While BCBS and IOSCO proposed these principles, regulators are/were required to write the specific regulatory requirements and technical standards applying to institutions in the countries under their supervision.

However, BCBS and IOSCO did offer specific guidance in respect of Requirements 2 and 4 as follows:

Requirement 2

2.1 All covered entities that engage in non-centrally cleared derivatives must exchange, on a bilateral basis, the full amount of variation margin (i.e. with a zero threshold) on a regular basis (i.e. every business day).

2.2 All covered entities must exchange, on a bilateral basis, initial margin with a threshold not to exceed EUR 50 million. The threshold is applied at a consolidated group level and is based on all non-centrally cleared derivatives between two consolidated groups.

2.3 All margin transfers between parties may be subject to a de-minimis minimum transfer amount not to exceed EUR 500,000.

2.4 Covered entities include all financial firms and systemically important non-financial firms. Central banks, sovereigns, multilateral development banks, the Bank for International Settlements, and non-systemic, non-financial firms are not covered entities.

2.5 Initial margin requirements will be phased-in, but at the end of the phase-in period there will be a minimum level of non-centrally cleared derivatives activity (EUR 8 billion of gross notional outstanding amount) necessary for covered entities to be subject to initial margin requirements described in the BCBS/IOSCO policy framework. The relevant initial margin phase-in date is determined by group entities' "average aggregate notional amount" (or "AANA") based on uncleared OTC derivatives trading.

2.6 The precise definition of financial firms, non-financial firms and systemically important non-financial firms will be determined by appropriate national regulation. Only non-centrally cleared derivatives transactions between two covered entities are governed by the requirements in the BCBS/IOSCO policy framework.

Requirement 4

4.1 National supervisors should develop their own list of eligible collateral assets based on this key principle, taking into account the conditions of their own markets. As a guide, examples of the types of eligible collateral that satisfy this key principle would generally include:

- Cash;
- High-quality government and central bank securities;
- High-quality corporate bonds;
- High-quality covered bonds;
- Equities included in major stock indices; and
- Gold.

In addition at the end of its document BCBS/IOSCO published a standardised haircut schedule. A haircut is a discount applied to the value of your collateral to cover the worst expected price movements over the mark to market frequency period and a holding period if collateral needs to be liquidated following a default. It provides a cushion of additional value to the collateral taker.

The ISDA collateral documents use the term Valuation Percentage. So, if the real value of a collateral asset is 100 and the agreed Valuation Percentage between the parties is 97% then the haircut is 3%.

Here is the standardised haircut schedule referred to above:

Figure 1.1

BCBS/IOSCO standardised haircut schedule

Asset class	Haircut percentage of market value (%)
Cash in same currency	0
High-quality government and central bank securities: residual maturity less than one year	0.5
High-quality government and central bank securities: residual maturity between one and five years	2
High-quality government and central bank securities: residual maturity greater than five years	4
High-quality corporate/covered bonds: residual maturity less than one year	1
High-quality corporate/covered bonds: residual maturity greater than one year and less than five years	4
High-quality corporate/covered bonds: residual maturity greater than five years	8
Equities included in major stock indices	15
Gold	15
Additional (additive) haircut on asset in which the currency of the derivatives obligation differs from that of the collateral asset	8

Despite these homogenous proposals some regulators have chosen to do things differently. One example is under Prudential Regulations in the USA physically settled FX forwards are not subject to margin requirements for non-cleared OTC derivatives while they are under EMIR from 3rd January 2018. However, this is subject to change under EMIR as we shall see later in this chapter.

Actual implementation deadlines for VM and IM under US and EU regulation

USA

There are three regulators who are responsible for implementing the uncleared margin rules in the United States i.e. the US Commodity Futures Trading Commission (the "CFTC"), the Prudential Regulators ("PR") and the US Securities and Exchange Commission (the "SEC").

The Prudential Regulators are the Federal Deposit Insurance Corporation, the Department of the Treasury (The Office of the Comptroller of the Currency), the Board of Governors of the Federal Reserve System, the Farm Credit System and the Federal Housing Finance Agency collectively.

The Prudential Regulators' final rules apply to registered swap dealers, major swap participants, security-based swap dealers and major security-based swap participants that are regulated by a Prudential Regulator.

The CFTC's final rules apply to swap dealers and major swap participants that are not regulated by a Prudential Regulator.

The CFTC's definition of a Swap Dealer is a person who:

- Holds itself out as a dealer in swaps.
- Makes a market in swaps.
- Regularly enters into swaps with counterparties for its own account.
- Is known in the industry as a dealer or market maker in swaps.

The CFTC's definition of a Major Swap Participant is:

- A person who maintains a substantial position in any of the main swap product categories except for hedging purposes; or
- A person whose outstanding swaps create substantial counterparty risk exposure which could have serious adverse effects on the financial stability of the US banking system or financial markets; or
- A financial entity which is highly leveraged against its capital base; maintains a substantial position in any of the major swap product categories; and is not subject to the capital requirements of any Federal banking agency.

Each regulator is therefore in charge of the adoption of uncleared margin rules for different entity types.

The PR jointly finalised their uncleared swap margin rules in October 2015 (the "PR Margin Rules"). The CFTC finalised its margin requirements for uncleared swap transactions on 16th December 2015 (the "CFTC Margin Rules").

The CFTC's adoption of final rules followed on those of the Prudential Regulators. Compliance with both sets of rules started to be phased in from 1st September 2016.

At the time of writing (January 2018) the SEC has not finalised their rules for uncleared derivative transactions.

The PR is responsible for the implementation of uncleared margin rules for bank holding companies, foreign banks treated as bank holding companies, bank subsidiaries of bank holding companies and of such foreign banks, federally insured deposit institutions, farm credit banks, federal home loan banks, the Federal Home Loan Mortgage Corporation and the Federal National Mortgage Corporation.

Technically the CFTC Margin Rules apply to "CFTC Covered Swap Entities" which capture swap dealers that are not subject to prudential regulation (including, *inter alia*, non-bank subsidiaries of bank holding companies), major swap participants and financial end-users.

As the CFTC Margin Rules largely track the PR Margin Rules, we will only be considering the key points in one set of rules, namely the CFTC Margin Rules, in this section.

Certain end-user types have been exempted from the CFTC's swap clearing requirements. These include non-financial corporations such as energy producers, manufacturing companies, small banks and financial cooperatives (see below).

CFTC Margin Rules

Following the recommended timeline of BCBS and IOSCO, the CFTC Margin Rules (like the PR Margin Rules) started being phased in on 1st September 2016 with the highest volume dealers that are CFTC Covered Swap Entities becoming subject to IM and VM requirements first. The following chart shows the timetable for the phasing in of VM and IM under the CFTC rules for all market participants apart from Exempted End-Users (see below):

Figure 1.2

Source: CFTC

Covered Swap Entities belonging to a group whose average aggregate notional amount of uncleared derivatives exceeds:	Variation margin (VM) implementation:	Initial margin (IM) implementation:
USD 3 trillion	1 September 2016	1 September 2016
USD 2.25 trillion	1 March 2017	1 September 2017
USD 1.5 trillion	1 March 2017	1 September 2018
USD 0.75 trillion	1 March 2017	1 September 2019
Any amount	1 March 2017	1 September 2020

All market participants, other than entities that are exempted from margining requirements "Exempted End-Users", were required to post VM from 1st March 2017 although regulatory forbearance deferred this in many cases until 1st September 2017.

An Exempted End-User is one of the following:

- Commercial end-users, including treasury affiliates (that do not otherwise qualify as Financial End-Users - see below under General Matters regarding CFTC Margin Rules) acting as agent and using the swaps to hedge commercial risk.
- Financial institutions (i.e. small banks, savings associations, Farm Credit System institutions, credit unions) with total assets of **USD 10 billion** or less and certain financial cooperatives hedging the risks associated with originating loans for their members.
- Captive finance companies (i.e. those whose primary business is providing financing and which use derivatives for the purposes of hedging underlying commercial risks relating to interest rate and FX exposures, 90% or more of which arise from financing that facilitates the purchase or lease of products, 90% or more of which are manufactured by the parent company or another subsidiary of the parent company).

As we have seen above, market players with IM requirements are subject to the rules in phases, with the final phase requiring all covered market participants to collect IM under the CFTC Margin Rules by 1st September 2020.

General matters regarding CFTC Margin Rules

The CFTC Margin Rules generally provide that:

- CFTC Covered Swap Entities entering into uncleared swaps with a person registered with the CFTC as a Swap Dealer or a Major Swap Participant or with Financial End-Users (a very wide ranging definition) with Material Swaps Exposure must collect and post IM and VM on every business day.
- CFTC Covered Swap Entities entering into uncleared swaps with Financial End-Users that **do not** have Material Swaps Exposure must collect and post VM on every business day, but **will not** be required to post or collect IM.
- CFTC Covered Swap Entities **are not** required to post or collect IM or VM with respect to uncleared swap transactions entered into with Exempted End-Users.
- For purposes of portfolio margining, uncleared swap counterparties may enter into Eligible Master Netting Agreements (like the ISDA Master Agreement or akin to it) that separately account for pre- and post-compliance date positions. While in most cases the parties will only have one Master Agreement they may have one CSA covering all trades or two CSAs (one for trades pre 1st March 2017 and one for trades post 1st March 2017).
- VM must be both collected and posted for uncleared swaps between a CFTC Covered Swap Entity and its Margin Affiliates.
- IM must be segregated with independent, non-affiliate custodians.
- For purposes of calculating IM, CFTC Covered Swap Entities may use approved proprietary margin models instead of the standardised margin schedule provided by the CFTC in the CFTC Margin Rules. This is a reference to the ISDA SIMM model.

    SIMM stands for Standard Initial Margin Model and is an ISDA proprietary system developed to create a standard IM methodology which can be used by market players globally. If adopted by both parties it can shorten disputes. In 2017 at the request of US regulators its product scope has been widened to cover CDO tranches, inflation swaps, cross-currency swaps, volatility indices, quanto credit default swaps and municipal swaps. This product expansion process is likely to recur regularly.
- The minimum transfer amount below which a CFTC Covered Swap Entity need not collect or post margin pursuant to the CFTC Margin Rules with respect to a particular counterparty has been set at **USD 500,000**. This maximum cap applies at a legal entity level. If a legal entity (e.g. a fund) has multiple investment managers that can enter into trades on behalf of the fund then it is important to ensure that the minimum transfer amount across all collateral agreements does not exceed this cap.

Eligible collateral

The scope of Eligible Collateral for VM under the CFTC Margin Rules varies depending on the identity of such CFTC Covered Swap Entity's counterparty:

- *Swap Entity Counterparties.* A CFTC Covered Swap Entity may only post and collect cash collateral to satisfy VM requirements imposed by the CFTC Margin Rules for uncleared swaps entered into with a Swap Entity counterparty.
- *Financial End-User Counterparties.* A CFTC Covered Swap Entity may post and collect the following forms of collateral to satisfy VM requirements under the CFTC Margin Rules for uncleared swaps entered into with a Financial End-User counterparty:
  - Cash collateral
  - Non-cash collateral i.e.
    - Securities issued by or guaranteed by a US government agency, the European Central Bank or certain sovereign entities.
    - Certain debt securities issued by, and asset-backed securities guaranteed by, US government-sponsored enterprises.
    - Certain redeemable securities in pooled investment funds that invest in US government securities or securities issued by the European Central Bank or certain sovereign entities.
    - Certain corporate debt securities.
    - Securities issued or guaranteed by the Bank for International Settlements, the International Monetary Fund or a multilateral development bank.
    - Certain listed equities.
    - Gold.

Many of these types of collateral are subject to significant haircuts.

Ineligible securities

The following securities are specifically **excluded** from the Eligible Collateral definition under the CFTC Margin Rules:

- Securities issued by (i) the party pledging such collateral (the posting counterparty) or (ii) a Margin Affiliate of the posting counterparty.
- Securities issued by a wide range of US and non-US financial entities and market intermediaries, including banks, bank holding companies, savings and loan holding companies and Margin Affiliates of the foregoing, and brokers, dealers, Swap Dealers and futures commission merchants.

Haircuts

The value of any Eligible Collateral collected or posted to satisfy the CFTC Margin Rules is subject to the sum of the following discounts:

Figure 1.3

CFTC Haircuts table

Asset Class	Discount (%)
Cash in same currency as swap obligation	0.0
Eligible government and related debt Residual maturity <1 year	0.5
Residual maturity 1-5 years	2.0
Residual maturity >5 years	4.0
Eligible corporate debt	
Residual maturity <1 year	1.0
Residual maturity 1-5 years	4.0
Residual maturity >5 years	8.0
Equity included in the S&P 500 or a related index	15.0
Equity included in the S&P 1500 Composite or a related index (but not the S&P 500 or related index)	25.0
Gold	15.0
Additional (additive) haircut on asset in which the currency of the swap obligation differs from that of the collateral asset.	8.0

Collateral Segregation

The CFTC Margin Rules require that IM posted or collected by a CFTC Covered Swap Entity be segregated at one or more custodians.

Collateral Valuation

The total value of all VM collateral collected or posted pursuant to the CFTC Margin Rules is calculated as the sum of the Collateral Values of each item of Eligible Collateral.

Netting Arrangements

The CFTC Margin Rules allow a CFTC Covered Swap Entity to net multiple uncleared swaps with a counterparty for purposes of calculating, posting or collecting IM and VM amounts provided that all uncleared swaps netted against each other have been executed under an Eligible Master Netting Agreement (like the ISDA Master Agreement) entered into between a CFTC Covered Swap Entity and its counterparty. IM amounts **may not** be netted against VM amounts (or vice versa) under the CFTC Margin Rules.

Eligible Master Netting Agreements

The CFTC Margin Rules define "Eligible Master Netting Agreement" as a legally enforceable agreement for which the following conditions are satisfied:
- Upon an event of default following any permitted stay, the agreement creates a single legal obligation for all transactions entered into under it.
- The agreement provides the CFTC Covered Swap Entity with the right (i) to accelerate, terminate and close out on a net basis all transactions under such agreement and (ii) to liquidate or set off collateral promptly upon an event of default. When this happens, the agreement shall provide that any exercise of rights under it will not be stayed or avoided (unless it is a permitted stay) under applicable law in the relevant jurisdictions, **except** in either of the following circumstances:
    - In receivership, conservatorship or resolution under the Federal Deposit Insurance Act, Title II of the Dodd-Frank Act, the Federal Housing Enterprises Financial Safety and Soundness Act of 1992, as amended, or the Farm Credit Act of 1971, as amended, or laws of foreign jurisdictions that are substantially similar to these Acts in order to facilitate the orderly resolution of the defaulting counterparty.
    - The agreement does not contain a walkaway clause (i.e. a provision that permits a non-defaulting counterparty to make a lower payment than it otherwise would make under the agreement, or no payment at all, to a defaulting party or its estate even if either of them is a net creditor under the agreement).

Uncleared Swaps can only be netted within the same portfolio

The CFTC Margin Rules permit a CFTC Covered Swap Entity to identify separate pre- and post-compliance date groups of uncleared swaps. Trades within each group will only be netted against the other uncleared swaps in the same group.

For example, if the uncleared swaps under a particular Eligible Master Netting Agreement entered into between two parties is divided into two netting portfolios:

1. uncleared swaps entered into before the compliance date (the pre-compliance portfolio) and
2. uncleared swaps entered into on or after the applicable compliance date (the post-compliance portfolio)

the CFTC Covered Swap Entity is permitted in the normal course of business to net the uncleared swaps in the post-compliance portfolio against only other post-compliance uncleared swaps, and the uncleared swaps in the pre-compliance portfolio against only other pre-compliance uncleared swaps.

Legacy Swaps

The CFTC expressly declined to exempt new swap transactions arising from amendments to, and novations or compressions of, uncleared swaps entered into before the applicable compliance date (legacy swaps) from the CFTC Margin Rules.

Therefore, the following transactions will be subject to the CFTC Margin Rules beginning on the applicable compliance date, despite their relationship to any legacy swap, to the extent such transactions give rise to a new swap transaction:

- Amendments to legacy swaps.
- Novations of legacy swaps.
- New derivatives resulting from portfolio compression of legacy swaps.

Divergence from International Standards

As mentioned earlier on pp. 11–13, the BCBS/IOSCO framework policy was prepared to set out a consistent approach to implementing the uncleared swap margin requirements globally. The CFTC Margin Rules have some deviations from this framework policy.

One example is that the applicable compliance date under the CFTC Margin Rules is determined based on the average **daily** aggregate notional amount of uncleared swaps, whereas the BCBS/IOSCO framework policy compliance dates are determined on an average **month-end** aggregate notional amount of non-centrally cleared derivatives.

Ongoing compliance obligations

Once a CFTC Covered Swap Entity and its counterparty are subject to the CFTC Margin Rules they will remain so until there is a material change in the aggregate volume of uncleared swaps entered into by the CFTC Covered Swap Entity with that counterparty. This might result in less strict margin requirements being applied to that counterparty under the CFTC Margin Rules.

For example, this might apply if the counterparty is a Financial End-User that previously had, but no longer has, Material Swaps Exposure. In that case the CFTC Covered Swap Entity may comply with the "less strict" margin requirements in relation to both:

i. any uncleared swaps entered into after such counterparty's status change; and
ii. any outstanding uncleared swaps entered into after the applicable compliance date and before such counterparty changed its status.

Please note that the opposite is true in that if a CFTC Covered Swap Entity's counterparty changes its status so that it would be subject to "stricter" margin rules, the CFTC Covered Swap Entity must comply with the "stricter" margin requirements for any uncleared swap entered into with that counterparty after its status change.

Cross Border application of the CFTC Rules

The CFTC Cross-Border Margin Rules subject all uncleared swap transactions entered into by US CFTC Covered Swap Entities to the CFTC Margin Rules. It also covers certain uncleared swaps entered into by non-US CFTC Covered Swap Entities where the risk flows back to a US entity. This is so where a non-US CFTC Covered Swap Entity is facing a counterparty that is a (i) non-US person whose relevant swap obligations are guaranteed by a US person, (ii) a US branch of a foreign bank, (iii) a foreign branch of a US CFTC Covered Swap Entity or (iv) a non-US CFTC Covered Swap Entity whose financials are consolidated in the annual report of an ultimate US parent.

EU

In the European Union, the recommendations of the WGMR were implemented through regulatory technical standards (RTS) under the European Market Infrastructure Regulation ("EMIR").

EMIR is the centrepiece of the EU post financial crisis reform of the OTC derivatives markets and seeks to reduce systemic risk and address perceived issues with counterparty credit risk and transparency which arose during the financial crisis. After a long and difficult consultation period and other similar initiatives like those of the CFTC in the USA, EMIR requires eligible counterparties to post margin on uncleared OTC derivative transactions.

Part of the aim of EMIR is to promote central clearing of OTC derivatives which is often cheaper than the new regulatory requirements for uncleared OTC derivatives. Another aim is to impose tougher margin requirements for uncleared OTC derivatives than previously existed.

These new requirements affect financial counterparties (which include EU banks, insurers, asset managers, investment managers, UCITS and pension funds) referred to as "FCs" and non-financial counterparties with OTC derivative portfolios above the EMIR thresholds referred to as "NFC+" entities. The requirements are included in Figure 1.4 below and result in major changes for these counterparties including the imposition of significant liquidity and operational burdens on their OTC derivative trading activities.

However, certain entities are specifically excluded viz:

• Members of the European System of Central Banks.
• Certain multilateral development banks.
• Public sector entities owned or guaranteed by governments.

Margin also does not need to be exchanged with a non-financial party (e.g. a corporate) with uncleared non-hedging OTC derivatives below the EMIR thresholds (technically referred to as "NFC-" entities) or if all its OTC derivatives are for hedging purposes. In addition, uncleared OTC derivatives between a non-financial counterparty and a CCP authorised as a credit institution in the EU are also exempted.

EMIR came into force on 16th August 2012 but its final RTS for uncleared OTC derivative margining were adopted by the European Commission on 4th October 2016 and published in the EU's Official Journal on 15th December 2016.

It is useful to outline the timelines for when a party is in scope for variation margin and initial margin under EMIR:

Figure 1.4

Source: ESMA

Covered entities belonging to a group whose aggregate average notional amount of uncleared derivatives exceeds:	Variation margin (VM) implementation:	Initial margin (IM) implementation:
EUR 3 trillion	4 February 2017	4 February 2017
EUR 2.25 trillion	1 March 2017	1 September 2017
EUR 1.5 trillion	1 March 2017	1 September 2018
EUR 0.75 trillion	1 March 2017	1 September 2019
EUR 8 billion	1 March 2017	1 September 2020
Below EUR 8 billion	1 March 2017	Not applicable

The focus of this part of Chapter 1 is on its margin rules which, like the CFTC Margin Rules, require eligible counterparties to exchange VM and IM when called upon to do so.

Only when both parties are in scope do the regulatory requirements apply. Where one party would be in scope at a lower tier than the other, the implementation date when margin is required to be exchanged would be on the date applicable for the party on the lower tier.

Many entities, who had not been required to put in place collateral arrangements in the past, are now required to post variation margin.

In addition many counterparties will need to provide initial margin on the phased basis described in Figure 1.4 above.

Whereas variation margin is taken to cover market risk arising from daily changes in the value of uncleared swap transactions, initial margin is a broader measure of a party's current and potential risk exposure between its last margin transfer and the liquidation of positions following that party's default or insolvency. It can therefore be seen as a collateral buffer.

In addition, there is a requirement under EMIR for "netting agreements" to be put in place. Quite often, FX had been traded on an undocumented basis (i.e. with just a confirmation but no master agreement). This can continue when parties are only trading spot FX but it is no longer possible for other FX products to trade without a netting agreement (like the ISDA Master Agreement).

Variation Margin (VM)

Because the EMIR margin rules came into force later than those of the CFTC, the requirement to exchange VM for the first phase of entities commenced on 4th February 2017 (rather than 1st September 2016). It applied to counterparties with a group aggregate average notional amount of non-cleared OTC derivatives in excess of EUR 3 trillion. For other eligible counterparties the VM implementation date was aligned with other jurisdictions where rules had been finalised i.e. on 1st March 2017 although regulatory forbearance deferred this in many cases until 1st September 2017.

EMIR requires collateral arrangements to be in place for new uncleared OTC derivative contracts. Existing contracts are not impacted unless there are lifecycle events (e.g. material amendments to the existing trade) which could bring the trades into scope under EMIR. The requirement to collateralise certain products (e.g. single stock equity options) is still under review and therefore the implementation date for these products has been extended.

Broadly in line with the recommendations under the BCBS/IOSCO framework policy, the EMIR RTS provide for the following for variation margin:

- It is permitted to net risk exposure in relation to variation margin (this is similar to what most market players already do).
- In almost all cases the arrangements need to be on a bilateral basis (i.e. both parties posting collateral). However, there are certain exemptions from two way margining under EMIR.
- No Threshold can be applied to variation margin.
- Valuations must be made on every business day.

Under the 1994/1995 versions of the CSAs both non-regulated IM and VM were typically documented under the same CSA. The new 2016 VM CSAs have been designed purely for variation margin and therefore a number of terms have been updated to reflect this as we shall see in Chapters 2 and 3.

Initial Margin (IM)

The requirement for eligible counterparties to exchange IM has a staggered implementation timeline as outlined in Figure 1.4 above, which depends on the size of the counterparties' portfolio of uncleared OTC derivative transactions measured as the aggregate average notional amount ("AANA") of the relevant party's portfolio on the last business day in each of March, April and May each year. AANA is calculated at the group level. Entities with an AANA below EUR 8 billion are exempt from exchanging IM.

IM is not just calculated on a one-off basis.

The RTS requires that IM is calculated using either:

i. the standardised approach set out in the RTS themselves where a fixed percentage of notional amount is used to calculate IM based on the product types and maturity of the trades; or

ii. a model which meets the detailed requirements of the RTS (including a confidence level of 99% with a risk horizon of at least 10 days, using data from a historical period of at least three years, including at least 25% of the overall data set from a period of stress). This is a reference to the ISDA SIMM model (as discussed in the CFTC section of this chapter on page 18).

A threshold can be applied before IM must be collected. The RTS permits a threshold of EUR 50 million for each group entity. If there are multiple legal entities within a group, the aggregate cannot exceed EUR 50 million when dealing with entities in another group. There is also a permitted threshold that can be applied to entities within the same group (i.e. intragroup entities). In this case a threshold of up to EUR 10 million can be agreed for each intragroup entity when dealing with another intragroup entity.

Counterparties are required to recalculate IM upon certain specified events happening including the execution of a new in-scope transaction, payments under a transaction or termination of a transaction with a minimum IM recalculation period of 10 days.

In addition, regulation requires IM models to be recalibrated on an annual basis.

As with VM, IM must be **provided** on the same business day on which it is calculated. With IM the third party custodian typically arranges for such collateral to settle on the same business day as the instructions were provided.

Initial margin must be posted on a gross basis. The RTS recognises that if both counterparties post IM to each other this would result in significant credit exposures between them. Therefore the RTS requires that any IM is segregated from the assets of both parties. This is likely to require them to use an unaffiliated third party custodian under a triparty relationship to protect against a collecting party's default or insolvency.

Cash IM must be deposited in an account with a central bank or an authorised third party credit institution. Typically cash is not agreed as eligible collateral under an IM arrangement.

Non-cash IM collateral may not be reused or rehypothecated.

Margin eligibility

The RTS details the types of collateral which can be exchanged. A full list is included in the RTS, which includes cash, gold, sovereign and quasi-sovereign bonds, supranational bonds, corporate bonds, senior tranches of eligible securitisations, equities included in main indices, convertibles and UCITS shares. For some non-cash collateral types there are minimum rating criteria (either internally ascribed or provided by an approved external credit rating agency).

In addition, a process must be included for the removal of any collateral which fails to meet those ratings requirements and becomes ineligible. Fire sales must be avoided too. Concentration limits are applied for some collateral types used for initial margin. Parties' own securities or those of entities in their group are excluded from being eligible collateral.

Haircuts

The RTS also contains the minimum haircuts which must be applied to the collateral. These depend on credit quality and maturity. The full list of haircuts for eligible collateral linked to minimum ratings, residual maturity and asset class type is outlined in Annex II of the RTS.

Cash collateral is valued at 100%. There is no haircut.

Some collateral types have a minimum rating requirement of Credit Quality Step 3 (equivalent to investment grade e.g. BBB- by S&P or Baa3 by Moody's). These include:

- Most senior tranches of securitisations.
- Regional government or local authority debt that is not listed by the European Banking Authority ("EBA listed").
- Public sector debt that is not EBA listed.
- Corporate bonds.

For other collateral types (e.g. government debt) there is no minimum rating but a 15% haircut would apply to these collateral types if they are rated below investment grade.

For variation margin, an 8% FX haircut is applied to non-cash collateral posted in a currency other than those agreed in a Confirmation, the Master Agreement or Credit Support Annex. As we shall see later in this book, typically whether the FX haircut is applied is determined by the Eligible Currencies or Major Currencies specified in the VM CSA concerned.

For IM, the application of the 8% FX haircut is determined by the Termination Currency used in a close-out situation.

Minimum Transfer Amount ("MTA")

Under the EMIR RTS this is a maximum of EUR 500,000 split between IM and VM on a counterparty <u>not</u> a group basis. If this MTA is exceeded, the entire amount of margin due must be exchanged and not just the excess. If a counterparty (e.g. a fund) has multiple managers who can execute trades on their behalf and these trading relationships are documented under separate collateral agreements, it is important to ensure that the MTA across all collateral agreements does not exceed this limit.

Operational processes

These must robustly support the margining process and include:

- Clear reporting within the organisation including at senior levels.
- Escalation procedures (internally and with counterparties).
- Dispute resolution procedures.
- Detailed authorisation procedures for deviations from collateral policies.
- Collateral eligibility verification procedures with a focus on the collateral's liquidity.
- Collateral valuation procedures.
- An efficient collateral management team.
- Margin segregation processes if needed.

Parties must formally test these procedures annually and present a report to regulators if required.

Legal agreements

The RTS requires an independent legal review to be performed to confirm netting and collateral enforceability and, where IM is concerned, the enforceability of segregation arrangements. This is to ensure the efficacy of the documentation in the normal course of business and in default situations. The review can be performed by either an independent internal unit or an independent third party. The use of ISDA documentation and ISDA commissioned legal opinions, where available, should meet these requirements.

Exemptions

The RTS contains several exemptions from both the VM and IM requirements.

Product exemptions

Physically-settled foreign exchange ("FX") forwards and physically-settled FX swaps and the exchange of principal in cross-currency swaps are excluded from the IM requirements.

However, the interest rate element in a cross-currency swap is not excluded and margin would be required for that.

Due to ongoing uncertainty over the definition of physically settled FX forwards in the EU there is a temporary exemption from the VM requirements for them until the earlier of (i) 31st December 2018 and (ii) the date on which the delegated regulation defining physically settled FX forwards is issued under MiFID II (which came into force on 3rd January 2018).

There is also a commercial purpose exemption under MiFID II which exempts a physically settled FX contract if:

- At least one of the parties is a non-financial party;
- it is for identifiable goods, services or investments; and
- it is not traded on any platform.

However, there are currently discussions under way to revise the types of entities that will be required to collateralise physically settled FX forwards as we shall see in the Delays and forbearance section of this chapter.

There is also a three year exemption from the VM and IM requirements for single stock equity options and index options until 4th January 2020.

In addition, there are exemptions for covered bond issuers to post VM where they enter into OTC derivatives for hedging purposes. In this case, they are still required to receive VM. This must be in the form of cash.

Pension funds are exempt from central clearing under EMIR until August 2018.

Spot FX (i.e. FX deals typically settling within T+2) is also excluded from EMIR.

Exemption for non-netting jurisdictions

The RTS contains an exemption for transactions with counterparties in non-EU jurisdictions where a legal review does not confirm that netting or IM segregation arrangements can be legally enforced.

Therefore, unless alternative processes are found, the RTS requirement is that there is no need for an EU counterparty to post VM or IM but it must collect it from its non-EU counterparty on a gross basis. Furthermore, there is no need for an EU counterparty to collect or post VM or IM if a legal review shows that collecting on a gross basis is not enforceable and the ratio of the notional amount of group OTC derivatives transactions for which no margin is collected in such jurisdictions is less than 2.5% of the total notional of all group OTC derivative transactions.

The upshot is that, if the 2.5% ratio is exceeded, the EU entity will probably be unable to trade with counterparties in non-netting jurisdictions unless it is willing to amend its documentation substantially.

Delays and forbearance

The original aim of global regulators was that the parties with OTC derivatives portfolios exceeding a notional currency amount of 3 trillion should perform their counterparty categorisation analysis, regulatory compliance, documentation repapering and start exchanging IM and VM on 1st September 2016. While the USA, Canada and Japan met this target through dealers prioritising agreements with their biggest counterparties and engaging hordes of lawyers and paralegals, the EU did not finalise its margin rules until later and did not reach the same point with parties with portfolios of more than EUR 3 trillion notional until 4th February 2017.

Another problem arose with the next regulatory deadline where all remaining counterparties in scope of uncleared margin rules were required to be ready to exchange variation margin with all their in-scope counterparties from 1st March 2017. As that time approached commentators estimated that only between 8% and 10.5% of collateral documents had been repapered and complied with the new regulations.

It has been estimated that globally about 160,000 existing collateral documents were subject to analysis and possible renegotiation in order for all the new regulatory requirements to be met.

On 7th February 2017 ISDA and some other trade bodies wrote an open letter to a number of regulators calling for regulatory forbearance in respect of the new rules on variation margin due to come into force on 1st March 2017.

ISDA and the other trade bodies argued that a large percentage of the market was unlikely to have made the necessary changes to their documentation to achieve compliance with the new rules by 1st March 2017 and that this could lead to market disruption. It gave several reasons specifically for this viz:

- The sheer scale of the exercise. Thousands of market players were subject to the new VM requirements.
- Complex renegotiations of existing Credit Support Annexes in many cases.
- Operational risk because the terms of the Credit Support Annexes needed to be updated in each party's systems.
- Possible risk that non-compliance with the full regulatory requirements would cut off firms from trading.

The letter called on the regulators in all jurisdictions where the new rules on variation margin were effective on 1st March 2017 to provide a transition period of six months for all market players to make the necessary amendments to their documentation. Regulators in Hong Kong, Singapore, South Korea and Australia had already provided for a six month transition period for this purpose until 1st September 2017.

On 13th February 2017 the CFTC issued a no-action letter which stated that from 1st March to 1st September 2017 it would not recommend enforcement action against dealers for failing to comply with the new rules. Canada essentially did the same. Japan limited its forbearance to certain foreign counterparties.

On 23rd February 2017 the European Supervisory Authorities ("ESAs") published a paper which indicated that neither they, nor the competent authorities ("CAs" i.e. individual country regulators) had the formal power to disapply directly applicable EU legislation, but that they expected the CAs in their day-to-day enforcement of applicable legislation to make a case-by-case assessment on the degree of compliance and progress made particularly by smaller counterparties. Regulators of other jurisdictions published similar statements including the Financial Conduct Authority in the UK.

On 30th March 2017 the Dutch Central Bank published a newsletter which indicated that the Dutch Central Bank would not directly enforce the 1st March compliance date against market participants subject to its supervision. Denmark decided the same.

Other regulators decided to adopt a risk based approach subject to regular supervision. These included France, Germany, Ireland and Spain.

Regulators indicated that while entities could continue to trade after 1st March there was an expectation that parties agreed **before** executing trades that they would expedite the negotiation of regulatory compliant CSAs during the forbearance window and that the CSAs would apply with retrospective effect back to 1st March so that trades executed during this forbearance window would be subject to uncleared margin requirements following the execution of the CSA.

As 1st September 2017 drew near, the US regulators indicated that if regulatory compliant collateral agreements were not in place by 1st September then trades entered into from 1st March 2017 that were still live and in scope for uncleared margin rules would need to be unwound. This was not necessarily a simple process because typically there was no unilateral mechanism to terminate trades and discussions needed to be held between the counterparties on the progress of the work to update their CSAs by the 1st September 2017 deadline or on the trade unwind process where completion of CSA updating was unlikely.

In general, the temporary relief or forbearance granted by regulators did come to an end on 1st September 2017 as expected. Where parties had still not made their collateral agreements regulatory compliant by that date, banks did and do have the option to stop trading with these counterparties and to unwind trades.

As mentioned earlier, the requirement to collateralise deliverable FX forwards was postponed/exempted under EMIR until a standard definition of what constitutes a physically settled FX forward could be agreed.

The transitional exemption was due to expire on the earlier of the implementation of MiFID 2 and 31st December 2018. MiFID 2 came into force on 3rd January 2018.

As this new deadline approached there was again a squeeze on resources required to repaper entities that only trade deliverable FX forwards and therefore had not yet put in place regulatory compliant VM CSAs.

Under CFTC and PR Margin Rules, deliverable FX forwards are not required to be collateralised. Due to the discrepancy between the US and EMIR rules, some US entities who only trade deliverable FX forwards decided that they would only deal with counterparties who were not captured by EMIR because there would be no requirement for them to put in place VM CSAs. Moreover, it was possible that European entities would be at a disadvantage because they would be required to collateralise trades and therefore bear operational costs that their US counterparts would not.

On 24th November 2017 the European Supervisory Authorities ("ESA") announced that a review of the EMIR RTS was currently under way with the expectation that a draft amendment to the EMIR RTS would be submitted to the European Commission with the intention of updating the entities that are required to collateralise deliverable FX forwards.

The ESA also recommends that CAs apply a risk based approach when considering how to enforce EMIR where parties do not have regulatory compliant collateral agreements in place.

The market has applied an approach whereby if an entity is captured by the definition of "institution" under the Capital Requirements Regulation (EU) No. 575/2013 (broadly speaking credit institutions (e.g. a bank) or investment firms acting on their own behalf rather than as an agent for a non-institution entity) then they would be required to collateralise physically settled FX forwards. If they are not captured by this definition then they are not required to do so.

However, a change in EU legislation takes time as all EU members are required to approve the terms. As mentioned earlier, neither the ESA nor CAs have the formal power directly to disapply EU legislation.

Taking the ESA's announcement on board, the UK's Financial Conduct Authority ("FCA") confirmed on 7th December 2017 that they supported the recommendation of the ESA to apply a risk based approach to supervision and they would not require firms who fall outside the institution definition to exchange variation margin. However, they do recognise that collateralisation is a "prudent risk management tool" and that the announcement is subject to any further statement issued by the ESA or themselves.

Many other regulators have issued similar statements.

On 18th December 2017, the ESA published draft regulatory technical standards to amend EMIR to address this matter which is consistent with the approach applied by the market. The amending RTS must now be considered by the European Commission and then by the European Parliament and the European Council.

Self-Disclosure Letter

In June 2016, ahead of the 1ˢᵗ March 2017 implementation date of the new variation margin requirements which would affect most financial end-users, ISDA released an informational Regulatory Margin Self-Disclosure Letter (the "SDL"). The SDL is essentially a standard form for sharing information on an entity's status under each applicable regulatory regime with that entity's uncleared swaps trading counterparties. Although market players are not required to complete and deliver an SDL to any of their non-cleared swaps counterparties, the information disclosed in the SDL is necessary to determine if and when the rules under a particular margin regime will apply to a trading relationship.

As a result of this analysis, the parties must determine the scope of application of each set of rules that apply.

This could result in the following scenarios:

- The party must post or collect VM only; or
- It must post or collect both IM and VM; or
- It does not need to post or collect either.

It is possible that one set of rules applies to one party to a swap and another applies to its counterparty. In that case each party must, of course, comply with the set of rules which applies to it. If more than one set of rules apply to a party it needs to comply with the strictest of those rules i.e. the most stringent of them because that would require more margin to be posted under it. This is known as the "strictest of" approach to margin compliance.

Since the initial publication of the SDL, additional supplements have been published relating to regimes that were not included in the original letter (e.g. Australia, Hong Kong, Singapore and Republic of Korea).

SDLs can be exchanged in hard copy form or can be completed and shared electronically on IHS Markit through ISDA Amend 2.0.

IHS Markit is a global company which provides independent market data. ISDA Amend 2.0 is a joint service by ISDA and IHS Markit which provides parties with an online tool to facilitate compliance with Dodd-Frank and EMIR requirements.

ISDA 2016 Variation Margin Protocol

In August 2016 ISDA published the ISDA 2016 Variation Margin Protocol (the "VM Protocol") which is intended to assist market players with compliance.

While parties can put in place regulatory compliant collateral agreements on a bilateral negotiation basis, some may find it most efficient to adhere to the VM

Protocol and exchange standardised questionnaires with each of their in-scope counterparties in order to amend existing or create new documentation.

The VM Protocol adopts a structure similar to previous ISDA protocols relating to OTC derivatives regulation and is designed to allow market players to establish new credit support documents or to amend existing ones for each of its uncleared OTC derivatives counterparties so as to implement the rules of various regulators for the exchange of margin for those derivatives.

When the VM Protocol was originally published it covered margin rules for uncleared OTC derivatives issued by the USA, Japan and Canada. Since then additional supplements have been added for EU, Swiss and Australian rules.

Adherence and matching questionnaires

The VM Protocol, like many of its predecessors, permits parties to amend its OTC derivatives contract documentation with multiple counterparties in one go. However, unlike past protocols, a number of elections are required to be "matched" by the parties in order to amend current documentation or to enter into a new agreement.

The VM Protocol is a two-step process. First the parties need to adhere to the VM Protocol by delivering an adherence letter to ISDA and paying a one-time fee of USD 1,000.

After delivering it, the party concerned can populate one or more questionnaires for delivery to each of its in-scope counterparties. The questionnaires include a number of elections. If parties exchange questionnaires and they fully match on elections, the parties will automatically create new, or amend existing, credit support documentation that is compliant with the new rules. If the parties do not match on any required elections, they may amend the questionnaires and redeliver them until those questionnaires match on those elections.

Questionnaires can be completed either on ISDA Amend 2.0 on IHS Markit's website or by exchanging paper, fax or email versions of the forms. Unlike past protocols, parties can exchange draft forms of questionnaires on ISDA Amend 2.0 prior to submitting final versions.

Elections under the VM Protocol

The VM Protocol offers three methods for parties to upgrade collateral documentation to comply with the uncleared margin rules viz:

- Amend.
- Replicate and Amend.
- New CSA.

Amend

Here market players can use exhibits included in the VM Protocol to amend Credit Support Annexes ("CSAs") to comply with the margin rules under different regulatory regimes. If this option is chosen, their existing trades prior to 1st March 2017 also become subject to the VM requirements as the amended CSAs cover all trades, existing and new, under the existing ISDA Master Agreement. Therefore all trades become subject to the regulatory compliant CSA. There can be no cherrypicking here. It is an all or nothing approach.

Replicate and Amend

This option creates a second CSA which is a copy of the existing CSA between the parties and which is then amended to make it regulatory compliant. Existing trades prior to 1st March 2017 remain under the existing unamended CSA while new trades are governed by the new amended CSA. VM Protocol adherents are responsible for ensuring that this method works with their existing CSAs. For example, if there are already two existing CSAs between the parties then it is not possible to use the Replicate and Amend approach to create a third CSA (because you cannot identify which of the two CSAs is being replicated). Under this option the existing and new trades cannot be netted off against each other in the normal course of business because they are governed by separate CSAs.

New CSA

Here parties enter into a new 2016 VM CSA with standard terms and elections based upon questionnaire responses. The new CSA can either govern only new trades entered into from 1st March 2017 or cover all trades (new and existing) governed by the ISDA Master Agreement. It depends whether the parties select "Import Legacy Transactions" or not.

It is also possible for a new ISDA Master Agreement to be created by the VM Protocol if there is no existing Agreement between the parties. In this case only the New CSA approach would be used as it is not possible to have an existing CSA without an ISDA Master Agreement.

Choices here are not "one size fits all". It is possible that parties may choose different options for different counterparties.

VM Protocol questionnaires are mainly exchanged on ISDA Amend 2.0 on IHS Markit's website.

ISDA Amend 2.0 allows parties to easily access and exchange documentation needed for margin rule compliance. This is an automated, online solution to this challenge.

Adherents to the VM Protocol

The VM Protocol is an open protocol with no fixed end date. However, ISDA has the option to designate an end date for the VM Protocol by giving 30 days' notice on its website.

As at 5th January 2018, 1164 parties had adhered to the VM Protocol. Despite this, a significant number of counterparties have instead undertaken bilateral negotiations with their counterparties. This approach works better where existing CSAs have customised provisions which do not fit into the VM Protocol.

Other key issues

Two other key issues need to be dealt with in this chapter viz:

1. Extraterritoriality
2. Substituted compliance

Extraterritoriality

On 29th June 2012 the CFTC released its cross border guidance on when the Dodd-Frank Act OTC derivatives legislation extends outside the USA. This included a proposal to regulate, to some extent, swaps entered into by anyone, wherever located, with a US person. Secondly, the CFTC expected registered swap dealers and major swap participants to operate in a Dodd-Frank compliant manner globally whether they are based in the USA or overseas. Initially this required both US and foreign parties to register with the CFTC.

The CFTC's cross-border rules relate to clearing, trading and reporting of OTC derivatives.

This proposed guidance would have required most counterparties trading on swap execution facilities with US counterparties to comply with US transaction rules. In addition, offshore branches of US banks would also be covered as would US hedge funds incorporated abroad. The CFTC cited the "London whale" incident in 2012 where JP Morgan Chase's London office lost USD 6.2 billion on credit default swaps and was fined USD 920 million by US and UK regulators for "unsafe and unsound practices". The CFTC did not want this sort of incident to flow back to the USA and therefore wanted authority over some trading outside the USA so that risks did not build up abroad for US banks. Indeed the CFTC considered it was following the Dodd-Frank Act's general broad authority to regulate any overseas swaps activity which had a "direct and significant" impact on US commerce.

Overseas regulators objected strongly to what they saw as the CFTC's overreach here which came to be known as extraterritoriality. They feared it would lead to fragmentation in the global market and liquidity shortages and not achieve a globally harmonised approach to cross border regulation which they considered to be of paramount importance. They were particularly concerned about the definition of "US person" which was very broad. They were also concerned that the market could face a costly compliance burden and conflicting and duplicative requirements if other regulators rolled out similar plans. Requiring non-US swap dealers or major swap participants to register with the CFTC if they met de minimis thresholds could stop such parties trading with US counterparties. Another fear was regulatory arbitrage – parties preferring to trade with counterparties in more lenient regulatory regimes.

Because most cross-border swaps trading was done between the USA and Europe a compromise was necessary and the route explored was substituted compliance.

Substituted compliance

Substituted compliance works if the regulatory regimes in two or more countries are deemed equally robust and comprehensive.

The CFTC's stance on substituted compliance was that it should apply on a firm by firm basis (i.e. between two non-US entities). Where a US counterparty was concerned it would always be subject to the Dodd-Frank Act even if another jurisdiction's regulations also applied.

ESMA preferred substituted compliance to be based on a jurisdiction basis i.e. on an individual country's regulations.

Overseas regulators wanted substituted compliance to exempt foreign swaps activity from falling under US rules so long as the CFTC deemed that those rules were sufficient and equivalent. Substituted compliance relies on local jurisdictions applying equivalent regulations.

In July 2013 the European Commission and the CFTC agreed the Common Path Forward on Derivatives. The CFTC and the European Commission shared the view that jurisdictions and regulators should be able to defer to each other when it is justified by the quality of their respective regulation and enforcement regimes. Where rules differ it was agreed that the stricter rule would apply.

For bilateral uncleared swaps, and because EU and US rules for risk mitigation are essentially identical, the CFTC agreed to issue no-action relief for certain transaction-based requirements.

However, in early December 2013 the CFTC was issuing further cross border guidance under the guise of advice and thus without the formal rule making statutory requirements for a public comment period and a cost-benefit analysis. Because of this ISDA and two other trade associations decided to sue the CFTC.

This was after a CFTC staff letter issued on 14th November 2013 stated that even trades between a non-US swap dealer and a non-US counterparty booked outside the US would be subject to the CFTC's transaction-level rules if those trades were regularly arranged, negotiated or executed by personnel or agents based in the USA. This was when ISDA and the other trade associations started to consider filing their lawsuit.

While the lawsuit was dismissed by the US court concerned on 16th September 2014, earlier in February 2014 the CFTC and EU regulators agreed that European approved swap execution facilities would be exempt from US trading rules until equivalent European rules came into force when MiFID II was implemented on 3rd January 2018. US banks also trading on such swap execution facilities would also be exempt.

On 18th September 2017 ISDA published a white paper entitled *Cross-border Harmonization of Derivatives Regulatory Regimes: A Risk-based Framework for Substituted Compliance via Cross-border Principles*.

In this white paper ISDA reviewed the current cross-border state of substituted compliance and tried to breathe new life into a slow if not stalled process. This process is the mutual international recognition of the robustness of the OTC derivatives regulation in major jurisdictions. The OTC derivatives regulation in each such jurisdiction does not need to be identical but closely comparable.

Taking the CFTC and the EU by way of example, so far the CFTC's analysis seems to have been a line by line, rule by rule approach while the EU prefers to analyse the objectives of a jurisdiction's derivatives regulations in what it calls an "outcomes approach". The priorities here for the EU are that the requirements being assessed are legally binding; they are subject to effective supervision and compliance by domestic authorities; and they achieve the same results as the corresponding EU provisions and supervision against which they are being assessed.

In its white paper ISDA believes that when examining the derivatives regulations of foreign jurisdictions for comparability, regulators should focus on whether the jurisdiction concerned has sufficient mechanisms in place to address or reduce systemic risk (i.e. the risk of a market collapse).

ISDA therefore favours adopting regulatory principles driven by the risk based measures referred to in its press release and white paper as follows:

- Foreign regulations that require firms to establish capital and margin requirements pursuant to the G-20 commitments.
- Foreign regulations that require firms to establish sound risk management policies to address risks posed by derivatives business.
- Foreign regulations that require firms to maintain an effective and accurate system of records.
- Foreign regulations that require firms to make swap data available to regulators.
- Foreign jurisdictions that have clearing and settlement services that comply with the Basel Committee on Banking Supervision / International Organization of Securities Commissions' principles and that have similar clearing mandates.

If a foreign jurisdiction meets these risk-based principles, ISDA believes it should be granted substituted compliance in full.

On page 12 of its white paper ISDA makes a good point on the groundwork of BCBS and IOSCO when it says that BCBS and IOSCO formulated a policy framework that reflected standard market practice and represented the consensus view of regulators across many jurisdictions. Therefore, rather than engage in a rule-by-rule analysis, ISDA proposes that the CFTC determines that the margin regime of a foreign jurisdiction is comparable to the CFTC's margin rules as long as the foreign jurisdiction is in compliance with the BCBS-IOSCO standards. On that basis ISDA believes that full substituted compliance could be granted to that regime.

It is hoped by the authors that ISDA's white paper may be the catalyst for full international agreement on this vexed and long standing issue.

Even more important is a MiFID 2 requirement for EU regulators to declare foreign trading platforms as "equivalent" so that European firms can continue to trade on them.

Fortunately there were 2 significant steps forward on this on 13th October 2017 when EU and US negotiators were reported as having come to agreements on recognising each other's trading platforms and the equivalence of their uncleared margin rules. These negotiators took the view that they were comparable in outcome and could be mutually regognised.

The recognition of equivalence for uncleared margin rules was voted on by the CFTC and the EU and passed to operate with immediate effect.

It should be noted that substituted compliance is only available where both the entity and the transaction are subject to both CFTC and EU uncleared margin regimes.

The second equivalence recognition concerned trading platforms and has become known as the Giancarlo-Dombrovskis Common Approach after its leading CFTC and EU negotiators. While the terms of this are agreed in principle and each key negotiator has committed to vote in favour of it, both the CFTC and the European Council need to have a formal vote on it in 2018.

However, on 6th December 2017 the European Commission determined that EU derivatives traders can do business on US trading platforms and remain in compliance with MiFID 2 from 3rd January 2018. The CFTC plans to issue a similar determination in early 2018 allowing US derivatives traders to use EU trading platforms and remain in compliance with the Dodd-Frank Act.

We hope this regulatory information has been useful to you as background as we now embark in Chapter 2 on the 2016 ISDA Credit Support Annex For Variation Margin under English law.

Chapter 2

The 2016 ISDA Credit Support Annex For Variation Margin (VM) under English Law

ISDA's suite of credit support documentation before 2016

Before 2016 there were 4 main ISDA Collateral Documents viz:

- 1994 ISDA Credit Support Annex under New York Law
- 1995 ISDA Credit Support Annex under English Law
- 1995 ISDA Credit Support Deed under English Law
- ISDA Credit Support Annexes under Japanese Law

Of course, these 4 documents are still used by counterparties who are not subject to the new uncleared margin regulations.

There were also 3 other ISDA Collateral Documents types which were used less frequently:

- 2001 ISDA Margin Provisions
- 2014 ISDA Standard Credit Support Annex under English Law
- 2014 ISDA Standard Credit Support Annex under New York Law

ISDA's new suite of credit support documentation

In April 2016, ISDA published updated versions of the English Law CSA and New York Law CSA for variation margin only. In July 2016 the first documentation for regulatory initial margin was published.

The list of available documentation which is expected to be used going forward is:

- 2016 ISDA Credit Support Annex under English Law For Variation Margin (VM)
- 2016 ISDA Credit Support Annex under New York Law For Variation Margin (VM)
- 2016 ISDA Credit Support Annexes under Japanese Law For Variation Margin (VM)

- 2016 ISDA Credit Support Deed under English Law For Initial Margin
- 2016 ISDA Credit Support Annex under New York Law For Initial Margin
- 2017 ISDA/Euroclear Collateral Transfer Agreement For Initial Margin
- 2016 ISDA/Clearstream Collateral Transfer Agreement For Initial Margin

Because IM is being phased in until 1st September 2020 it is possible ISDA may issue further IM Credit Support Annexes, Deeds and Collateral Transfer Agreements until then.

In this book we are only studying the 2016 ISDA Credit Support Annexes For Variation Margin (VM) under English and New York Law.

This chapter provides a paragraph by paragraph review of the provisions in the English Law VM CSA and an interpretation of each clause.

Introduction

Following the changing regulatory landscape as outlined in Chapter 1, it was determined that a new version of the English law Credit Support Annex should be prepared which would provide parties with a quick way to put in place regulatory compliant collateral documentation rather than analysing any existing CSA to determine if it was regulatory compliant and if not, what changes would be needed to it. As there is a lot of optionality in the 1995 ISDA Credit Support Annex under English law ("1995 English Law CSA") with a number of elections being made in Paragraph 11, this analysis was no mean task and typically needed to be undertaken for each CSA separately.

Given the strict timings imposed for putting in place regulatory compliant collateral documents as we saw in Chapter 1, when the updated version of the CSA was being formulated it was agreed to focus purely on two key matters viz:

1. The minimum updates required in order to ensure that the English Law VM CSA was regulatory compliant; and
2. Updates to interest rate provisions to incorporate changes required where negative interest rates apply.

Any other "nice to have" updates or amendments made in Paragraph 11 that were often seen in the market were not considered in composing the English Law VM CSA.

The English Law VM CSA is a title transfer document and is divided into 11 Paragraphs.

Similar to the ISDA Master Agreement Schedule, Paragraph 11 is what negotiators negotiate and is where elections are made and provisions are amended or added.

It is useful to remember that when you see the word "Paragraph" in the document it refers to a paragraph of the English Law VM CSA. When you see the word "Section" it relates to a Section of the ISDA Master Agreement.

Paragraph by paragraph analysis

Footnotes

(Bilateral Form - Transfer)[1]   (ISDA Agreements Subject to English Law)[2]

[1] This document is not intended to create a charge or other security interest over the assets transferred under its terms. Persons intending to establish a collateral arrangement based on the creation of a charge or other security interest should consider using the ISDA Credit Support Deed (English law) or the ISDA Credit Support Annex (New York law), as appropriate.

[2] This Credit Support Annex has been prepared for use with ISDA Master Agreements subject to English law. Users should consult their legal advisers as to the proper use and effect of this form and the arrangements it contemplates. In particular, users should consult their legal advisers if they wish to have the Credit Support Annex made subject to a governing law other than English law or to have the Credit Support Annex subject to a different governing law than that governing the rest of the ISDA Master Agreement (e.g., English law for the Credit Support Annex and New York law for the rest of the ISDA Master Agreement).

The top left hand corner of the first page of the English Law VM CSA, clearly identifies that the document, in its standard form, is supposed to be a two way agreement and that it has been prepared on the basis of a title transfer structure.

Title transfer means that the collateral giver transfers outright legal title and ownership of the collateral to the collateral taker who can deal with it as he sees fit. His only obligation is to return equivalent collateral at a future date if there is a change to the mark-to-market value of the portfolio of trades or if no trades are outstanding.

The first footnote reinforces this point by stating that no charge or security interest is created under the terms of the English Law VM CSA. It also provides guidance for alternative ISDA collateral documents which could be used if the intention is to put in place a collateral agreement on a security interest basis (i.e. a Credit Support Deed under English law or a Credit Support Annex under New York law).

Security interest is the other main approach that is used for taking collateral. Under this arrangement the collateral giver (known as the Pledgor) retains an ownership interest in the collateral pledged to the collateral taker (known as the Secured Party).

In the top right hand corner of the English Law VM CSA the governing law of the agreement is identified. Footnote 2 stipulates that the English Law VM CSA is to be used with an ISDA Master Agreement subject to English Law. Legal advice should be sought if the English Law VM CSA is to be added to an ISDA Master Agreement governed by any other law.

Dating of the VM CSA and identification of the parties

International Swaps and Derivatives Association, Inc.

2016 CREDIT SUPPORT ANNEX FOR VARIATION MARGIN (VM)

dated as of ....
to the Schedule to the

ISDA Master Agreement
dated as of ....
between
.... and ....
("Party A")   ("Party B")

The English Law VM CSA makes references to two dates. The first is the date to be applied to the VM CSA itself and the second is the date of the ISDA Master Agreement.

In the 1995 English Law CSA market convention was for the date to match the date of the ISDA Master Agreement even if the CSA was executed at a later date (often many years later).

One of the reasons for the dating the English Law VM CSA is that there may be multiple CSAs linked to the same ISDA Master Agreement. This makes it easier to identify the CSAs in the future particularly if an amendment is required.

Uncleared margin rules require that new trades entered into after the relevant implementation date (generally 1st March 2017 for Variation Margin) need to be collateralised in accordance with the relevant rules applicable to the parties concerned. Unless there is a life cycle event (e.g. a material amendment to a trade or a novation), existing trades before the implementation date do not need to be regulatory compliant. Parties may agree to keep the existing collateralised trades under their 1995 English Law CSA and only use the new English Law VM CSA for new trades. This would be the situation where multiple CSAs apply.

After the English Law VM CSA and ISDA Master Agreement to which it relates are identified, the parties include their full legal names. In general if a party is identified as Party A in the ISDA Master Agreement then they will also be Party A under the English Law VM CSA. While this is not absolutely necessary it is good practice to follow this convention to reduce any confusion or misinterpretation in the future.

Preamble

> This Annex supplements, forms part of, and is subject to, the ISDA Master Agreement referred to above and is part of its Schedule. For the purposes of this Agreement, including, without limitation, Sections 1(c), 2(a), 5 and 6, the credit support arrangements set out in this Annex constitute a Transaction (for which this Annex constitutes the Confirmation).

In this provision the collateral under the English Law VM CSA is defined as a "Transaction". The ISDA Master Agreement itself only governs Transactions between the parties. Defining the English Law VM CSA in this way, makes it part of and subject to the Agreement itself.

As the term "Transaction" is not specifically defined in the ISDA Master Agreement, it is necessary to have a "Confirmation" in place where it is defined. For Transactions in general a Confirmation will outline the terms of the trade and make reference to the ISDA Master Agreement that governs it. Confirmations can be in electronic or in paper form. Therefore, in order to link the two documents together the English Law VM CSA is defined as the Confirmation for the Transaction (i.e. the collateral held under it).

As the English Law VM CSA is not a Credit Support Document, various references to Sections of the ISDA Master Agreement are stated in order to ensure that it correctly interacts with the Agreement. In a default situation such Sections are taken into consideration for close-out purposes.

The first Section referenced (Section 1(c)) is the single agreement concept. It stops a liquidator cherrypicking (i.e. making payments under those Transactions profitable to his insolvent client and refusing to pay on others unprofitable to it but insisting that you as the Non-defaulting Party make your payments under those Transactions). Section 1(c) of the Agreement prevents this by effectively collapsing all the Transactions into a single net termination payment due to one party or the other.

Section 2(a) of the Agreement relates to payments in the ordinary course of business and what happens if an event occurs (e.g. a Potential Event of Default) where payments could be suspended for a specific period of time. After this time either payments will recommence or close-out will occur.

References to the Events of Default and Termination Events clauses (Section 5) and the close-out netting mechanism (Section 6) of the Agreement help to identify that any collateral balance will be taken into account in a close-out situation.

In the normal course of business, collateral calculations and transfers are made based on the terms of the English Law VM CSA. In a close-out situation the collateral held becomes an "Unpaid Amount" under the ISDA Master Agreement and is included in the calculations in the close-out process in its Section 6(e).

Therefore, in a close-out situation the collateral balance is part of the Early Termination Amount calculated. It cannot be treated separately. We will look at this matter again when reviewing the terms of Paragraph 6 of the English Law VM CSA.

Paragraph 1. Interpretation

Paragraph 1. Interpretation

(a) *Definitions and Inconsistency*. Capitalised terms not otherwise defined in this Annex or elsewhere in this Agreement have the meanings specified pursuant to Paragraph 10, and all references in this Annex to Paragraphs are to Paragraphs of this Annex. In the event of any inconsistency between this Annex and the other provisions of this Schedule, this Annex will prevail, and in the event of any inconsistency between Paragraph 11 and the other provisions of this Annex, Paragraph 11 will prevail. For the avoidance of doubt, references to "transfer" in this Annex mean, in relation to cash, payment and, in relation to other assets, delivery.

Paragraph 1(a) states that if there is any inconsistency between the Annex and the other provisions of the ISDA Schedule, the Annex will prevail. However, Paragraph 11 (the Elections and Variables Paragraph) will prevail if it conflicts with the other provisions of the Annex.

Paragraph 1(a) also clarifies certain basic matters e.g. that the term "transfer" covers both the payment of cash and the delivery of securities and other assets as appropriate.

(b) *Scope of this Annex and the Other CSA.* The only Transactions which will be relevant for the purposes of determining "Exposure" under this Annex will be the Covered Transactions specified in Paragraph 11. Each Other CSA, if any, is hereby amended such that the Transactions that will be relevant for purposes of determining "Exposure" thereunder, if any, will exclude the Covered Transactions and the Transaction constituted by this Annex. Except as provided in Paragraph 9(h), nothing in this Annex will affect the rights and obligations, if any, of either party with respect to "independent amounts" or initial margin under each Other CSA, if any, with respect to Transactions that are Covered Transactions.

Paragraph 1(b) is new in the English Law VM CSA. In many cases, except for new relationships, the two parties will have already entered into a 1995 English Law CSA. For regulatory reasons, they may be required to enter into an English Law VM CSA. This provision is designed to address the issue that the original CSA may have been drafted to include all "Transactions" governed by the ISDA Master Agreement and makes it clear that the English Law VM CSA will only include "Covered Transactions" as defined in Paragraph 11. All other Transactions would be covered by the original CSA. There could very well be economic reasons why the parties would not want the English Law VM CSA to cover all trades that have been executed under an ISDA Master Agreement but only to include trades executed from the date that variation margin applied to uncleared swaps under the new regulations e.g. from 1st March 2017. If independent amounts are already included under an existing 1995 English Law CSA or regulatory initial margin applies (which is documented under one or more separate collateral agreements), they do not affect the exposure calculation for variation margin for Covered Transactions under the English Law VM CSA.

If the parties agreed to apply Credit Support Offsets, as outlined in Paragraph 9(h) and elected in Paragraph 11(h), there is a possibility that the English Law VM CSA and Other CSAs (e.g. a 1995 English Law CSA executed between the parties) could interact. Where Credit Support Offsets do not apply, they would be treated separately.

Paragraph 2. Credit Support Obligations

Paragraph 2. Credit Support Obligations

(a) *Delivery Amount (VM).* Subject to Paragraphs 3 and 4, upon a demand made by the Transferee on or promptly following a Valuation Date, if the Delivery Amount (VM) for that Valuation Date equals or exceeds the Transferor's Minimum Transfer Amount, then the Transferor will transfer to the Transferee Eligible Credit Support (VM) having a Value as of the date of transfer at least equal to the applicable Delivery Amount (VM) (rounded pursuant to Paragraph 11(c)(vi)(B)). Unless otherwise specified in Paragraph 11(c), the *"Delivery Amount (VM)"* applicable to the Transferor for any Valuation Date will equal the amount by which:

(i) the Transferee's Exposure

exceeds

(ii) the Value as of that Valuation Date of the Transferor's Credit Support Balance (VM) (adjusted to include any prior Delivery Amount (VM) and to exclude any prior Return Amount (VM) , the transfer of which, in either case, has not yet been completed and for which the relevant Regular Settlement Day falls on or after such Valuation Date).

Basically this Paragraph concerns collateral calls and returns and how they are calculated.

The Transferee compares his risk exposure to the collateral he holds and calls for more, returns any surplus, if requested, or does nothing depending upon his calculations after taking into account any Minimum Transfer Amounts.

In Paragraph 2(a) the collateral taker (the Transferee) can call for collateral from the collateral giver (the Transferor) where his OTC derivatives risk exposure on the Transferor is greater than the Transferor's Minimum Transfer Amount.

When called upon and provided there is no dispute, the Transferor will transfer the requested amount of collateral (the "Delivery Amount (VM)") to the Transferee. Any transfers for previous collateral calls already on their way (whether for earlier Delivery Amounts (VM) or Return Amounts (VM)) are also taken into account in the calculation of the latest Delivery Amount (VM).

(b) *Return Amount (VM)*. Subject to Paragraphs 3 and 4, upon a demand made by the Transferor on or promptly following a Valuation Date, if the Return Amount (VM) for that Valuation Date equals or exceeds the Transferee's Minimum Transfer Amount, then the Transferee will transfer to the Transferor Equivalent Credit Support (VM) specified by the Transferor in that demand having a Value as of the date of transfer as close as practicable to the applicable Return Amount (VM) (rounded pursuant to Paragraph 11(c)(vi)(B)) and the Credit Support Balance (VM) will, upon such transfer, be reduced accordingly. Unless otherwise specified in Paragraph 11(c)(i)(B), the *"Return Amount (VM)"* applicable to the Transferee for any Valuation Date will equal the amount by which:

(i) the Value as of that Valuation Date of the Transferor's Credit Support Balance (VM) (adjusted to include any prior Delivery Amount (VM) and to exclude any prior Return Amount (VM), the transfer of which, in either case, has not yet been completed and for which the relevant Regular Settlement Day falls on or after such Valuation Date)

exceeds

(ii) the Transferee's Exposure.

As we might expect Paragraph 2(b) is the mirror image of Paragraph 2(a) and covers the position where the Transferee holds surplus collateral which it must return to the Transferor if it is above the Transferee's Minimum Transfer Amount and the Transferor calls for the return of the collateral. Please note that if the Transferor does not make a call, the Transferee is not obliged to transfer the collateral or point this out to the Transferor.

A Return Amount (VM) arises where the value of the collateral held by the Transferee is greater than its risk exposure on the Transferor and is also above the Transferee's agreed Minimum Transfer Amount.

Again with a Return Amount (VM), any Delivery Amounts (VM) or Return Amounts (VM) from previous collateral calls and which are already in transit will be taken into account in calculating the collateral amount to be returned.

Paragraph 3. Transfers, Calculations and Exchanges

Paragraph 3. Transfers, Calculations and Exchanges

(a) *Transfers.* All transfers under this Annex of any Eligible Credit Support (VM), Equivalent Credit Support (VM), Interest Payment (VM) or Equivalent Distributions will be made in accordance with the instructions of the Transferee or Transferor, as applicable, and will be made:

(i) in the case of cash, by transfer into one or more bank accounts specified by the recipient;
(ii) in the case of certificated securities which cannot or which the parties have agreed will not be delivered by book-entry, by delivery in appropriate

physical form to the recipient or its account accompanied by any duly executed instruments of transfer, transfer tax stamps and any other documents necessary to constitute a legally valid transfer of the transferring party's legal and beneficial title to the recipient; and

(iii) in the case of securities which the parties have agreed will be delivered by book-entry, by causing the relevant depository institution(s) or other securities intermediaries to make changes to their books and records sufficient to result in a legally effective transfer of the transferring party's legal and beneficial title to the recipient or its agent.

Subject to Paragraph 4, and unless otherwise specified in Paragraph 11, if a demand for the transfer of Eligible Credit Support (VM) or Equivalent Credit Support (VM) is received by the Notification Time, then the relevant transfer will be made not later than the close of business on the Regular Settlement Day relating to the date such demand is received; if a demand is received after the Notification Time, then the relevant transfer will be made not later than the close of business on the Regular Settlement Day relating to the day after the date such demand is received.

All transfers are to be made in line with the instructions of the Transferor or the Transferee. Paragraph 3(a) states how transfers will be made under the Annex for cash and securities in certificate form (rare now) and electronic book entry. It also provides through the definition of Regular Settlement Day in Paragraph 10 that transfer will be made on the same Local Business Day as the demand is made. This update to the settlement timing in the English Law VM CSA is again due to regulation. Typically same day settlement applies. There are some exceptions under certain uncleared margin regulation (for example under EMIR) where the settlement timings for variation margin could be extended. An example is where there are time zone issues related to the collateral management locations of the two parties. If this applies then the definition of Regular Settlement Day would need to be amended in Paragraph 11.

Delivery is adjusted to the next Regular Settlement Day if the demand is made after the stated Notification Time in Paragraph 11(d)(iv).

(b) *Calculations.* All calculations of Value and Exposure for purposes of Paragraph 2 and Paragraph 4(a) will be made by the relevant Valuation Agent as of the relevant Valuation Time, *provided* that, the Valuation Agent may use, in the case of any calculation of (i) Value, Values most recently reasonably available for close of business in the relevant market for the relevant Eligible Credit Support (VM) as of the Valuation Time and (ii)

Exposure, relevant information or data most recently reasonably available for close of business in the relevant market(s) as of the Valuation Time. The Valuation Agent will notify each party (or the other party, if the Valuation Agent is a party) of its calculations not later than the Notification Time on the Local Business Day following the applicable Valuation Date (or, in the case of Paragraph 4(a), following the date of calculation).

Paragraph 3(b) provides for the calculation of risk exposure and the value of collateral held to be made by the relevant Valuation Agent stated in Paragraph 11(d)(i) for the purposes of calculating Delivery Amounts (VM) and Return Amounts (VM) both in the normal course of business and in disputes. Collateral values and risk exposure rates as at the close of business in the relevant market will be used for this purpose. The Valuation Agent will notify its calculations to the other party by the deadline (Notification Time) on the Local Business Day after it makes its calculations. With a dispute (Paragraph 4(a)) this will be the date following a recalculation by the Valuation Agent.

(c) *Exchanges.*

(i) Unless otherwise specified in Paragraph 11, the Transferor may on any Local Business Day by notice inform the Transferee that it wishes to transfer to the Transferee Eligible Credit Support (VM) specified in that notice (the *"New Credit Support (VM)"*) in exchange for certain Eligible Credit Support (VM) (the *"Original Credit Support (VM)"*) specified in that notice comprised in the Transferor's Credit Support Balance (VM).

(ii) If the Transferee notifies the Transferor that it has consented to the proposed exchange, (A) the Transferor will be obliged to transfer the New Credit Support (VM) to the Transferee on the first Settlement Day following the date on which it receives notice (which may be oral telephonic notice) from the Transferee of its consent and (B) the Transferee will be obliged to transfer to the Transferor Equivalent Credit Support (VM) in respect of the Original Credit Support (VM) not later than the Settlement Day following the date on which the Transferee receives the New Credit Support (VM), unless otherwise specified in Paragraph 11(e) (the *"Exchange Date"*); *provided* that the Transferee will only be obliged to transfer Equivalent Credit Support (VM) with a Value as of the date of transfer as close as practicable to, but in any event not more than, the Value of the New Credit Support (VM) as of that date.

Paragraph 3(c) is about substitutions of collateral. Whenever you see the word "exchange" in the English Law VM CSA it means substitution.

(i) Unless forbidden in Paragraph 11, the Transferor (the collateral giver) may request by notice to the Transferee (the collateral taker) a substitution of part or all of the collateral it has previously transferred to the collateral taker in exchange for new collateral acceptable to the collateral taker. This would relate to bond collateral.

(ii) If the collateral taker consents to this then the collateral giver must transfer the new collateral to the collateral taker on the first trade settlement date after it receives the consent notice from the collateral taker. After it has received the new collateral, the collateral taker must return the original collateral which has been substituted no later than the trade settlement date after he has received the new collateral from the collateral giver. This will normally be on the following Local Business Day. In any case on the transfer date the collateral must be worth the same or nearly the same and in no circumstances is he obliged to retransfer original collateral worth more than the new collateral.

The final sentence of Paragraph 3(c) stipulates that the Transferee is only obliged to return collateral whose value is as close as possible to the value of the new collateral but not any higher. This is because with some bonds they can only be transferred in specific integral amounts.

It is useful to note that while transfers under Paragraph 3(a) require same day settlement, substitutions do not. The definition of Settlement Day from the 1995 English Law CSA is retained here meaning (a) each transfer of cash collateral will be made on the next Local Business Day and (b) each transfer of bond collateral will be made on the number of days after demand customary for settlement through the agreed clearing system or otherwise in the relevant local market. This Settlement Day definition is intended to be sufficiently flexible to cover various settlement periods for different types of bonds in different international and European domestic markets and settlement systems.

The reason for the distinction is that when a margin call is made it is to cover a change in mark to market risk exposure and therefore settlement should be same day. When a substitution takes place this exposure is already collateralised and it is more of an operational point on what collateral is substituted to cover this exposure.

There is another risk with substitutions.

The Transferor's potential credit risk on the Transferee increases during the short period when the Transferee holds both the old and new collateral. If he goes bankrupt in that short window then the Transferor can only rank as an unsecured creditor in his liquidation. The market knows this risk and accepts it because it regards it as very remote if it considers its counterparty to be creditworthy.

Paragraph 4. Dispute Resolution

Paragraph 4. Dispute Resolution

(a) *Disputed Calculations or Valuations.* If a party (a *"Disputing Party"*) reasonably disputes (I) the Valuation Agent's calculation of a Delivery Amount (VM) or a Return Amount (VM) or (II) the Value of any transfer of Eligible Credit Support (VM) or Equivalent Credit Support (VM), then:

(1) the Disputing Party will notify the other party and the Valuation Agent (if the Valuation Agent is not the other party) not later than the close of business on the date that the transfer is due in respect of such Delivery Amount (VM) or Return Amount (VM) in the case of (I) above, or, in the case of (II) above, the Local Business Day following the date of transfer;

(2) in the case of (I) above, the appropriate party will transfer the undisputed amount to the other party not later than the close of business on the date that the transfer is due in respect of such Delivery Amount (VM) or Return Amount (VM);

(3) the parties will consult with each other in an attempt to resolve the dispute; and

(4) if they fail to resolve the dispute by the Resolution Time, then:

(i) in the case of a dispute involving a Delivery Amount (VM) or Return Amount (VM), unless otherwise specified in Paragraph 11, the Valuation Agent will recalculate the Exposure and the Value as of the Recalculation Date by:

(A) utilising any calculations of that part of the Exposure attributable to the Covered Transactions that the parties have agreed are not in dispute;

(B) (I) if this Agreement is a 1992 ISDA Master Agreement, calculating the Exposure for the Covered Transactions in dispute by seeking four actual quotations at midmarket from Reference Market-makers for purposes of calculating Market Quotation, and taking the arithmetic average of those obtained, or (II) if this Agreement is an ISDA 2002 Master Agreement or a 1992 ISDA Master Agreement in which the definition of Loss and/or Market Quotation has been amended (including where such amendment has occurred pursuant to the terms of a separate agreement or protocol) to reflect the definition of Close-out Amount from the pre-printed form of the ISDA 2002 Master Agreement as published by ISDA, calculating that part of the Exposure attributable to the Covered Transactions in dispute by seeking four actual quotations at mid-market from third parties for purposes of calculating the relevant Close-out Amount, and taking the arithmetic average of those obtained; *provided* that, in either case, if four quotations are not available for a particular Covered Transaction, then fewer than four quotations may be used for that Covered Transaction, and if no quotations are available for a particular Covered Transaction, then the Valuation Agent's original calculations will be used for the Covered Transaction; and

(C) utilising the procedures specified in Paragraph 11(f)(ii) for calculating the Value, if disputed, of the outstanding Credit Support Balance (VM);

(ii) in the case of a dispute involving the Value of any transfer of Eligible Credit Support (VM) or Equivalent Credit Support (VM), the Valuation Agent will recalculate the Value as of the date of transfer pursuant to Paragraph 11(f)(ii).

Following a recalculation pursuant to this Paragraph, the Valuation Agent will notify each party (or the other party, if the Valuation Agent is a party) as soon as possible but in any event not later than the Notification Time on the Local Business Day following the Resolution Time. The appropriate party will, upon demand following such notice given by the Valuation Agent or a resolution pursuant to (3) above and subject to Paragraph 3(a), make the appropriate transfer.

(a) If a party disputes the Valuation Agent's calculation of risk exposure or the value of collateral held, Paragraph 4 provides a structure for resolving the dispute if it cannot be settled informally. Most such disputes are normally settled informally between the parties.

Collateral disputes <u>always</u> relate to these two matters and the calculation of risk exposure is the more common sort of dispute. Disputes may also arise over the valuation of collateral if illiquid collateral is being transferred.

Please note in Paragraph 4(a) the Disputing Party has to observe a standard of reasonableness in starting a dispute with its counterparty.

The steps for the dispute resolution procedure are outlined in Paragraph 4(a)(1)-(4) and involve:

(1) A requirement for the Disputing Party to notify its counterparty that it wishes to dispute (1) the risk exposure calculation no later than the close of business on the date the transfer is due or (2) the collateral valuation no later than the close of business on the Local Business Day after the date of

the collateral transfer. This would cover the situation where a Transferor had transferred the wrong amount of collateral to the Transferee.

(2) In the case of disputes over the risk exposure calculation for collateral calls, the Disputing Party agrees to transfer the undisputed amount of the call to the other party not later than the close of business on the date the transfer is due. Under EMIR this is a regulatory requirement.

(3) The parties will attempt to resolve the dispute by the deadline stated in Paragraph 11(f)(i) – the Resolution Time.

(4) If they fail then:

(i) (A) if the dispute involves the amount of collateral called for, the Valuation Agent will recalculate his figures for risk exposure and collateral value (including any haircut) by reusing any calculation of the undisputed part of the risk exposure of the Covered Transactions. In fact this dispute resolution provision only relates to Covered Transactions. It is important to bear this in mind.

(B) It will then approach 4 Reference Market-makers or third parties for mid market quotations (i.e. the average of the bid and offer prices of the Coveered Transactions involved). Provided 4 quotations are received the arithmetic mean of these quotations is used. To this is added the risk exposure calculation which is not in dispute. However, fewer than 4 quotations may be used in the recalculation of risk exposure but if no quotations are available for a particular Covered Transaction then the Valuation Agent's original calculation will be used for that Covered Transaction because it is the only reasonable thing to do in the circumstances.

This sub-paragraph has been substantially revised from the 1995 English Law CSA version in a positive way. The 1995 English Law CSA only made reference to the term "Market Quotation" which is used in the 1992 version of the ISDA Master Agreement. However, many parties are nowadays entering into the 2002 version of the Agreement which uses "Close-out Amount". Many parties also incorporate Close-out Amount terms into their 1992 Agreements or via the ISDA Close-out Amount Protocol. The clause has been updated to deal with both situations.

(C) The Valuation Agent will also follow the method stated in Paragraph 11(f)(ii) for calculating the value of collateral held. This method has to be stated in Paragraph 11(f)(ii) or the dispute resolution provisions in Paragraph 4 will not work. There is no fallback.

(ii) The Valuation Agent will directly home in on Paragraph 11(f)(ii) where the dispute solely involves the value of collateral held.

When all the recalculations have been done the Valuation Agent will notify the other party of the revised figures not later than the deadline (Notification Time) on the Local Business Day after the Resolution Time (i.e. the dispute resolution deadline agreed in the English Law VM CSA's Paragraph 11(f)(i)).

Once all is agreed a revised collateral call notice is sent and the necessary collateral transfer is made.

> (b) *No Event of Default.* The failure by a party to make a transfer of any amount which is the subject of a dispute to which Paragraph 4(a) applies will not constitute an Event of Default for as long as the procedures set out in this Paragraph 4 are being carried out. For the avoidance of doubt, upon completion of those procedures, Section 5(a)(i) of this Agreement will apply to any failure by a party to make a transfer required under the final sentence of Paragraph 4(a) on the relevant due date.

Paragraph 4(b) clarifies that failure to transfer a disputed amount does not count as an Event of Default under Paragraph 6 while the dispute resolution process is being carried out. However, when it ends and the transfer is still not made then Section 5(a)(i) of the Master Agreement – the Failure to Pay or Deliver Event of Default – comes into play and an Event of Default will be called if the transfer is not made within three Local Business Days with a 1992 Agreement or one Local Business Day with a 2002 Agreement following notice to the party who has failed to transfer the collateral. This assumes the standard grace periods apply in these Agreements. This is another way in which the English Law VM CSA links into the ISDA Master Agreement.

Paragraph 5. Transfer of Title, No Security Interest, Distributions and Interest Amount (VM)

> Paragraph 5. Transfer of Title, No Security Interest, Distributions and Interest Amount (VM)
>
> (a) *Transfer of Title.* Each party agrees that all right, title and interest in and to any Eligible Credit Support (VM), Equivalent Credit Support (VM), Equivalent Distributions or Interest Payment (VM) which it transfers to the other party under the terms of this Annex will vest in the recipient free and clear of any liens, claims, charges or encumbrances or any other interest of the transferring party or of any third person (other than a lien routinely imposed on all securities in a relevant clearance system).

Paragraph 5(a) clearly states that each party when making transfers under the Annex thereby transfers outright ownership to the collateral concerned or any distributions or interest on it to the other party free of all encumbrances except for any liens (charges to cover custody fees) routinely imposed on all bonds by clearing systems.

(b) *No Security Interest*. Nothing in this Annex is intended to create or does create in favour of either party any mortgage, charge, lien, pledge, encumbrance or other security interest in any cash or other property transferred by one party to the other party under the terms of this Annex.

Paragraph 5(b) expressly states that no security interest of any kind is being created under the Annex. In other words it is a pure title transfer document.

(c) *Distributions and Interest Amount.*

(i) *Distributions*. The Transferee will transfer to the Transferor not later than the Settlement Day following each Distributions Date cash, securities or other property of the same type, nominal value, description and amount as the relevant Distributions (*"Equivalent Distributions"*) to the extent that a Delivery Amount (VM) would not be created or increased by the transfer, as calculated by the Valuation Agent (and the date of calculation will be deemed a Valuation Date for this purpose).

(c)(i) A key principle of collateral arrangements is that the collateral giver should not be disadvantaged by them. While ownership of the collateral clearly passes to the collateral taker it is anticipated that at some point in the future the collateral taker will be obliged to return the collateral to the collateral giver e.g. when risk exposure moves in favour of the collateral giver or when the transactions covered by the collateral expire.

During this period coupons will be paid on bonds to the Transferee (the collateral taker) because he will be registered as their owner in the books of the bond issuer. Once the coupon has been received, the Transferee then makes a separate payment to the Transferor equivalent to 100% of the coupon payment received from the bond issuer. This is what is stipulated in Paragraph 5(c)(i). This payment is known in the market as a manufactured dividend or a manufactured coupon.

Where, for tax reasons, a collateral taker is reluctant or concerned about doing this, parties provide for this in Paragraph 11(k) Other Provisions and arrange a bond substitution before the coupon payment date.

However, such payments are not made if they give rise to creating or increasing a collateral call. In these circumstances they will remain part of the collateral balance held by the collateral taker. This is because part of a bond's price is the interest accrued upon it and when that is paid to the holder, the bond's price normally falls. If the payment of that accrued interest via a manufactured dividend is made it could result in a collateral call but in this case the call is not made and the accrued interest is added to the Credit Support Balance (VM).

(ii) *Interest Payment (VM)*. Unless otherwise specified in Paragraph 11(g)(iv):

(A) if "Interest Transfer" is specified as applicable in Paragraph 11(g)(ii), the Interest Payer (VM) will transfer to the Interest Payee (VM), at the times specified in Paragraph 11(g)(ii) and on any Early Termination Date referred to in Paragraph 6, the relevant Interest Payment (VM), *provided* that if "Interest Payment Netting" is specified as applicable in Paragraph 11(g)(ii):

(I) if the Interest Payer (VM) is entitled to demand a Delivery Amount (VM) or Return Amount (VM) in respect of the date such Interest Payment (VM) is required to be transferred:

(a) such Delivery Amount (VM) or Return Amount (VM) will be reduced (but not below zero) by the Interest Payment (VM), *provided* that, in case of such Return Amount (VM), if the amount in the Credit Support Balance (VM) which is comprised of cash in the Base Currency is less than such Interest Payment (VM), such reduction will only be to the extent of the amount of such cash comprised in the Credit Support Balance (VM) (the *"Eligible Return Amount (VM)"*); and

(b) the Interest Payer (VM) will transfer to the Interest Payee (VM) the amount of the excess, if any, of such Interest Payment (VM) over such Delivery Amount (VM) or Eligible Return Amount (VM), as applicable;

(II) if under Paragraph 5(c)(ii)(A)(I)(a) a Delivery Amount (VM) is reduced (the amount of such reduction, the *"Delivery Amount Reduction (VM)"*) or a Return Amount (VM) is reduced (the amount of such reduction, the *"Return Amount Reduction (VM)"*), then for purposes of calculating the Credit Support Balance (VM) only, the Transferee will be deemed to have received an amount in cash in the Base Currency equal to any Delivery Amount Reduction (VM) and will be deemed to have transferred an amount in cash in the Base Currency equal to any Return Amount Reduction (VM), as applicable, in each case on the day on which the relevant Interest Payment (VM) was due to be transferred; and

(B) if "Interest Adjustment" is specified as applicable in Paragraph 11(g)(ii), the Credit Support Balance (VM) will be adjusted by the Transferee, at the times specified in Paragraph 11(g)(ii) and on any Early Termination Date referred to in Paragraph 6 as follows:

(I) if the Interest Amount (VM) for an Interest Period is a positive number, the Interest Amount (VM) will constitute an addition of an amount of cash in the Base Currency comprised in the Credit Support Balance (VM); and

(II) if the Interest Amount (VM) for an Interest Period is a negative number, the Interest Amount (VM) will constitute a reduction to the amount of cash in the Base Currency comprised in the Credit Support Balance (VM) in an amount (such amount, the *"Interest Adjustment Reduction Amount (VM)"*) equal to the absolute value of the Interest Amount (VM); *provided* that if the amount in the Credit Support Balance (VM) which is comprised of cash in the Base Currency is less than the Interest Adjustment Reduction Amount (VM), such reduction will only be to the extent of the amount of such cash comprised in the Credit Support Balance (VM) and the Transferor will be obliged to transfer the remainder of the Interest Adjustment Reduction Amount (VM) to the Transferee on the day that such reduction occurred.

In Paragraph 5(c)(ii) Interest Payment (VM) is the interest amount payable by the collateral taker on cash deposits he holds as collateral from the collateral giver. The frequency at which cash interest is paid over to the collateral giver or adjusted as part of the Credit Support Balance (VM) is stated in Paragraph 11(g)(ii). It is usually monthly.

The interest provisions in the English Law VM CSA have been substantially amended from those in the 1995 English Law CSA.

New defined terms such as "Interest Transfer", "Interest Payment Netting" and "Interest Adjustment" have been introduced.

In addition, "Interest Payer (VM)" and "Interest Payee (VM)" have been added as defined terms. In the 1995 English Law CSA it was assumed that the Transferee would always be the party who would be required to pay interest. However, this is not necessarily the case where negative interest rates apply and the Transferor may in fact be the party who is required to do so.

Paragraph 5(c)(ii)(A) outlines the procedure when Interest Transfer applies. The Interest Payer (VM) will transfer interest to the Interest Payee (VM) on the frequency specified in Paragraph 11(g)(ii). Typically such interest is paid in arrears on the first, second or third Local Business Day of the month depending upon a party's operational capability. If an Early Termination Date has been designated under the ISDA Master Agreement then any outstanding interest will also be paid then.

When Interest Transfer applies, the parties will also choose whether Interest Payment Netting is applied. This is a process whereby the parties can net any interest payments that are due against any Delivery Amount (VM) or Return Amount (VM) payable on the same day. It is only possible to offset these amounts if:

1. the Interest Payment (VM) is less than the Delivery Amount (VM) or Return Amount (VM); or
2. the amount of cash held as part of the Credit Support Balance (VM) is less than the Interest Payment (VM) i.e. this can only be offset against the cash held (and not against the value of any securities collateral).

If the value of the Interest Payment (VM) is more than the Delivery Amount (VM) or the Return Amount (VM) compared with the cash in the Credit Support Balance (VM), the additional amount of interest is payable.

Paragraph 5(c)(ii)(A)(II) clarifies that while the Delivery Amount (VM) / Return Amount (VM) and Interest Payment (VM) are offset and therefore a single net payment is made, the two payments are deemed to have been made separately for the purposes of calculating the Credit Support Balance (VM).

Please note that it is not common in the market for parties to apply Interest Payment Netting. Typically interest transfers are handled separately from collateral transfers.

Paragraph 5(c)(ii)(B) details the process when Interest Adjustment applies. In this case, interest is not transferred to the other party but instead the Credit Support Balance (VM) is adjusted. The provision looks at two scenarios:

1. The Interest Amount (VM) is positive and therefore added to the Credit Support Balance (VM).
2. The Interest Amount (VM) is negative and therefore a reduction is made to the Credit Support Balance (VM). If the Interest Amount (VM) is more that the amount of cash held as part of the Credit Support Balance (VM) then only the cash portion can be offset. Any additional Interest Amount (VM) will need to be transferred to the other party on the same day as the partial reduction of the Credit Support Balance (VM) takes place.

Paragraph 6. Default

Paragraph 6. Default

If an Early Termination Date is designated or deemed to occur as a result of an Event of Default in relation to a party, an amount equal to the Value of the Credit Support Balance (VM), determined as though the Early Termination Date were a Valuation Date, will be deemed to be an Unpaid Amount due to the Transferor (which may or may not be the Defaulting Party) for purposes of Section 6(e). For the avoidance of doubt (a) any Market Quotation determined under Section 6(e) in relation to the Transaction constituted by this Annex will be deemed to be zero, (b) any Loss determined under Section 6(e) in relation to the Transaction constituted by this Annex will be limited to the Unpaid Amount representing the Value of the relevant Credit Support Balance (VM) and any unsatisfied obligations with respect to the transfer of an Interest Payment (VM); (c) any Close-out Amount determined under Section 6(e) in relation to the Transaction constituted by this Annex will be deemed to be zero; and (d) no Unpaid Amount will be determined with respect to an unsatisfied obligation under Paragraph 2 and Paragraph 3(c).

This is a technical Paragraph but very important. First of all in a close-out situation under the Master Agreement the date on which termination calculations are made (the Early Termination Date) will be treated as if it were Valuation Date under the English Law VM CSA. In addition the collateral previously transferred by the collateral giver to the collateral taker becomes an Unpaid Amount under the early termination provisions of Section 6 of the Master Agreement.

Close-out involves the netting off of the termination values of all Transactions under Section 6 of the ISDA Master Agreement and bringing Unpaid Amounts into the close-out calculations.

The Credit Support Balance (VM) held by the collateral taker is deemed to be an Unpaid Amount owing to the collateral giver (who could be but need not be the Defaulting Party). The Master Agreement works whether the Transferee is the Defaulting Party or the Non-defaulting Party.

Of course, the Unpaid Amount needs to be valued.

This part of Paragraph 6 has been updated from the 1995 English Law CSA version to address the different payment measures included in the 1992 and 2002 versions of the ISDA Master Agreement.

In Part 1(f) of the 1992 Master Agreement Schedule the payment measure for calculating termination payments is chosen. Market Quotation involves obtaining close-out quotations for Transactions from up to four leading dealers and taking the arithmetic mean of the two remaining quotations after discarding the highest and the lowest. Loss is a more subjective measure and is the Non-defaulting Party's good faith calculation of its losses and costs minus its gains.

Here there is no need to obtain four quotations on the likely value of the collateral and so Market Quotation is jettisoned as inappropriate. It will be deemed to be zero which is no help at all in calculating the Unpaid Amount's value. Loss is fallen back on to value the Unpaid Amount requested by the Non-defaulting Party. However, Loss is limited to 100% of the collateral's value because in a termination situation the collateral is valued at 100% of its market value and all haircuts are ignored. Unpaid Interest Payments (VM) are also taken into account if relevant.

Reference to Close-out Amount is now also included in this provision on the same basis as Market Quotation (i.e. it is deemed to be zero). This is because information under Close-out Amount is weighted towards quotations from third party dealers or other market sources or internal valuation sources and is therefore seen as inappropriate.

Finally unfulfilled delivery or return obligations in Paragraph 2 or unfulfilled substitutions in Paragraph 3(c) shall not constitute Unpaid Amounts for the purposes of Paragraph 6.

This whole process is another way in which the English Law VM CSA links into the ISDA Master Agreement.

Paragraph 7. Representation

Paragraph 7. Representation

Each party represents to the other party (which representation will be deemed to be repeated as of each date on which it transfers Eligible Credit Support (VM), Equivalent Credit Support (VM) or Equivalent Distributions) that it is the sole owner of or otherwise has the right to transfer all Eligible Credit Support (VM), Equivalent Credit Support (VM) or Equivalent Distributions it transfers to the other party under this Annex, free and clear of any security interest, lien, encumbrance or other restriction (other than a lien routinely imposed on all securities in a relevant clearance system).

This is a representation that each transferring party confirms to the other that it is the sole owner or has the sole right to transfer the relevant collateral and any distributions on it. It repeats that transfers are free of encumbrances in the same manner as in Paragraph 5(a).

Paragraph 8. Expenses

> **Paragraph 8. Expenses**
>
> Each party will pay its own costs and expenses (including any stamp, transfer or similar transaction tax or duty payable on any transfer it is required to make under this Annex) in connection with performing its obligations under this Annex, and neither party will be liable for any such costs and expenses incurred by the other party.

This is a simple statement that each party will pay its own costs and expenses (including any stamp or transfer taxes payable on transfers made under the English Law VM CSA) and will not be liable for any incurred by the other party.

Paragraph 9. Miscellaneous

This contains a number of protective boilerplate provisions.

> **Paragraph 9. Miscellaneous**
>
> (a) *Default Interest*. Other than in the case of an amount which is the subject of a dispute under Paragraph 4, if a Transferee fails to make, when due, any transfer of Equivalent Credit Support (VM) or Equivalent Distributions, it will be obliged to pay the Transferor (to the extent permitted under applicable law) an amount equal to interest at the Default Rate multiplied by the Value on the relevant Valuation Date of the items of property that were required to be transferred, from (and including) the date that the Equivalent Credit Support (VM) or Equivalent Distributions were required to be transferred to (but excluding) the date of transfer of the Equivalent Credit Support (VM) or Equivalent Distributions. This interest will be calculated on the basis of daily compounding and the actual number of days elapsed. Other than in the case of an amount which is the subject of a dispute under Paragraph 4, if an Interest Payer (VM) fails to make, when due, any transfer of an Interest Payment (VM), it will be obliged to pay the Interest Payee (VM) (to the extent permitted under applicable law) an amount equal to interest at the Default Rate (and for such purposes, if the Default Rate is less than zero, it will be deemed to be zero) multiplied by that Interest Payment (VM), from (and including) the date that Interest Payment (VM) was required to be transferred to (but excluding) the date of transfer of that Interest Payment (VM). This interest will be calculated on the basis of daily compounding and the actual number of days elapsed.

Paragraph 9(a) states that the Transferee will pay default interest to the Transferor for any overdue return of securities collateral or interest or dividends on it. Similarly the Interest Payer (VM) will also pay default interest to the Interest Payee (VM) for any overdue payment of interest on cash collateral. This default interest is calculated at the Default Rate (1% over the Transferor's or Interest Payee (VM)'s cost of funds) from and including the date the transfer was due to be made to but excluding the date that it was made. It will also be subject to daily compounding in both cases.

If the Default Rate is a negative figure, it will be deemed to be zero.

> (b) *Good Faith and Commercially Reasonable Manner.* Performance of all obligations under this Annex, including, but not limited to, all calculations, valuations and determinations made by either party, will be made in good faith and in a commercially reasonable manner.

(b) Each party must perform all its obligations under the English Law VM CSA in good faith and in a commercially reasonable manner.

> (c) *Demands and Notices.* All demands and notices given by a party under this Annex will be given as specified in Section 12 of this Agreement.

(c) All demands and notices under the English Law CSA will be given in one of the traditional or electronic means referred to in Section 12 of the Master Agreement.

> (d) *Specifications of Certain Matters.* Anything referred to in this Annex as being specified in Paragraph 11 also may be specified in one or more Confirmations or other documents and this Annex will be construed accordingly.

(d) This relatively inconspicuous provision enables any matters referred to in a Confirmation or other document which could alternatively be stated in the English Law VM CSA's Paragraph 11, to be interpreted as being a provision of the English Law VM CSA itself. If any such use of a Confirmation is made it should state that the provision will survive the maturity of the Transaction which is the subject of the Confirmation. How an Operations Department would monitor such usage of a Confirmation in a long dated Transaction is another question.

(e) *Legally Ineligible Credit Support (VM)*.

Unless otherwise specified in Paragraph 11, upon delivery of a Legal Ineligibility Notice by a party, each item of Eligible Credit Support (VM) (or a specified amount of such item) identified in such notice (i) will cease to be Eligible Credit Support (VM) for purposes of transfers to such party as the Transferee hereunder as of the applicable Transfer Ineligibility Date, (ii) will cease to be Eligible Credit Support (VM) for the other party as the Transferor for all purposes hereunder (other than for the purposes of the definitions of Credit Support Balance (VM) and Equivalent Credit Support (VM)) as of the Total Ineligibility Date and (iii) will have a Value of zero on and from the Total Ineligibility Date, other than for the purposes of Paragraph 6.

"Legal Ineligibility Notice" means a written notice from the Transferee to the Transferor in which the Transferee (i) represents that the Transferee has determined that one or more items of Eligible Credit Support (VM) (or a specified amount of any such item) either has ceased to satisfy, or as of a specified date will cease to satisfy, collateral eligibility requirements under law applicable to the Transferee requiring the collection of variation margin (the *"Legal Eligibility Requirements"*), (ii) lists the item(s) of Eligible Credit Support (VM) (and, if applicable, the specified amount of such item) that have ceased to satisfy, or as of a specified date will cease to satisfy, the Legal Eligibility Requirements, (iii) describes the reason(s) why such item(s) of Eligible Credit Support (VM) (or the specified amount thereof) have ceased to satisfy, or will cease to satisfy, the Legal Eligibility Requirements and (iv) specifies the Total Ineligibility Date and, if different, the Transfer Ineligibility Date.

"Total Ineligibility Date" means the date on which the relevant item of Eligible Credit Support (VM) (or a specified amount of such item) has ceased to satisfy, or will cease to satisfy, the Legal Eligibility Requirements applicable to the Transferee for all purposes hereunder, *provided* that, unless otherwise specified in Paragraph 11, if such date is earlier than the fifth Local Business Day following the date on which the Legal Ineligibility Notice is delivered, the Total Ineligibility Date will be the fifth Local Business Day following the date of such delivery.

"Transfer Ineligibility Date" means the date on which the relevant item of Eligible Credit Support (VM) (or a specified amount of such item) has ceased to satisfy, or will cease to satisfy, the Legal Eligibility Requirements for purposes of transfers to the Transferee hereunder, *provided* that, unless otherwise specified in Paragraph 11, if such date is earlier than the fifth Local

> Business Day following the date on which the Legal Ineligibility Notice is delivered, the Transfer Ineligibility Date will be the fifth Local Business Day following the date of such delivery.

Paragraphs (e)-(h) are new to the English Law VM CSA.

(e) Introduces the concept of Legally Ineligible Credit Support (VM) and how it should be handled. Uncleared OTC derivative margin regulations in various countries provide a list of types of collateral that are allowed for variation margin requirements. Sometimes there will be restrictions on certain collateral types. For example this could be a minimum credit rating.

In these cases, existing collateral held may become legally ineligible. If the Transferee identifies that this has happened, it is required to notify the Transferor by delivering a Legal Ineligibility Notice.

This written notice must include the following:

- A representation that one or more types of collateral (in whole or in part) do not or will not on a future specified date meet the collateral eligibility requirements under the relevant uncleared OTC derivative margin law(s) applicable to the Transferee;
- A list of the types of collateral that are impacted;
- The reason why such collateral no longer fulfils or will not fulfil the Legal Eligibility Requirements; and
- The date on which the collateral has or will become ineligible. This can be one of two dates viz:
  - *Transfer Ineligibility Date*: the date on which certain collateral items have or will no longer meet the Legal Eligibility Requirements for the purposes of **transfers to the Transferee** (i.e. no more collateral of this type can be transferred to the Transferee but collateral of this type that is currently held by the Transferee is still eligible and valued);
  - *Total Ineligibility Date*: the date on which certain collateral items have or will no longer meet the Legal Eligibility Requirements applicable to the Transferee for **all other purposes** (i.e. all collateral of this type is now ineligible and valued at zero except for close-out purposes under Paragraph 6); in each case provided that if the ineligibility date is earlier than the fifth Local Business Day after the notice is received then the Transfer Ineligibility Date or the Total Ineligibility Date will be the fifth Local Business Day following delivery of the notice.

As mentioned above, once a Legal Ineligibility Notice has been delivered, the impacted collateral will no longer be eligible following the Total Ineligibility Date and will be valued at zero except in a close-out situation under Paragraph 6.

However, existing collateral of this type that is already held before the Transfer Ineligibility Date will retain its value until the Total Ineligibility Date.

> (f) *Return of Equivalent Credit Support (VM).* The Transferee will, promptly upon demand (but in no event later than the time at which a transfer would be due under Paragraph 3(a) with respect to a demand for the transfer of Eligible Credit Support (VM) or Equivalent Credit Support (VM)), transfer to the Transferor Equivalent Credit Support (VM) in respect of any item comprised in the Credit Support Balance (VM) (or the specified amount of such item) that as of the date of such demand has a Value of zero; *provided* that the Transferee will only be obligated to transfer any Equivalent Credit Support (VM) in accordance with this Paragraph 9(f), if, as of the date of transfer of such item, the Transferor has satisfied all of its transfer obligations under this Annex, if any.

(f) If any collateral has a Value of zero (i.e. if it is no longer eligible) then the Transferee is required to return such collateral upon demand by the Transferor provided that he has satisfied all of his transfer obligations under the English Law VM CSA. It is likely that if an item of Eligible Credit Support (VM) is valued at zero then the Transferee would be undercollateralised and would need to call for more collateral in a form that is eligible. The Return of Equivalent Credit Support (VM) outlined in Paragraph 9(f) is likely to follow a process similar to that used for substitution as outlined in Paragraph 3(c).

> (g) *Reinstatement of Credit Support Eligibility.* Upon a reasonable request by the Transferor, the Transferee will determine whether an item (or a specified amount of such item) of Eligible Credit Support (VM) that was the subject of a prior Legal Ineligibility Notice would currently satisfy the Legal Eligibility Requirements applicable to the Transferee. If the Transferee determines that as of such date of determination such item (or specified amount of such item) satisfies the Legal Eligibility Requirements applicable to the Transferee, the Transferee will promptly following such determination rescind the relevant Legal Ineligibility Notice with respect to such item (or specified amount of such item) by written notice to the Transferor. Upon the delivery of such notice, the relevant item (or specified amount of such item) will constitute Eligible Credit Support (VM) hereunder.

This sub-paragraph deals with the situation where the Transferor believes that collateral that was previously categorised as legally ineligible has become eligible again. He can request that the Transferee reviews and determines if it is still ineligible or not. If it is eligible then the Transferee will promptly provide a written notice withdrawing his previous relevant Legal Ineligibility Notice and the collateral will become legally eligible again.

> (h) **Credit Support Offsets.** If the parties specify that "Credit Support Offsets" is applicable in Paragraph 11 and on any date:
>
> (i) a transfer of Eligible Credit Support (VM) or Equivalent Credit Support (VM) is due under this Annex to satisfy a Delivery Amount (VM) or a Return Amount (VM) obligation, and a transfer of credit support (other than any Other CSA Excluded Credit Support) is also due under any Other CSA;
> (ii) the parties have notified each other of the credit support that they intend to transfer under this Annex and transfer under such Other CSA (other than any Other CSA Excluded Credit Support) to satisfy their respective obligations; and
> (iii) in respect of Paragraph 9(h)(ii), each party intends to transfer one or more types of credit support that is fully fungible with one or more types of credit support the other party intends to transfer (each such credit support, a *"Fungible Credit Support Type"*),
> then, on such date and in respect of each such Fungible Credit Support Type, each party's obligation to make a transfer of any such Fungible Credit Support Type hereunder or under such Other CSA will be automatically satisfied and discharged and, if the aggregate amount that would have otherwise been transferred by one party exceeds the aggregate amount that would have otherwise been transferred by the other party, replaced by an obligation hereunder or under such Other CSA, as applicable, upon the party by which the larger aggregate amount would have been transferred to transfer to the other party the excess of the larger aggregate amount over the smaller aggregate amount. If a party's obligation to make a transfer of credit support under this Annex or an Other CSA is automatically satisfied and discharged pursuant to this Paragraph 9(h), then for purposes of this Annex or the Other CSA, as applicable, the other party will be deemed to have received credit support of the applicable Fungible Credit Support Type in the amount that would otherwise have been required to be transferred, in each case on the day on which the relevant transfer was due.

(h) If Credit Support Offsets are chosen to apply in Paragraph 11(h) the parties are able to offset collateral deliveries between different CSAs which are due to be made on the same day. In many cases the parties may have two CSAs in place – an existing 1995 English Law CSA for trades entered into before the relevant margin regulatory implementation date and a new English Law VM CSA for trades after this date. This effectively means that there are two collateral pools existing at the same time. Depending on market movements, it is possible that one party is required to post collateral under the old CSA and the other party is required to post collateral under the new English Law VM CSA. Rather than two transfers taking place, the parties can agree to offset the amounts due and only one transfer will be made by the party with the higher amount to transfer to cover the excess. However, this is only possible if the types of collateral being transferred are fully fungible (e.g. (a) cash or (b) bonds issued by the same issuer, of the same issue and the same nominal value).

Therefore, Credit Support Offsets allow parties effectively to settlement net transfers of collateral between CSAs provided that the collateral in question is fully fungible and does not need to be segregated.

Most parties would like to implement Credit Support Offsets to reduce operational burdens and risks but currently very few entities have the systems or operational capability do to this. This point therefore needs to be carefully considered during negotiation of the terms of their English Law VM CSA.

Paragraph 10. Definitions

This Paragraph provides an extensive list of definitions used throughout the English Law VM CSA.

Paragraph 10. Definitions

As used in this Annex:

"Base Currency" means the currency specified as such in Paragraph 11(a)(i).

"Base Currency Equivalent" means, with respect to an amount on a Valuation Date, in the case of an amount denominated in the Base Currency, such Base Currency amount and, in the case of an amount denominated in a currency other than the Base Currency (the *"Other Currency"*), the amount of Base Currency required to purchase such amount of the Other Currency at the spot exchange rate on such Valuation Date as determined by the Valuation Agent.

"Covered Transaction" has the meaning specified in Paragraph 11(b).

"Credit Support Balance (VM)" means, with respect to a Transferor on a Valuation Date, the aggregate of all Eligible Credit Support (VM) that has

been transferred to or received by the Transferee under this Annex, together with any Distributions and all proceeds of any such Eligible Credit Support (VM) or Distributions, as reduced pursuant to Paragraph 2(b), 3(c)(ii) or 6 and as adjusted pursuant to Paragraph 5(c)(ii). Any Equivalent Distributions (or portion thereof) not transferred pursuant to Paragraph 5(c)(i) will form part of the Credit Support Balance (VM).

"Credit Support Eligibility Condition (VM)" means, with respect to any item specified for a party as Eligible Credit Support (VM) in Paragraph 11(c)(ii), any condition specified for that item in Paragraph 11(c)(iv).

"Delivery Amount (VM)" has the meaning specified in Paragraph 2(a).

"Delivery Amount Reduction (VM)" has the meaning specified in Paragraph 5(c)(ii)(A)(II).

"Disputing Party" has the meaning specified in Paragraph 4.

"Distributions" means, with respect to any Eligible Credit Support (VM) comprised in the Credit Support Balance (VM) consisting of securities, all principal, interest and other payments and distributions of cash or other property to which a holder of securities of the same type, nominal value, description and amount as such Eligible Credit Support (VM) would be entitled from time to time.

"Distributions Date" means, with respect to any Eligible Credit Support (VM) comprised in the Credit Support Balance (VM) other than cash, each date on which a holder of such Eligible Credit Support (VM) is entitled to receive Distributions or, if that date is not a Local Business Day, the next following Local Business Day.

"Eligible Credit Support (VM)" means, with respect to a party, the items, if any, specified as such for that party in Paragraph 11(c)(ii) including, in relation to any securities, if applicable, the proceeds of any redemption in whole or in part of such securities by the relevant issuer.

"Eligible Currency" means each currency specified as such in Paragraph 11(a)(ii), if such currency is freely available.

"Eligible Return Amount (VM)" has the meaning specified in Paragraph 5(c)(ii)(A)(I)(a).

"Equivalent Credit Support (VM)" means, in relation to any Eligible Credit Support (VM) comprised in the Credit Support Balance (VM), Eligible Credit Support (VM) of the same type, nominal value, description and amount as that Eligible Credit Support (VM).

"Equivalent Distributions" has the meaning specified in Paragraph 5(c)(i).

"Exchange Date" has the meaning specified in Paragraph 11(e).

"Exposure" means, unless otherwise specified in Paragraph 11 for any Valuation Date or other date for which Exposure is calculated and subject to Paragraph 4 in the case of a dispute:

(i) if this Agreement is a 1992 ISDA Master Agreement, the amount, if any, that would be payable to that party by the other party (expressed as a positive number) or by that party to the other party (expressed as a negative number) pursuant to Section 6(e)(ii)(1) of this Agreement if all Covered Transactions (other than the Transaction constituted by this Annex) were being terminated as of the relevant Valuation Time on the basis that (A) that party is not the Affected Party and (B) the Base Currency is the Termination Currency; *provided* that Market Quotations will be determined by the Valuation Agent on behalf of that party using its estimates at mid-market of the amounts that would be paid for Replacement Transactions (as that term is defined in the definition of "Market Quotation"); and

(ii) if this Agreement is an ISDA 2002 Master Agreement or a 1992 ISDA Master Agreement in which the definition of Loss and/or Market Quotation has been amended (including where such amendment has occurred pursuant to the terms of a separate agreement or protocol) to reflect the definition of Close-out Amount from the pre-printed form of the ISDA 2002 Master Agreement as published by ISDA, the amount, if any, that would be payable to that party by the other party (expressed as a positive number) or by that party to the other party (expressed as a negative number) pursuant to Section 6(e)(ii)(1) (but without reference to clause (3) of Section 6(e)(ii)) of this Agreement as if all Covered Transactions (other than the Transactions constituted by this Annex) were being terminated as of the relevant Valuation Time on the basis that (A) that party is not the Affected Party and (B) the Base Currency is the Termination Currency; *provided* that the Close-out Amount will be determined by the Valuation Agent on behalf of that party using its estimates at mid-market of the amounts that would be paid for transactions providing the economic equivalent of (X) the material terms of the Covered Transactions, including the payments and deliveries by the parties under Section 2(a)(i) in respect of the Covered Transactions that would, but for the occurrence of the relevant Early Termination Date, have been required after that date (assuming satisfaction of the conditions precedent in Section 2(a)(iii) of this Agreement); and (Y) the option rights of the parties in respect of the Covered Transactions.

"Fungible Credit Support Type" has the meaning specified in Paragraph 9(h)(iii).

"FX Haircut Percentage" means, for any item of Eligible Credit Support (VM), the percentage specified as such in Paragraph 11(c)(v).

"Interest Adjustment Reduction Amount (VM)" has the meaning specified in Paragraph 5(c)(ii)(B)(II).

"Interest Amount (VM)" means with respect to an Interest Period, the aggregate sum of the Base Currency Equivalents of the amounts of interest determined for each relevant currency and calculated for each day in that Interest Period on the portion of the Credit Support Balance (VM) comprised of cash in such currency, determined by the Valuation Agent for each such day as follows:

(i) the amount of cash in such currency on that day plus, only if "Daily Interest Compounding" is specified as applicable in Paragraph 11(g)(iii), the aggregate of each Interest Amount (VM) determined for each preceding day, if any, in that Interest Period; multiplied by

(ii) the relevant Interest Rate (VM) in effect for that day; divided by

(iii) 360 (or, in the case of pounds sterling or any other currency specified as an "A/365 Currency" in Paragraph 11(g)(i), 365),

provided that, unless "Negative Interest" is specified as applicable in Paragraph 11(g)(iii), if the Interest Amount (VM) for an Interest Period would be a negative amount, it will be deemed to be zero.

"Interest Payee (VM)" means, in relation to an Interest Payer (VM), the other party.

"Interest Payer (VM)" means the Transferee, *provided* that if "Negative Interest" is specified as applicable in Paragraph 11(g)(iii) and an Interest Payment (VM) is determined in respect of a negative Interest Amount (VM), the Interest Payer (VM) in respect of such Interest Payment (VM) will be the Transferor.

"Interest Payment (VM)" means, with respect to an Interest Period, the Interest Amount (VM) determined in respect of such Interest Period, *provided* that in respect of any negative Interest Amount (VM), the Interest Payment (VM) will be the absolute value of such negative Interest Amount (VM).

"Interest Period" means the period from (and including) the last day on which (i) a party became obliged to transfer an Interest Payment (VM) or (ii) an Interest Amount (VM) was added to the Credit Support Balance (VM) (or, if no Interest Payment (VM) or Interest Amount (VM) has yet fallen due or been added to the Credit Support Balance (VM), respectively, the day on which Eligible Credit Support (VM) or Equivalent Credit Support (VM) in the form of cash was transferred to or received by the Transferee) to (but excluding) the day on which (i) a party is obliged to transfer the current Interest Payment (VM) or (ii) the current Interest Amount (VM) is added to the Credit Support Balance (VM).

"Interest Rate (VM)" means, with respect to an Eligible Currency, the rate specified in Paragraph 11(g)(i) for that currency.

"Legal Eligibility Requirements" has the meaning specified in Paragraph 9(e).

"Legal Ineligibility Notice" has the meaning specified in Paragraph 9(e).

"Local Business Day", unless otherwise specified in Paragraph 11(k), means:

(i) in relation to a transfer of cash or other property (other than securities) under this Annex, a day on which commercial banks are open for business (including dealings in foreign exchange and foreign currency deposits) in the place where the relevant account is located and, if different, in the principal financial centre, if any, of the currency of such payment;

(ii) in relation to a transfer of securities under this Annex, a day on which the clearance system agreed between the parties for delivery of the securities is open for the acceptance and execution of settlement instructions or, if delivery of the securities is contemplated by other means, a day on which commercial banks are open for business (including dealings in foreign exchange and foreign currency deposits) in the place(s) agreed between the parties for this purpose;

(iii) in relation to the Resolution Time, a day on which commercial banks are open for business (including dealings in foreign exchange and foreign currency deposits) in at least one Valuation Date Location for Party A and at least one Valuation Date Location for Party B; and

(iv) in relation to any notice or other communication under this Annex, a day on which commercial banks are open for business (including dealings in foreign exchange and foreign currency deposits) in the place specified in the address for notice most recently provided by the recipient.

"Minimum Transfer Amount" means, with respect to a party, the amount specified as such for that party in Paragraph 11(c)(vi)(A) or if no amount is specified, zero.

"New Credit Support (VM)" has the meaning specified in Paragraph 3(c)(i).

"Notification Time" has the meaning specified in Paragraph 11(d)(iv).

"Original Credit Support (VM)" has the meaning specified in Paragraph 3(c)(i).

"Other CSA" means, unless otherwise specified in Paragraph 11, any other credit support annex or credit support deed that is in relation to, or that is a Credit Support Document in relation to, this Agreement.

"Other CSA Excluded Credit Support" means, with respect to an Other CSA, any amounts and items transferred as credit support under such Other CSA, which, pursuant to the terms of such Other CSA, Party A and Party B have agreed must be segregated in an account maintained by a third-party custodian or for which offsets are prohibited.

"Recalculation Date" means the Valuation Date that gives rise to the dispute under Paragraph 4; *provided, however,* that if a subsequent Valuation Date occurs under Paragraph 2 prior to the resolution of the dispute, then the *"Recalculation Date"* means the most recent Valuation Date under Paragraph 2.

"Regular Settlement Day" means, unless otherwise specified in Paragraph 11, the same Local Business Day on which a demand for the transfer of Eligible Credit Support (VM) or Equivalent Credit Support (VM) is made.

"Resolution Time" has the meaning specified in Paragraph 11(f)(i).

"Return Amount (VM)" has the meaning specified in Paragraph 2(b).

"Return Amount Reduction (VM)" has the meaning specified in Paragraph 5(c)(ii)(A)(II).

"Settlement Day" means, in relation to a date, (i) with respect to a transfer of cash or other property (other than securities), the next Local Business Day and (ii) with respect to a transfer of securities, the first Local Business Day after such date on which settlement of a trade in the relevant securities, if effected on such date, would have been settled in accordance with customary practice when settling through the clearance system agreed between the parties for delivery of such securities or, otherwise, on the market in which such securities are principally traded (or, in either case, if there is no such customary practice, on the first Local Business Day after such date on which it is reasonably practicable to deliver such securities).

"Total Ineligibility Date" has the meaning specified in Paragraph 9(e), unless otherwise specified in Paragraph 11.

"Transferee" means, in relation to each Valuation Date, the party in respect of which Exposure is a positive number and, in relation to a Credit Support Balance (VM), the party which, subject to this Annex, owes such Credit Support Balance (VM) or, as the case may be, the Value of such Credit Support Balance (VM) to the other party.

"Transferor" means, in relation to a Transferee, the other party.

"Transfer Ineligibility Date" has the meaning specified in Paragraph 9(e), unless otherwise specified in Paragraph 11.

"Valuation Agent" has the meaning specified in Paragraph 11(d)(i).

"Valuation Date" means, unless otherwise specified in Paragraph 11, each day from, and including, the date of this Annex, that is a day on which commercial banks are open for business (including dealings in foreign

exchange and foreign currency deposits) in at least one Valuation Date Location for Party A and at least one Valuation Date Location for Party B.

"Valuation Date Location" has the meaning specified in Paragraph 11(d)(ii).

"Valuation Percentage" means, for any item of Eligible Credit Support (VM), the percentage specified as such in Paragraph 11(c)(v).

"Valuation Time" means, unless otherwise specified in Paragraph 11, the time as of which the Valuation Agent computes its end of day valuations of derivatives transactions in the ordinary course of its business (or such other commercially reasonable convenient time on the relevant day as the Valuation Agent may determine).

"Value" means, for any Valuation Date or other date for which Value is calculated, and subject to Paragraph 4 in the case of a dispute, with respect to:

(i) Eligible Credit Support (VM) comprised in a Credit Support Balance (VM) or Equivalent Credit Support (VM) that is:

(A) an amount of cash, the Base Currency Equivalent of such amount multiplied by $(VP - H_{FX})$, *provided* that, in the case of a determination of a Value for the purposes of Paragraph 6, the Value will be the Base Currency Equivalent of such amount; and
(B) a security, the Base Currency Equivalent of the bid price obtained by the Valuation Agent multiplied by $(VP - H_{FX})$, where:

VP equals the applicable Valuation Percentage; and

H_{FX} equals the applicable FX Haircut Percentage,

provided that, in the case of a determination of a Value for the purposes of Paragraph 6, the Value will be the Base Currency Equivalent of the bid price obtained by the Valuation Agent; and

(ii) items that are comprised in a Credit Support Balance (VM) and are not Eligible Credit Support (VM) (including any item or any portion of any item that fails to satisfy any (A) Credit Support Eligibility Conditions (VM) applicable to it or (B) applicable Legal Eligibility Requirements), zero *provided* that any items that are comprised in a Credit Support Balance (VM) that are not Eligible Credit Support (VM) will, in the case of a determination of a Value for the purposes of Paragraph 6, have a Value determined in accordance with (i) above as if they were Eligible Credit Support (VM).

No doubt with a big government health warning from lawyers and others we set out below a simplified glossary of all terms in Paragraph 10 of the English Law VM CSA.

Glossary of terms in Paragraph 10

Base Currency	The currency into which risk exposure and collateral already held is converted to calculate if a collateral call needs to be made by either party.
Base Currency Equivalent	If collateral is denominated in another currency, the amount in the Base Currency needed to purchase the other currency at the spot rate of exchange so as to convert it into the Base Currency as determined by the Valuation Agent on the Valuation Date.
Covered Transaction	The OTC derivative and FX type trades covered in Paragraph 11(b) of the English Law VM CSA.
Credit Support Balance (VM)	The actual amount of collateral held at any one time by the collateral taker under the English Law VM CSA.
Credit Support Eligibility Condition (VM)	Any restrictions or conditions relating to collateral specified in Paragraph 11(c)(iv) that must be considered when assessing whether that collateral is eligible or not under the English Law VM CSA.
Delivery Amount (VM)	The amount of collateral the collateral giver must deliver if he agrees with a collateral call from the collateral taker under the English Law VM CSA.
Delivery Amount Reduction (VM)	The amount by which a Delivery Amount (VM) is reduced by an offsetting interest payment where the parties have agreed that Interest Transfer and Interest Payment Netting apply.

Disputing Party	A party who reasonably disputes the Valuation Agent's calculation of Covered Transaction values in determining risk exposure and/or the value of collateral held or to be returned under the English Law VM CSA.
Distributions	Periodic payments of interest on bonds or dividends on shares by their issuers to their holders. Interest on cash collateral is excluded from this definition.
Distributions Date	The date, which must be a Local Business Day, upon which holders of bonds or shares are entitled to receive interest or dividends from their issuers.
Eligible Credit Support (VM)	The types of eligible collateral with haircuts applied which may be transferred by the parties under Paragraph 11(c)(ii) of the English Law VM CSA.
Eligible Currency	The freely available currencies specified in Paragraph 11(a)(ii) for cash collateral transferable under the English Law VM CSA.
Eligible Return Amount (VM)	The amount of cash collateral held which is taken into account when calculating whether an interest payment can be netted or offset and if so, how much of it can be offset or netted.
Equivalent Credit Support (VM)	The collateral which the collateral taker is obliged to return to the collateral giver when its risk exposure on the collateral giver reduces or when the collateral taker agrees a substitution. The returned collateral must be of the same issuer, class, type and issue but need not be the identically numbered bonds or shares originally received.
Equivalent Distributions	The separate payment or manufactured dividend the collateral taker makes to the collateral giver equal to 100% of the interest or dividend he has received from the bond or share issuer.
Exchange Date	The deadline for the collateral taker to return previously delivered collateral to the collateral giver following an agreed substitution.

Exposure	The estimated termination value of all Covered Transactions so as to calculate risk exposure. The calculation is made as if the Covered Transactions were being closed out as at the Valuation Time using the methodologies in Section 6(e) of either the 1992 ISDA Master Agreement or the 2002 ISDA Master Agreement.
Fungible Credit Support Type	Collateral of the same type (e.g. (a) cash or (b) bonds issued by the same issuer, of the same issue and the same nominal value) which one party wishes to transfer to the other party for settlement netting purposes.
FX Haircut Percentage	An additional haircut (typically 8%) which may be applied to collateral if certain conditions apply under the relevant uncleared margin regulations applicable to the party concerned typically if the currency concerned is not an Eligible Currency or not a defined Major Currency depending on the relevant regulatory regime.
Interest Adjustment Reduction Amount (VM)	The amount by which cash collateral held is reduced by offsetting interest (which may be at a negative rate) where the parties have agreed that Interest Adjustment applies.
Interest Amount (VM)	The aggregate sum of interest due on cash collateral in the Base Currency. If Negative Interest rates do not apply and the interest amount for an interest period is negative, it shall be deemed to be zero.
Interest Payee (VM)	The party due to receive an interest payment on cash collateral.
Interest Payer (VM)	The party required to make an interest payment on cash collateral. Normally this is the Transferee but if negative interest rates apply and are not deemed to be zero, the Transferor.
Interest Payment (VM)	The amount of interest that has accrued during an Interest Period. Where Negative Interest applies, the absolute value of the negative Interest Amount (VM) is used.

Interest Period	Basically the period from and including the date when interest was last paid on cash collateral to but excluding the date on which it is next due to be paid.
Interest Rate (VM)	The particular benchmark interest rate (e.g. EONIA) stated in Paragraph 11(g) of the English Law VM CSA which the parties agree shall be paid on cash deposited as collateral. It may also include a spread.
Legal Eligibility Requirements	The minimum requirements under the law applicable to the collateral taker for collateral to be eligible under the English Law VM CSA.
Legal Ineligibility Notice	A written notice from the Transferee to the Transferor providing details of why one or more types of Eligible Credit Support (VM) are no longer eligible as collateral.
Local Business Day	A normal business day for commercial banks in the location required for the valuation of Covered Transactions and collateral under the English Law VM CSA. With securities transfers it is a normal business day when securities clearance systems are open. Where there is a dispute, it is where commercial banks are open in at least one business centre for each party.
Minimum Transfer Amount	The minimum amount that the Delivery Amount (VM) or Return Amount (VM) must reach before a party can be called to deliver or return collateral.
New Credit Support (VM)	Where agreed by the collateral taker, collateral transferred by the collateral giver in substitution for other collateral already held by the collateral taker.
Notification Time	The agreed deadline for making a collateral call so that same day transfer of collateral can be achieved.
Original Credit Support (VM)	Collateral held by the Transferee which the Transferor would like to substitute with New Credit Support (VM).
Other CSA	Any other credit support annex or credit support deed linked to the same ISDA Master Agreement.

Other CSA Excluded Credit Support	Any amounts of collateral posted under an Other CSA which must be kept segregated in an account with a third party custodian or which cannot be offset.
Recalculation Date	In a dispute, the date or dates upon which recalculation of Covered Transactions and collateral values are made under the English Law VM CSA.
Regular Settlement Day	The day on which collateral must be provided following a collateral call. This is the same Local Business Day as the demand unless amended in Paragraph 11(c)(vii).
Resolution Time	The deadline for resolving disputes i.e. one Local Business Day after the date on which the party receives a notice that it disputes.
Return Amount (VM)	The collateral amount to be returned by the collateral taker to the collateral giver because it is surplus to the collateral taker's risk exposure on the collateral giver.
Return Amount Reduction (VM)	The amount by which a Return Amount (VM) is reduced by an offsetting interest payment where the parties have agreed that Interest Transfer and Interest Payment Netting apply under the English Law VM CSA.
Settlement Day	This definition is used in relation to substitutions and distributions. For cash collateral transfers, the following Local Business Day. For securities collateral, the next Local Business Day when transfer of such securities can be completed in their normal settlement cycle.
Total Ineligibility Date	Following the delivery of a Legal Ineligibility Notice, the date upon which collateral that is already held will be deemed ineligible under the English Law VM CSA.
Transferee	The collateral taker.
Transferor	The collateral giver.

Transfer Ineligibility Date	The date upon which collateral in the form specified in a Legal Ineligibility Notice will no longer be accepted by the Transferee. Collateral of this type that is already held will still be considered eligible and will continue to be valued until the Total Ineligibility Date.
Valuation Agent	The relevant party to the English Law VM CSA performing their valuations of Covered Transactions and collateral and making calls as appropriate or a third party doing this for them. For example, a Transferor would be the Valuation Agent if it were making a demand for a return of collateral.
Valuation Date	The date upon which risk exposure calculations and collateral valuations are made (based upon those amounts as at the Valuation Time) to determine if a collateral delivery or return is needed. This is each day on which commercial banks are open for business in at least one Valuation Date Location for each party.
Valuation Date Location	The location(s) specified in Paragraph 11(d)(ii) for each party which must be open in order for a Valuation Date to be effective.
Valuation Percentage	The remaining value of collateral expressed in percentage terms after the agreed haircut has been deducted.
Valuation Time	The reference time at which calculations for collateral calls are made. This is the time when the Valuation Agent normally calculates its end of day valuations for OTC derivative trades.
Value	The agreed valuation bases for cash and securities collateral required to value collateral in the normal course of business. The revised language in the English Law VM CSA takes into account any FX Haircut Percentage. It is confirmed that in a Paragraph 6 close-out situation all collateral including ineligible collateral which is still held will have a full market valuation without haircuts or FX Haircut Percentages.

Paragraph 11. Elections and Variables

Paragraph 11 is the English Law VM CSA's Elections and Variables Paragraph where parties can make various choices for their margining relationship. However great care is needed in its completion if the parties are to gain the protection they seek.

> ### Paragraph 11. Elections and Variables
>
> (a) *Base Currency and Eligible Currency.*
>
> (i) *"Base Currency"* means [•] unless otherwise specified here:
> ....
> (ii) *"Eligible Currency"* means the Base Currency and each other currency specified here: ....
> ....

Base Currency

The Base Currency is the currency into which the calculation of collateral and the risk exposure are converted in order to determine if a collateral call is needed.

Eligible Currency

These are the currencies the parties are willing to accept as cash collateral from each other.

> (b) *"Covered Transactions"; "Exposure"*
>
> The term *"Covered Transactions"* as used in this Annex includes any Transaction specified below that is entered into on or after [....................][3], except as otherwise provided in the Confirmation of such Transaction:
>
> For purposes of the foregoing, the term *"Covered Transactions"* includes: [Any Transaction [that is any of the following] [Swap], [Security-Based Swap], [OTC Derivative], [Physically Settled FX Forward] or [Physically Settled FX Swap]] [and is not any of the following: [Swap], [Security-Based Swap], [OTC Derivative], [Physically Settled FX Forward] or [Physically Settled FX Swap]][4] ....]

As used above:

["OTC Derivative" means an "OTC derivative" or "OTC derivative contract" as defined in Article 2(7) of Regulation (EU) No 648/2012 of the European Parliament and of the Council of 4 July 2012 on OTC derivatives, central counterparties and trade repositories ("EMIR") other than one which constitutes (i) a "foreign exchange forward" as defined in Article 7(1)(a) of the final draft regulatory technical standards on risk-mitigation techniques for OTC-derivative contracts not cleared by a CCP under Article 11(15) of EMIR dated March 8, 2016 (the "EMIR RTS") for so long as such transactions are subject to the transitional exemption from the variation margin requirements under Article 39(6) of the EMIR RTS or (ii) a single stock equity option or index option transaction as referred to in Article 39(7) of the EMIR RTS for so long as such transactions are subject to the transitional exemption from the variation margin requirements under Article 39(7) of the EMIR RTS.]

["Physically Settled FX Forward" means [.................................]]

["Physically Settled FX Swap" means [.................................]]

["Security-Based Swap" means a "security-based swap" as defined in Section 3(a)(68) of the U.S. Securities Exchange Act of 1934, as amended ("SEA"), and the rules adopted thereunder. For the avoidance of doubt, the term "Security-Based Swap" does not include a security-based swap that has been cleared by a "clearing agency" as such term is defined in Section 3(a)(23) of the SEA and the rules adopted thereunder.]

["Swap" means a "swap" as defined in Section 1a(47) of the U.S. Commodity Exchange Act, as amended ("CEA"), and the regulations adopted thereunder. For the avoidance of doubt, the term "Swap" does not include a swap that has been cleared by a "derivatives clearing organization" as such term is defined in Section 1a(15) of the CEA and the regulations adopted thereunder.]

[For the purposes of the foregoing, a Transaction will be deemed to be entered into on or after the date specified in this Paragraph 11(b)(i) if an amendment, novation or other lifecycle event with respect to such Transaction would cause such Transaction to be entered into after such date under law applicable to either party requiring the collection or delivery of variation margin.][5]

(ii) *"Exposure"* has the meaning specified in Paragraph 10, unless otherwise specified here: ....

Footnotes:
[3] Insert the relevant date.
[4] Parties may retain, delete or revise any of these definitions or add any additional definitions as applicable.
[5] Parties may retain, delete or revise the bracketed language, as applicable.

Covered Transactions

These are types of transactions covered by the VM CSA and the date on which the VM CSA comes into force.

Not all products are required to be collateralised under different regulations (e.g. spot FX is generally excluded under all uncleared margin regulations).

In addition to new trades entered into on or after the date the VM CSA comes into force, existing trades that have lifecycle events (e.g. material amendments or novations) on or after this date would also be captured under the VM CSA.

Covered Transactions under the English Law VM CSA are specifically excluded when calculating risk exposure under any Other CSA.

Footnotes 4-5 here indicate that this provision may be customised to reflect the product coverage the parties agree between them.

Exposure

There is now a specific place where amendments to the definition of Exposure can be made. This is, however, less likely to occur nowadays due to the introduction of the wide-ranging Covered Transactions definition.

(c) *Credit Support Obligations.*

(i) *Delivery Amount (VM) and Return Amount (VM).*

(A) *"Delivery Amount (VM)"* has the meaning specified in Paragraph 2(a), unless otherwise specified here:
....

(B) *"Return Amount (VM)"* has the meaning specified in Paragraph 2(b), unless otherwise specified here:
....

Delivery Amount (VM)/Return Amount (VM)

If you amend either of these definitions you must change the other since they are mirror images of each other.

(ii) *Eligible Credit Support (VM)*. Subject to Paragraph 9(e), if applicable, and each Credit Support Eligibility Condition (VM) applicable to it specified in Paragraph 11, if any, the following items will qualify as *"Eligible Credit Support (VM)"* for the party specified (as the Transferor):

	Party A	Valuation Percentage	Party B	Valuation Percentage
(A) cash in an Eligible Currency	[ ]	[ ]%	[ ]	[ ]%
(B) other:	[ ]	[ ]%	[ ]	[ ]%

Eligible Credit Support (VM)

The list of eligible collateral for each party when acting as Transferor is stated here.

Nowadays bond collateral is measured on its remaining maturity and not from its date of issuance for the purpose of setting Valuation Percentages as was previously stated in the 1995 English law CSA.

(iii) *Legally Ineligible Credit Support (VM)*. The provisions of Paragraph 9(e) will not apply to the [party/parties] specified here (as the Transferee):[6]

[ ] Party A
[ ] Party B
(A) *"Total Ineligibility Date"* has the meaning specified in Paragraph 9(e), unless otherwise specified here:
....
(B) *"Transfer Ineligibility Date"* has the meaning specified in Paragraph 9(e), unless otherwise specified here:
....

Footnote:

6 Parties should leave the relevant box below unmarked unless they agree to disapply Paragraph 9(e) with respect to a party as the Transferee.

Legally Ineligible Credit Support (VM)

You can state here if the Legally Ineligible Credit Support (VM) terms in Paragraph 9(e) will not apply to Party A or Party B when acting as Transferee by ticking the box concerned. As described in the commentary in Paragraph 9(e), Legally Ineligible Credit Support (VM) provides a process for handling collateral which, from a regulatory perspective, becomes ineligible (e.g. it no longer has the minimum rating required under the relevant uncleared margin regime).

This provision is typically disapplied when only cash collateral is eligible but applies when securities are included. As clarified in footnote 6, if is this not stated in Paragraph 11 then it is deemed to apply to both parties. There is an opportunity to redefine Total Ineligibility Date and Transfer Ineligibility Date in Paragraph 11 (c)(iii)(A) and (B) if the parties wish to amend their meaning from that in Paragraph 9(e) of the English Law VM CSA. If Legally Ineligible Credit Support does not apply then the Total Ineligibility Date and Transfer Ineligibility Date will also not apply either.

It may be useful to note that this provision only deals with the situation where collateral is no longer **legally** eligible under the relevant uncleared margin regulation. If the parties have negotiated Credit Support Eligibility Conditions (VM) that are more strict that the minimum required under the relevant uncleared margin rules and collateral becomes ineligible under the terms agreed in the VM CSA but would still technically be legally eligible under such relevant rules then the process in this provision would not apply. It would need to be handled separately.

In addition, this provision in its standard form only relates to collateral that **becomes** ineligible. Many parties include an additional provision to expand the definition also to cover the situation where collateral was (incorrectly) agreed in the VM CSA that **never would have been legally eligible** in the first place.

(iv) *Credit Support Eligibility Conditions (VM)*. The following conditions will each be a *"Credit Support Eligibility Condition (VM)"* for the party specified. Any item will not qualify as Eligible Credit Support (VM) if such item does not satisfy each Credit Support Eligibility Condition (VM) applicable to it.

[...]
[...]

Credit Support Eligibility Conditions (VM)

This is where you state if any additional eligibility criteria applies to your collateral (e.g. minimum credit rating requirements or concentration limits). This is typically not applicable for cash collateral.

> (v) *"Valuation Percentage"*; *"FX Haircut Percentage"*
>
> *"Valuation Percentage"* means, with respect to each party (as the Transferor) and item of Eligible Credit Support (VM), the percentage (expressed as a decimal) specified in Paragraph 11(c)(ii), *provided* that if nothing is specified in Paragraph 11(c)(ii), the Valuation Percentage will be 100% unless otherwise specified below. The Valuation Percentage for either party and any item of Eligible Credit Support (VM) will further be subject to the terms and conditions, if any, specified below as applicable to such party and item:
>
> ....
>
> [If at any time the Valuation Percentage assigned to an item of Eligible Credit Support (VM) with respect to a party (as the Transferor) under this Annex is greater than the maximum permitted valuation percentage (prescribed or implied) for such item of collateral under any law requiring the collection of variation margin applicable to the other party (as the Transferee), then the Valuation Percentage with respect to such item of Eligible Credit Support (VM) and such party will be such maximum permitted valuation percentage.][7]
>
> Footnote:
> [7] Parties may retain, delete or revise the bracketed language, as applicable.

Valuation Percentage

This is a new Paragraph 11 provision in the English Law VM CSA.

Sometimes there is confusion over the terms Valuation Percentage and "haircut". A haircut is a discount on the value of your collateral which reduces its value. Therefore a 3% haircut will result in a 97% Valuation Percentage for the collateral concerned.

If a Valuation Percentage is not stated in the Eligible Credit Support (VM) table in Paragraph 11(c)(ii) then it is deemed to be 100%.

The provision also provides an opportunity for further terms and conditions to be applied to Valuation Percentages for eligible collateral.

However, there is also an optional "catch all" provision available so that Valuation Percentages can be automatically amended if the ones stated in the English Law VM CSA are not acceptable under applicable regulation.

For example, if you have agreed that a certain bond collateral type can have a 1% haircut (99% Valuation Percentage) but under the regulation applicable to a party there is a minimum haircut requirement of 2% then the Valuation Percentage would automatically be amended from 99% to 98% as this is the maximum permitted valuation percentage under such regulation.

While this is useful provision to ensure that your documentation is always regulatory compliant, there can be operational issues with agreeing language which would automatically update haircuts because it may not be easy to monitor such changes and to ensure an Operations Department can apply the amended Valuation Percentage at the relevant time.

(B) *"FX Haircut Percentage"* means, with respect to each party (as the Transferor) and item of Eligible Credit Support (VM), [[8%], unless the Eligible Credit Support (VM) or Equivalent Credit Support (VM) is in the form of cash [in a Major Currency] or is denominated in a currency that matches [an Eligible Currency], in which case the FX Haircut Percentage will be 0%.]

[As used above, *"Major Currency"* means any of: (1) United States Dollar; (2) Canadian Dollar; (3) Euro; (4) United Kingdom Pound; (5) Japanese Yen; (6) Swiss Franc; (7) New Zealand Dollar; (8) Australian Dollar; (9) Swedish Kronor; (10) Danish Kroner; (11) Norwegian Krone or any other currency specified below:
[...]][8]

Footnote:
[8] Parties may revise the bracketed language and the related definitions, as applicable.

FX Haircut Percentage

Depending on the relevant regulation and the types of collateral involved, there may be a requirement to apply an additional FX haircut to your collateral. This is typically 8% under regulation but your credit officer could ask for a higher percentage.

Under EMIR there is a 0% FX haircut for variation margin where cash collateral applies. An 8% FX haircut applies to all non-cash collateral posted in a currency other than those agreed in a confirmation, Master Agreement or CSA.

Here in Paragraph 11(c)(v)(B) footnote 8 states that the parties may retain, delete or revise the bracketed language. Where a party is not subject to CFTC or PR Margin Rules, the Major Currency definition is often deleted. Where a party is subject to one of these rules then it is typically retained but the list of currencies may be reduced.

(vi) **Thresholds.**

"Minimum Transfer Amount" means with respect to Party A:
....

"Minimum Transfer Amount" means with respect to Party B:
....

Minimum Transfer Amount

Minimum Transfer Amounts should prevent costly transfers of small amounts of collateral. Nowadays this is typically a fixed amount and, as mentioned before in Chapter 1, there is a limit on the aggregate value that can be agreed for Minimum Transfer Amounts for variation margin and initial margin permitted under regulation. For EMIR, this is EUR 500,000. If a Minimum Transfer Amount is not stated it is deemed to be zero.

Because the use of a Minimum Transfer Amount only establishes a "floor", it does not itself prevent the delivery of uneven amounts of Eligible Credit Support (VM) or Equivalent Credit Support (VM). Applying a rounding convention overcomes this.

(B) **Rounding.** The Delivery Amount (VM) and the Return Amount (VM) will be rounded up and down respectively to the nearest integral multiple of ....

Rounding

In the past parties could choose how Rounding was to apply and typically rounded the Delivery Amount (VM) up and the Return Amount (VM) down to the nearest integral multiple stated. This is now clearly stated here. It avoids undercollateralisation which could happen where both Delivery Amounts and Return Amounts were elected to be rounded up. Now there is no choice offered.

If no rounding convention is stated, then the Delivery Amount (VM) and the Return Amount (VM) will not be rounded.

> (vii) *Transfers.* *"Regular Settlement Day"* has the meaning specified in Paragraph 10, unless otherwise specified here:
>
> ....

Transfers, Regular Settlement Day

The standard Regular Settlement Day definition is the same day as the margin call.

The regulatory requirements for settlement of collateral vary depending on the applicable jurisdiction. For example, CFTC rules state that same day settlement is required, although this is currently under review (January 2018). The Japanese rules state that settlement should be "without delay" (e.g. as soon as practicable).

In relation to EMIR, originally there was a same day settlement requirement (with certain exceptions). When the final draft EMIR RTS was published the language changed from "Valuation margins shall be **collected** within one of the following: (a) within the business day of calculation...." to "The posting counterparty shall **provide** the variation margin as follows: (a) within the same business day of the calculation date..." (see Article 12.1).

This change from "collect" to "provide" caused much debate in the market and it took some time before a general consensus was reached. It was determined that as long as the instruction to transfer the collateral had been made, then the "provide" condition had been met. This means that settlement timing can be longer.

ISDA published language in the EMIR Supplement to the VM Protocol on 16th December 2016 to address this which outlined that next day settlement can apply provided that the parties have initiated the transfer on the same day as the demand was received.

When parties have collateral management units in different locations (e.g. one party in Asia Pacific ("APAC") and one in the USA) this can cause significant issues when same day settlement is required (e.g. under CFTC rules). With respect to the CFTC rules, a compromise was agreed whereby the definition of "close of business" in the final sub-paragraph of Paragraph 3(a) is extended to "23.59 Eastern Standard Time / New York time". This allows the party in APAC time to meet the same day settlement requirement.

(d) *Valuation and Timing.*

(i) **"Valuation *Agent*"** means, for purposes of Paragraphs 2 and 4, the party making the demand under Paragraph 2, and, for purposes of Paragraph 5(c), the Transferee, as applicable, unless otherwise specified here:

Valuation Agent

The Valuation Agent calculates the Delivery Amount (VM) and the Return Amount (VM) and reports its calculations to its counterparty so that they can fulfil their obligations under Paragraph 2 of the English Law VM CSA by transferring or returning collateral if needed.

The parties may nominate one of themselves as the Valuation Agent. If no Valuation Agent is stated here then the party calling for the collateral (the Transferee) under Paragraph 2(a) will be the Valuation Agent. The Transferee will also be the Valuation Agent for transferring Distributions or any Interest Amount (VM) under Paragraph 5(c). The Transferor will be the Valuation Agent if he is calling for a Return Amount (VM) under Paragraph 2(b) because he knows how much he needs to call.

(ii) **"*Valuation Date*"** has the meaning specified in in Paragraph 10, unless otherwise specified here: ....

For purposes of determining the Valuation Date and clause (iii) of the definition of "Local Business Day" in Paragraph 10, **"*Valuation Date Location*"**[9] means, with respect to each party, each city, region or country specified below: Party A: .... Party B: ....

Footnote:
[9] If applicable, a party can specify more than one Valuation Date Location.

Valuation Date and Valuation Date Location

Valuation Date states the frequency at which risk exposure and collateral are revalued under the English Law VM CSA.

Valuation every business day is a requirement under regulation.

With Valuation Date Location the parties each state at least one location. This is typically the location where their collateral management unit is based. Valuations are only undertaken when a least one location for each party is open for business.

Footnote 9 clarifies that a party may specify more than one Valuation Date Location if necessary. Please note that if more than one Valuation Date Location is specified for a party, only one needs to be open for a Valuation Date to be valid.

For example, if a party selects London and New York as their Valuation Date Locations then only London or New York needs to be open because the Valuation Date definition in Paragraph 10 refers to "at least one Valuation Date Location for Party A and at least one Valuation Date Location for Party B". If you require both locations to be open then the definition of Valuation Date should be amended here.

> (iii) *"Valuation Time"* has the meaning specified in Paragraph 10, unless otherwise specified here:
>
> ....

Valuation Time

The Valuation Time is the time as at which the Valuation Agent calculates Exposure and the value of collateral held to decide if a Delivery Amount (VM) or Return Amount (VM) call is needed. The Valuation Agent will also factor in any Distributions or Interest Amounts (VM) due to the Transferor at the Valuation Time.

The definition of Valuation Time in Paragraph 10 of the English Law VM CSA has been broadly drafted. It is normally the time when the Valuation Agent makes its end of day valuations. As parties may make their calculations at different times, this can lead to disputes.

> (iv) *"Notification Time"* means 12 noon, London time, on a Local Business Day, unless otherwise specified here:
>
> ....

Notification Time

This is the time by which, among other things, (1) the Valuation Agent must notify its counterparty of its calculations under Paragraph 3(b) on the Local Business Day following a Valuation Date and (2) a party must make a demand for a transfer of Eligible Credit Support (VM) or Equivalent Credit Support (VM) so that the other party makes the appropriate transfer not later than the close of business on the Regular Settlement Day. If a demand for a transfer is made after the Notification Time then the transfer can be made up to the close of business on the next Regular Settlement Day following the day on which the demand was made. Such transfers are subject to no dispute arising.

The Notification Time is now stated as 12 noon London time on the appropriate Local Business Day unless the parties agree otherwise. In the 1995 English Law CSA it was 1.00 p.m. London time. This amendment indicates that regulators want notification to take place earlier in the market to facilitate same day transfer of collateral.

> (e) *Exchange Date.* *"Exchange Date"* has the meaning specified in Paragraph 3(c)(ii), unless otherwise specified here:

Exchange Date

This concerns the timing of collateral substitutions.

This is sometimes amended to reduce the time period in which the Transferee must return Equivalent Credit Support (VM). This is because there will be a short period when the Transferee will hold both Original Credit Support (VM) and New Credit Support (VM) and the Transferor may want to reduce the unlikely risk of Transferee becoming insolvent at that juncture.

> (f) *Dispute Resolution.*
>
> (i) *"Resolution Time"* means 1:00 p.m., London time, on the Local Business Day following the date on which the notice is given that gives rise to a dispute under Paragraph 4, unless otherwise specified here:
> ....

Dispute Resolution

Resolution Time

The Resolution Time is the deadline for the parties to resolve their dispute under Paragraph 4. The template states 1.00 p.m. London time but the parties can agree otherwise. If they fail to resolve their dispute the Valuation Agent will make certain recalculations under Paragraph 4(a)(4)(i).

> (ii) *Value.* For the purpose of Paragraphs 4(a)(4)(i)(C) and 4(a)(4)(ii), the Value of the outstanding Credit Support Balance (VM) or of any transfer of Eligible Credit Support (VM) or Equivalent Credit Support (VM), as the case may be, will be calculated as follows:
>
> ....

Value

Paragraph 4 requires that the parties provide a means for the Valuation Agent to recalculate the Value of the outstanding Credit Support Balance (VM) and the Value of any collateral transfer in a dispute. If this provision is not completed, the Valuation Agent will be unable to resolve such disputes. Therefore this provision must be completed.

The simplest Value provision where only cash collateral is involved is:
   "(ii) **The Value of Cash will be the face value thereof multiplied by the applicable Valuation Percentage.**"

The most common method for valuing bond collateral is to obtain two or three bid quotations from leading dealers and take their arithmetic mean e.g.:
   "(ii) *Value.* **For the purpose of Paragraphs 4(a)(4)(i)(C) and 4(a)(4)(ii), the Value of the outstanding Credit Support Balance (VM) or of any transfer of Eligible Credit Support (VM) or Equivalent Credit Support (VM), as the case may be, will be calculated as follows: disputes over value will be resolved by the Valuation Agent seeking three bid quotations as of the relevant Valuation Date or date of transfer from parties that regularly act as dealers in the securities or other property in question. The value will be the arithmetic mean of the quotations received by the Valuation Agent multiplied by the applicable Valuation Percentage.**"

(iii) *Alternative*. The provisions of Paragraph 4 will apply, unless an alternative dispute resolution procedure is specified here:

Alternative

This provision allows the parties to adopt a different dispute resolution procedure to that contained in Paragraph 4. However, normally parties adopt Paragraph 4.

Other alternatives include agreeing tolerances or splitting the difference below an agreed figure. These are unlikely to be agreed in the future given the rigour of current regulation.

(g) *Distributions and Interest Amount (VM)*.

(i) *Interest Rate (VM)*. The *"Interest Rate (VM)"* in relation to each Eligible Currency specified below will be:

Eligible Currency	Interest Rate (VM)	A/365 Currency
....	....	....
....	....	....
....	....	....

Distributions and Interest Amount (VM)

Interest Rate (VM)

The Interest Rate (VM) is the interest which will be paid on the cash collateral received from the Transferor flat or minus a spread. Typically the relevant OIS (overnight index swap) rate is used. For example EONIA (Euro Overnight Index Average) would be used if interest was in the Euro.

This sub-paragraph must be completed as there is no ISDA fallback.

There is now an option to state the relevant day count fraction for a specific currency. Most currencies use A/360 (actual number of days in the period divided by 360 days). GBP, JPY, AUD, NZD and CAD use A/365.

(ii) *Transfer of Interest Payment (VM) or application of Interest Amount (VM).*

Interest Transfer: [Applicable/Not Applicable]

Interest Payment Netting: [Applicable/Not Applicable]

[The transfer of an Interest Payment (VM) by the Interest Payer (VM) will be made on [the last Local Business Day of each calendar month] [and on any Local Business Day that a Return Amount (VM) consisting wholly or partly of cash is transferred to the Transferor pursuant to Paragraph 2(b)]. The transfer of an Interest Payment (VM) by the Interest Payer (VM) will be made on [the last Local Business Day of each calendar month] [and on any Local Business Day that a Delivery Amount (VM) consisting wholly or partly of cash is transferred to the Transferee pursuant to Paragraph 2(a)].]

Interest Adjustment: [Applicable/Not Applicable]

[The accrued Interest Amount (VM) will be added to the Credit Support Balance (VM) on [the last Local Business Day of each calendar month] [each day].]

Transfer of Interest Payment (VM) or application of Interest Amount (VM)

This is where the parties identify whether Interest Transfer or Interest Adjustment applies. Only one should be selected.

If Interest Transfer applies, then the parties can select whether Interest Payment Netting also applies.

The parties could choose for the Interest Amount (VM) to be added to the Credit Support Balance (VM) rather than being transferred to the Interest Payee (VM) by applying Interest Adjustment.

Most parties are only able operationally to support Interest Transfer. Interest Payment Netting is normally not applicable.

The parties then specify the frequency that the transfer or adjustment will take place.

Many parties prefer interest transfers to take place on the second Local Business Day of the following calendar month because they can take the first

Local Business Day of that month to check calculations and prepare the necessary electronic transfers.

> (iii) *Other Interest Elections.*
>
> Negative Interest: [Applicable/Not Applicable]
>
> Daily Interest Compounding: [Applicable/Not Applicable]

Other Interest Elections

There is now an option to state whether Negative Interest and Daily Interest Compounding apply.

> (iv) *Alternative to Interest Amount (VM).* The provisions of Paragraph 5(c) (ii) will apply, unless otherwise specified here:
> ....

Alternative to Interest Amount (VM)

This provision gives the Transferee, with the Transferor's agreement, the opportunity to invest part of the cash collateral in other financial instruments (e.g. money market funds or commercial paper) rather than just paying over an agreed interest return. It is very rarely used.

> (h) *Credit Support Offsets.*
>
> If specified here as applicable, then the "Credit Support Offsets" provisions in Paragraph 9(h) of this Annex will apply: [Applicable/Not Applicable].

Credit Support Offsets

This is where the parties state if offsetting across different CSAs will apply. This is not typically used at present. Many parties currently lack the operational capability to do this.

(i) *Addresses for Transfers.*

Party A:

....
....

Party B:

....
....

Addresses for Transfers

This provision must be completed if collateral transfers, interest payments and Distributions are to be correctly routed to their recipient.

That said, parties often do not provide their standard settlement instructions in the English Law VM CSA itself but instead issue separate payment instructions to each other for this purpose. Paragraph 11(i) may be completed, if necessary, with generic language e.g. "To be provided at the time of transfer".

(j) *Other CSA. "Other CSA"* has the meaning specified in Paragraph 10, unless otherwise specified here:

....

Other CSA

Normally the standard Paragraph 10 definition applies. If the parties look to apply Credit Support Offsets then they may decide to amend this to identify the Other CSA(s) in more detail.

(k) *Other Provisions.*

Other provisions

Paragraph 11(k) is similar to Part 5 of the ISDA Master Agreement Schedule – a place where other provisions desired by the parties may be inserted.

Potentially Negotiated Terms

1. Eligible Credit Support (VM) can sometimes be heavily negotiated both in terms of what collateral is acceptable and the Credit Support Eligibility Conditions (VM) that may be applied. It is key that you ensure that the types of securities collateral agreed are acceptable under the relevant uncleared margin regulations applicable to you and your counterparty. However, the parties' credit departments may also have additional conditions that they would want to apply.

2. Your credit department may require the inclusion of Independent Amounts in your English Law VM CSA. This is different from regulatory "initial margin". The Independent Amount referred to here is an additional buffer that your credit department may require based on the entity type (e.g. hedge funds). It can mean additional collateral taken at the start of a collateral relationship and not counted in the collateral balance or a sum taken later in the relationship and which is counted in it.

    It is typically taken to address the estimated volatility of a particular Transaction; the time gap between a collateral call and the delivery of the collateral itself or in relation to credit concerns relating to one or both parties. Independent Amount can be a fixed money sum or be expressed as a formula (e.g. as a percentage of the Transaction's notional amount). It can even be based upon low credit ratings.

    The English Law VM CSA is not drafted to allow for the inclusion of "non-regulatory" Independent Amounts. ISDA has produced wording that can be used for this purpose. This includes reintroducing the definition of Credit Support Amount which appears in the 1995 English Law CSA but has been removed from the English Law VM CSA.

3. Rounding is usually to the nearest 10,000 in the Base Currency.

4. Notification Time is often changed. Many parties seek to agree a time earlier than 12 noon London time in order to meet the same day settlement requirements (where applicable).

5. The interest rate payable on cash collateral is sometimes fought over as rates are currently so low. The important thing here is to choose a rate matching the frequency of marking to market.

6. The interest rate source definition (e.g. Reuters, Bloomberg) is also often negotiated. It is important that you agree a source that your collateral team can readily access and possibly specify it in Paragraph 11(g)(i).

7. Often the transfer of interest amount is changed from the last Local Business Day of each calendar month to suit parties' operational preferences.

8. Daily interest compounding is also often fought over. The general move in the market it to apply compounding because clearing houses (CCPs) now apply compounding as standard. However, not all counterparties are able

operationally to support it and often operational constraints will win the argument.

9. Some parties seek to amend the definition of Regular Settlement Day to increase the settlement period. This needs to be carefully assessed to ensure it does not breach relevant regulation.

10. It is also fairly common to extend Paragraph 6 to include Termination Events which close out all Affected Transactions. This can be done as follows:

Paragraph 6. Default.

Paragraph 6 shall be amended by the insertion of: (i) in the first line after the words "Event of Default" the words "or a Termination Event resulting in the termination of all (but not less than all) Transactions"; and (ii) in the fourth line after the words "Defaulting Party" the words "or the Affected Party as the case may be".

11. **Minimum Transfer Amount**

The two most common amendments with Minimum Transfer Amount are (i) in relation to Events of Default where the Minimum Transfer Amount will fall to zero if one of the parties commits an Event of Default and (ii) where the Transferee's risk exposure falls to zero. The Transferor will want to call for the return of his collateral and in those circumstances the Transferee's Minimum Transfer Amount will fall to zero. Here is an example which combines both in one provision:

"Minimum Transfer Amount" means with respect to Party A and Party B: EUR 100,000 provided that if (i) an Event of Default has occurred with respect to a party, the Minimum Transfer Amount for that party shall be zero; and (ii) where the Transferee's Exposure is zero, for the purposes of calculating any Return Amount, the Minimum Transfer Amount with respect to the Transferee shall be zero and Rounding shall not apply.

It is fair to say that fewer matters are negotiated with VM CSAs than with ISDA Master Agreements but negotiation can be just as intense despite this.

Principal differences between the 1995 English Law CSA and 2016 English Law VM CSA

Definitions

Independent Amounts

The 1995 English Law CSA includes Independent Amount provisions. The English Law VM CSA is designed for variation margin only and therefore this definition and related provisions have been deleted or revised. It is possible to reinsert these terms if necessary and, as mentioned before, ISDA has published wording for this.

Threshold

The definition of Threshold has been removed in the English Law VM CSA as it should always be zero.

Covered Transactions

While the 1995 English Law CSA was designed to cover all Transactions under an ISDA Master Agreement, the English Law VM CSA is only required to include Covered Transactions as defined in Paragraph 11.

Valuation Date

Under the 1995 English Law CSA, the parties specify the frequency of valuations in Paragraph 11. Daily valuation is hardcoded in Paragraph 10 of the English Law VM CSA.

Close-out Amount updates

The 1995 English Law CSA is not compatible with the 2002 ISDA Master Agreement unless amendments are made to incorporate Close-out Amount. This can be done in a number of ways. The parties could have adhered to the 2002 Master Agreement Protocol when it was open; they parties can adhere to Close-out Amount Protocol where they have a 1992 ISDA Master Agreement in place; they can incorporate the relevant wording directly in Paragraph 11(h) of their 1995 English Law CSA; or make reference to the 2002 Master Agreement Protocol and incorporate its terms by reference in the 2002 ISDA Master Agreement Schedule.

The English Law VM CSA includes the language in the relevant provisions of Paragraphs 1-10 and so no further updates are required.

Settlement Timings

The English Law 1995 CSA allows for longer settlement timings following a collateral call or request for substitution.

The English Law VM CSA has short time periods (same day settlement if the standard Regular Settlement Day definition is used) for collateral calls. It allows a longer period where substitutions are involved. This longer period is the same as that under the 1995 English Law CSA.

Interest Rate provisions

Substantial changes have been made to the interest rate provisions in the English Law VM CSA. This is mainly due to changes in market practice and takes account of negative interest rate environments.

Scope of Annex / Credit Support Offsets / Other CSAs

A scope clause has been added as Paragraph 1(b) of the English Law VM CSA so that only certain trades are captured by it. It amends any existing "Other CSA" at the same time so that trades are only collateralised once from a variation margin perspective.

The addition of the Credit Support Offsets provision provides the option to "link" CSAs and offset across them. However, parties must have the operational capability to do this.

Legal Ineligibility provisions

Clauses have been added in Paragraph 9 of the English Law VM CSA to deal with:

- The situation where collateral becomes ineligible due to the relevant uncleared margin rules.
- How to value such ineligible collateral.
- How ineligible collateral is returned/substituted.
- The situation where collateral that was previously legally ineligible becomes eligible again.

In Chapter 3 we perform a similar clause by clause analysis of the 2016 Credit Support Annex For Variation Margin (VM) under New York Law.

The 2016 ISDA Credit Support Annex For Variation Margin (VM) under New York Law

Introduction

The 1994 ISDA Credit Support Annex under New York Law was the first of ISDA's stable of Credit Support Annexes.

An updated version of the New York Law Annex was published in April 2016 and was designed to cover variation margin only and to comply with new uncleared margin regulations.

The Credit Support Annex has been prepared on the basis that it is governed by the laws of the State of New York. It is expected that this New York Law VM CSA will be appended to an ISDA Master Agreement governed by New York law.

The New York Law VM CSA is a hybrid document for two reasons:

a. In the preamble it states that it supplements, forms part of and is subject to the ISDA Master Agreement, is part of its Schedule like the English Law VM CSA but is also a Credit Support Document which the English Law Annex VM CSA is not.
b. In Paragraph 2 the Pledgor grants the Secured Party a first priority continuing security interest in, lien on and right of set off against all Posted Collateral (VM) and in Paragraph 6(c)(i) it has the right to reuse it freely.

Commentary on the New York Law CSA For Variation Margin

(Bilateral Form)   (ISDA Agreements Subject to New York Law Only)

ISDA. Safe, Efficient Markets

International Swaps and Derivatives Association, Inc.

2016 CREDIT SUPPORT ANNEX FOR VARIATION MARGIN (VM)

dated as of ....

to the Schedule to the

....

dated as of ....

between

.... and ....
("Party A")   ("Party B")

Similar to the English Law VM CSA, there are two dates that are included at the start of the New York Law VM CSA. The first is the date for the New York Law VM CSA itself. This is used to help easily identify this VM CSA particularly if there is a 1994 ISDA Credit Support Annex subject to New York Law also linked to the same ISDA Master Agreement.

The second date is in relation to the ISDA Master Agreement itself.

The legal names of each contracting party are then specified.

Preamble

This Annex supplements, forms part of, and is subject to, the above-referenced Agreement, is part of its Schedule and is a Credit Support Document under this Agreement with respect to each party.

The New York Law VM CSA is hybrid in nature. Firstly it is described as part of the Schedule to the ISDA Master Agreement and like it supplements, forms part of and is subject to the Master Agreement itself. However, it is also a Credit Support Document under the ISDA Master Agreement. Unlike in the English Law VM CSA, it is not a Confirmation in relation to a "Transaction" under the Master Agreement.

Paragraph 1. Interpretation

Accordingly, the parties agree as follows:—

Paragraph 1. Interpretation

(a) *Definitions and Inconsistency*. Capitalized terms not otherwise defined herein or elsewhere in this Agreement have the meanings specified pursuant to Paragraph 12, and all references in this Annex to Paragraphs are to Paragraphs of this Annex. In the event of any inconsistency between this Annex and the other provisions of this Schedule, this Annex will prevail, and in the event of any inconsistency between Paragraph 13 and the other provisions of this Annex, Paragraph 13 will prevail.

This provision clarifies that terms that are capitalised in the New York VM CSA but are not defined in the ISDA Master Agreement will have the meanings stated in Paragraph 12, the Definitions Paragraph, of the New York Law VM CSA. It is useful to remember that references to "Paragraphs" relate to paragraphs in the New York Law VM CSA and references to "Sections" are to Sections in the ISDA Master Agreement.

If there is any inconsistency between the New York Law VM CSA and the other provisions of the ISDA Schedule, the New York Law VM CSA will prevail. However, any elections or amendments made in Paragraph 13 (the Elections and Variables Paragraph) will prevail they are inconsistent with the other provisions of the New York Law VM CSA.

(b) *Secured Party and Pledgor*. All references in this Annex to the "Secured Party" will be to either party when acting in that capacity and all corresponding references to the "Pledgor" will be to the other party when acting in that capacity; *provided, however*, that if Other Posted Support (VM) is held by a party to this Annex, all references herein to that party as the Secured Party with respect to that Other Posted Support (VM) will be to that party as the beneficiary thereof and will not subject that support or

> that party as the beneficiary thereof to provisions of law generally relating to security interests and secured parties.

(b) As the New York Law VM CSA is drafted as a bilateral agreement, it is possible either party may be the Secured Party or the Pledgor at any point in time during their trading relationship depending on the mark-to-market risk exposure of the deal portfolio at that time.

The party that is posting the collateral (or receiving collateral that is being returned) is called the Pledgor. The party receiving the pledged collateral (or holding or returning collateral) is referred as the Secured Party.

In respect of Other Posted Support (VM) the Secured Party will be considered to hold it as a beneficiary rather than as a secured party.

> (c) *Scope of this Annex and the Other CSA.* The only Transactions which will be relevant for the purposes of determining "Exposure" under this Annex will be the Covered Transactions specified in Paragraph 13. Each Other CSA, if any, is hereby amended such that the Transactions that will be relevant for purposes of determining "Exposure" thereunder, if any, will exclude the Covered Transactions. Except as provided in Paragraphs 8(a), 8(b) and 11(j), nothing in this Annex will affect the rights and obligations, if any, of either party with respect to "independent amounts" or initial margin under each Other CSA, if any, with respect to Transactions that are Covered Transactions.

Paragraph 1(c) is new in the New York Law VM CSA.

It has been included to handle the situation where the parties already have an existing CSA and are now entering into a New York Law VM CSA to cover new trades. The 1994 New York Law CSA and 1995 English Law CSA were drafted to capture all Transactions entered into under the ISDA Master Agreement (although this was often amended in Paragraph 13 or Paragraph 11 respectively, typically to exclude spot FX). Paragraph 1(c) makes it clear that the New York Law VM CSA will only incorporate "Covered Transactions" as defined in Paragraph 13. All other Transactions would be covered by the original CSA, if any.

The clause also covers the possibility that non-regulatory independent amounts or regulatory initial margin exist under an Other CSA. If so, except in a close-out situation or if Credit Support Offsets apply (see Paragraph 11(j)), there will be no effect on the Covered Transactions under the New York Law VM CSA from a variation margin perspective.

Paragraph 2. Security Interest

Paragraph 2. Security Interest

Each party, as the Pledgor, hereby pledges to the other party, as the Secured Party, as security for its Obligations, and grants to the Secured Party a first priority continuing security interest in, lien on and right of Set-off against all Posted Collateral (VM) Transferred to or received by the Secured Party hereunder. Upon the Transfer by the Secured Party to the Pledgor of Posted Collateral (VM), the security interest and lien granted hereunder on that Posted Collateral (VM) will be released immediately and, to the extent possible, without any further action by either party.

Paragraph 2 which is governed by the New York Uniform Commercial Code (the "NYUCC"), is known as a granting clause.

A security interest is granted by the Pledgor in the collateral that is pledged to the Secured Party. The Pledgor grants "a first priority continuing security interest, lien and right of set off" in the collateral to the Secured Party.

Under the NYUCC, this means that the Secured Party generally has a claim to the pledged collateral which is superior to any other creditor provided that the Secured Party perfects its rights in its pledge. Where the Pledgor is pledging cash or U.S. Treasury securities, the security interest in the pledged collateral is perfected by the Secured Party taking possession (although not ownership) of the pledged collateral.

The Secured Party also agrees here that when it returns the Posted Collateral (VM) to the Pledgor, its security interest in that collateral is automatically released. Because attachment and perfection of Posted Collateral (VM) is normally achieved by possession, the surrender of that possession will also normally release the Secured Party's lien on the surrendered collateral under the NYUCC.

Paragraph 3. Credit Support Obligations

Paragraph 3. Credit Support Obligations

(a) *Delivery Amount (VM)*. Subject to Paragraphs 4 and 5, upon a demand made by the Secured Party on or promptly following a Valuation Date, if the Delivery Amount (VM) for that Valuation Date equals or exceeds the Pledgor's Minimum Transfer Amount, then the Pledgor will Transfer to the Secured Party Eligible Credit Support (VM) having a Value as of the date of Transfer at least equal to the applicable Delivery Amount (VM) (rounded pursuant to Paragraph 13). Unless otherwise specified in Paragraph 13, the *"Delivery Amount (VM)"* applicable to the Pledgor for any Valuation Date will equal the amount by which:

(i) the Secured Party's Exposure

exceeds

(ii) the Value as of that Valuation Date of all Posted Credit Support (VM) held by the Secured Party.

This Paragraph outlines when collateral calls and returns are made and how they are calculated.

Promptly following a Valuation Date (typically the next Local Business Day) the Secured Party compares his risk exposure against the amount of collateral he holds. Based on this calculation, he determines:

- if a call is required for more collateral;
- if he is required to return any surplus collateral; or
- if nothing needs to be done.

This analysis takes into account Minimum Transfer Amounts. The amount of the call must be greater than the Pledgor's Minimum Transfer Amount otherwise a call cannot be made.

In Paragraph 3(a) the Secured Party can call for collateral when its Exposure exceeds the value of any Posted Collateral (VM) (i.e. pledged collateral already held by the Secured Party). The call relates to the Delivery Amount (VM).

Assuming there is no dispute, when called upon the Pledgor will transfer the requested Delivery Amount (VM) to the Secured Party.

(b) *Return Amount (VM)*. Subject to Paragraphs 4 and 5, upon a demand made by the Pledgor on or promptly following a Valuation Date, if the Return Amount (VM) for that Valuation Date equals or exceeds the Secured Party's Minimum Transfer Amount, then the Secured Party will Transfer to the Pledgor Posted Credit Support (VM) specified by the Pledgor in that demand having a Value as of the date of Transfer as close as practicable to the applicable Return Amount (VM) (rounded pursuant to Paragraph 13). Unless otherwise specified in Paragraph 13, the *"Return Amount"* applicable to the Secured Party for any Valuation Date will equal the amount by which:

> (i) the Value as of that Valuation Date of all Posted Credit Support (VM) held by the Secured Party
>
> exceeds
>
> (ii) the Secured Party's Exposure.

In Paragraph 3(b), where the amount of collateral held by the Secured Party is greater than the Secured Party's risk exposure on the Pledgor, the Pledgor can request that the surplus collateral is returned to him. In this case the Secured Party's Minimum Transfer Amount is taken into consideration.

It is useful to note that if the Pledgor fails to make a call, the Secured Party is not obliged to transfer the collateral or point this out to the Pledgor. The Secured Party only needs to act "upon a demand" from the Pledgor.

The Secured Party's Exposure is calculated by assessing the total population of Covered Transactions between the parties and using mid-market prices to determine the amount that would be owed to the Secured Party if all Covered Transactions were terminated on the Valuation Date.

The reference to Posted Credit Support (VM) being as close as practicable to the Return Amount (VM) covers the situation where bond collateral is only transferable in specific integral amounts.

Paragraph 4. Conditions Precedent, Transfer Timing, Calculations and Substitutions

> **Paragraph 4. Conditions Precedent, Transfer Timing, Calculations and Substitutions**
>
> (a) *Conditions Precedent.* Unless otherwise specified in Paragraph 13, each Transfer obligation of the Pledgor under Paragraphs 3, 5 and 6(d) and of the Secured Party under Paragraphs 3, 4(d)(ii), 5, 6(d) and 11(h) is subject to the conditions precedent that:
>
> (i) no Event of Default, Potential Event of Default or Specified Condition has occurred and is continuing with respect to the other party; and

Paragraph 4(a)(i) outlines conditions that must apply in order for the general day to day operations of the New York Law VM CSA to run smoothly. A party is not obliged to transfer collateral under the New York Law VM CSA if:

- an Event of Default,
- Potential Event of Default or
- a Specified Condition

has occurred and is continuing to its counterparty.

This protects a party from having to transfer collateral to a counterparty in difficulties. This provision may result in one of the two parties being either under or overcollateralised during the time period when a Conditions Precedent arises and is implemented.

The party impacted by the Conditions Precedent is not allowed to:

- call for or substitute collateral.
- receive dividends or interest on pledged collateral.
- call for or return (depending on the party) Posted Credit Support (VM) that has a zero Value (i.e. posted collateral that is now ineligible).

The occurrence of a Specified Condition also permits a Secured Party to exercise its remedies under the New York Law VM CSA.

A Specified Condition is one or more Termination Events in the ISDA Master Agreement that is selected in Paragraph 13(e)(ii) of the New York Law VM CSA as being subject to the Conditions Precedent outlined above.

> (ii) no Early Termination Date for which any unsatisfied payment obligations exist has occurred or been designated as the result of an Event of Default or Specified Condition with respect to the other party.

Paragraph 4(a)(ii) specifies that neither party is obliged to transfer collateral after an Early Termination Date has been declared regardless of who designated it, why it was designated or when the termination payment is due.

This is because one of the parties will soon be making the early termination payment. If a Non-defaulting Party or a Non-affected Party is worried about being exposed during that period, the Early Termination Date should occur as soon as possible after it gives notice of one.

> (b) *Transfer Timing*. Subject to Paragraphs 4(a) and 5 and unless otherwise specified in Paragraph 13, if a demand for the Transfer of Eligible Credit Support (VM) or Posted Credit Support (VM) is made by the Notification Time, then the relevant Transfer will be made not later than the close of business on the Regular Settlement Day; if a demand is made after the

Notification Time, then the relevant Transfer will be made not later than the close of business on the next Local Business Day following the Regular Settlement Day.

Under Paragraph 4(b), a party is required to deliver collateral by the close of business on the Regular Settlement Day if it receives a call notice by the Notification Time. If it receives the call notice after the Notification Time, it is required to deliver collateral by the close of business on the next Regular Settlement Day.

Regular Settlement Day is defined in Paragraph 12 as the same Local Business Day as the demand for the transfer of collateral is made. Under CFTC and PR Margin Rules it is a requirement for settlement to occur on the same business day as the call is made, although this is currently under review (January 2018). Under regulation in other jurisdictions the settlement timings could be extended (e.g. under EMIR where settlement can be longer provided that the party has initiated the transfer on the same business day as the demand is made).

(c) *Calculations*. All calculations of Value and Exposure for purposes of Paragraphs 3 and 6(d) will be made by the Valuation Agent as of the Valuation Time; *provided* that the Valuation Agent may use, in the case of any calculation of (i) Value, Values most recently reasonably available for close of business in the relevant market for the relevant Eligible Credit Support (VM) as of the Valuation Time and (ii) Exposure, relevant information or data most recently reasonably available for close of business in the relevant market(s) as of the Valuation Time. The Valuation Agent will notify each party (or the other party, if the Valuation Agent is a party) of its calculations not later than the Notification Time on the Local Business Day following the applicable Valuation Date (or in the case of Paragraph 6(d), following the date of calculation).

Paragraph 4(c) requires the Valuation Agent to make the calculations of the value of collateral and risk exposure as of the Valuation Time (normally the time when the Valuation Agent makes its end of day valuations). The Valuation Agent then notifies the other party of its calculations not later than the Notification Time on the Local Business Day following the Valuation Date or in respect of payments of interest on bonds or cash on the next Local Business Day following the date of calculation.

The language in the New York Law VM CSA has been extended from that in the 1994 New York Law CSA to clarify what information can be used for calculations. In the case of the value of collateral this is the most recently available Values as at the close of business in the relevant market for that collateral. For

Exposure it is the most recently available relevant information or data in the appropriate market.

(d) *Substitutions.*

(i) Unless otherwise specified in Paragraph 13, upon notice to the Secured Party specifying the items of Posted Credit Support (VM) to be exchanged, the Pledgor may, on any Local Business Day, Transfer to the Secured Party substitute Eligible Credit Support (VM) (the *"Substitute Credit Support (VM)"*); and

(ii) subject to Paragraph 4(a), the Secured Party will Transfer to the Pledgor the items of Posted Credit Support (VM) specified by the Pledgor in its notice not later than the Local Business Day following the date on which the Secured Party receives the Substitute Credit Support (VM), unless otherwise specified in Paragraph 13 (the *"Substitution Date"*); *provided* that the Secured Party will only be obligated to Transfer Posted Credit Support (VM) with a Value as of the date of Transfer of that Posted Credit Support (VM) equal to the Value as of that date of the Substitute Credit Support (VM).

Paragraph 4(d) outlines the process to be followed if the Pledgor wants to substitute another form of Eligible Credit Support (VM) for collateral that it had previously posted to the Secured Party. There could be various reasons why the Pledgor needs the collateral that was previously provided to the Secured Party. He therefore requests a substitution.

Unless an election is made in Paragraph 13(f)(ii) stating that consent is required, the Secured Party has to agree the substitution request. An instance where a Secured Party may want to have a consent clause in Paragraph 13(f)(ii) is where the Pledgor becomes a nuisance by making too many substitutions of Eligible Credit Support (VM). While the Secured Party is not in a weaker position after a substitution, frequent substitutions of collateral by the Pledgor can prove to be time consuming and operationally onerous for the Secured Party and would involve transfer costs.

The Secured Party is not required to transfer the previously Posted Credit Support (VM) to the Pledgor until it has received the substitute collateral. Once the new collateral is received, the Secured Party must transfer the previous Posted Credit Support (VM) on the next Local Business Day and then only in an amount which is not greater than the Value of the Substitute Credit Support (VM). This wording is included because some bonds can only be transferred in specific integral amounts and therefore it may not be possible to transfer the exact amount required.

Paragraph 5. Dispute Resolution

Paragraph 5. Dispute Resolution

If a party (a *"Disputing Party"*) disputes (I) the Valuation Agent's calculation of a Delivery Amount (VM) or a Return Amount (VM) or (II) the Value of any Transfer of Eligible Credit Support (VM) or Posted Credit Support (VM), then:

(i) the Disputing Party will notify the other party and the Valuation Agent (if the Valuation Agent is not the other party) not later than the close of business on (X) the date that the Transfer is due in respect of such Delivery Amount (VM) or Return Amount (VM) in the case of (I) above, or (Y) the Local Business Day following the date of Transfer in the case of (II) above,

(ii) subject to Paragraph 4(a), the appropriate party will Transfer the undisputed amount to the other party not later than the close of business on (X) the date that the Transfer is due in respect of such Delivery Amount (VM) or Return Amount (VM) in the case of (I) above, or (Y) the Local Business Day following the date of Transfer in the case of (II) above,

(iii) the parties will consult with each other in an attempt to resolve the dispute, and

(iv) if they fail to resolve the dispute by the Resolution Time, then:

(A) In the case of a dispute involving a Delivery Amount (VM) or Return Amount (VM), unless otherwise specified in Paragraph 13, the Valuation Agent will recalculate the Exposure and the Value as of the Recalculation Date by:

(1) utilizing any calculations of Exposure for the Covered Transactions that the parties have agreed are not in dispute;

(2) (I) if this Agreement is a 1992 ISDA Master Agreement, calculating the Exposure for the Covered Transactions in dispute by seeking four actual quotations at mid-market from Reference Market-makers for purposes of calculating Market Quotation, and taking the arithmetic average of those obtained, or (II) if this Agreement is an ISDA 2002 Master Agreement or a 1992 ISDA Master Agreement in which the definition of Loss and/or Market Quotation has been amended (including where such amendment

has occurred pursuant to the terms of a separate agreement or protocol) to reflect the definition of Close-out Amount from the pre-printed form of the ISDA 2002 Master Agreement as published by ISDA, calculating the Exposure for the Covered Transactions in dispute by seeking four actual quotations at mid-market from third parties for purposes of calculating the relevant Close-out Amount, and taking the arithmetic average of those obtained; *provided* that, in either case, if four quotations are not available for a particular Covered Transaction, then fewer than four quotations may be used for that Covered Transaction, and if no quotations are available for a particular Covered Transaction, then the Valuation Agent's original calculations will be used for that Covered Transaction; and

(3) utilizing the procedures specified in Paragraph 13 for calculating the Value, if disputed, of Posted Credit Support (VM).

(B) In the case of a dispute involving the Value of any Transfer of Eligible Credit Support (VM) or Posted Credit Support (VM), the Valuation Agent will recalculate the Value as of the date of Transfer pursuant to Paragraph 13.

Following a recalculation pursuant to this Paragraph, the Valuation Agent will notify each party (or the other party, if the Valuation Agent is a party) not later than the Notification Time on the Local Business Day following the Resolution Time. The appropriate party will, upon demand following that notice by the Valuation Agent or a resolution pursuant to (iii) above and subject to Paragraphs 4(a) and 4(b), make the appropriate Transfer.

Paragraph 5 provides a resolution procedure where a party disputes the Valuation Agent's calculation of Exposure or the Value of Eligible Credit Support (VM) or of Posted Credit Support (VM), if it cannot be settled informally. Most disputes are resolved informally.

Collateral disputes always relate to these two matters and the calculation of risk exposure is the more common kind of dispute. Parties often disagree on the calculation of Exposure if the underlying Transactions are illiquid and difficult to value.

Disputes may also arise over the valuation of collateral if illiquid securities that are difficult to value are being pledged.

The steps are outlined in Paragraph 5(i) to (iv) and involve:

(i) (1) if the Disputing Party wishes to dispute the calculation of risk exposure, it must notify its counterparty or the Valuation Agent (if a separate one exists) by the close of business on the Local Business Day the collateral call notice is due or (2) if the Disputing Party wants to dispute the calculation of the value of the collateral transferred, it must notify its counterparty or the third party Valuation Agent on the Local Business Day after the date that the collateral transfer has been made. This covers the situation of a Pledgor sending the wrong amount of collateral.

(ii) the Disputing Party is required to transfer the undisputed amount to the other party not later than (1) in the case of disputes over risk exposure, the close of business on the Local Business Day the collateral call is due or (2) in the case of disputes on collateral value, the Local Business Day after the date the collateral is transferred.

(iii) The parties will attempt to resolve the dispute by the deadline nominated in Paragraph 13(g)(i) - the Resolution Time.

(iv) If they fail then:

(A)(1) if the dispute involves the amount of collateral called for, the Valuation Agent will recalculate his figures by reusing any calculation of the amount of Exposure which is undisputed.

(2) The Valuation Agent will then approach four Reference Market-makers (i.e. major dealers) for mid-market quotations (i.e. the average of the bid and offer prices for the Covered Transactions concerned). Provided four quotations are received the arithmetic average of these quotations is taken. If four quotations are not available to calculate the amount for a particular Covered Transaction, fewer may be used. If no quotations are available, then the Valuation Agent's original calculation will be used for that Covered Transaction as it is probably the only reasonable thing to do in the circumstances although it is not totally precise and may result in under or overcollateralisation.

This sub-paragraph has been significantly revised from the 1994 New York Law CSA version but the revisions are positive. Because the 1994 New York Law CSA was published before the 2002 ISDA Master Agreement, it only makes reference to the term "Market Quotation" which is used in the 1992 version of the ISDA Master Agreement. "Close-out Amount" is now also incorporated which is a defined term in the 2002 ISDA Master Agreement as well as many 1992 Agreements either via a party's adherence to the ISDA Close-out Amount Protocol or by negotiating the inclusion of the terms directly in their 1992 Agreements.

(3) For calculating the value of collateral held, the Valuation Agent will directly home in on the method specified in Paragraph 13(g)(ii). A method has to be stated in Paragraph 13(g)(ii) or the dispute resolution provisions with respect to the calculation of Value will not work. There is no fallback.

(B) This sub-paragraph underlines that the Valuation Agent will directly focus on Paragraph 13(g)(ii) where the dispute solely involves the Value of a new transfer of collateral or of collateral already held.

When all the recalculations have been made the Valuation Agent will notify its counterparty of the revised figures not later than the deadline (Notification Time) on the Local Business Day after the Resolution Time (i.e. the dispute resolution deadline agreed in Paragraph 13(g)(i) of the New York Law VM CSA).

Once the amount of Exposure and the Value of collateral have been agreed, a revised collateral call notice is sent and the necessary collateral transfer is made.

There is no linkage in to Section 5(a)(i) of the Master Agreement - the Failure to Pay or Deliver Event of Default - as there is in the English Law VM CSA where a party due to pay a resolved disputed amount fails to do so.

Paragraph 6. Holding and Using Posted Collateral (VM)

Paragraph 6. Holding and Using Posted Collateral (VM)

(a) *Care of Posted Collateral (VM).* Without limiting the Secured Party's rights under Paragraph 6(c), the Secured Party will exercise reasonable care to assure the safe custody of all Posted Collateral (VM) to the extent required by applicable law, and in any event the Secured Party will be deemed to have exercised reasonable care if it exercises at least the same degree of care as it would exercise with respect to its own property. Except as specified in the preceding sentence, the Secured Party will have no duty with respect to Posted Collateral (VM), including, without limitation, any duty to collect any Distributions, or enforce or preserve any rights pertaining thereto.

Paragraph 6(a) generally imposes a duty of care on the Secured Party in holding pledged collateral. He will be deemed to have met that duty if he uses the same care that he would have used in holding his own property. Please note that the Secured Party is under no obligation to collect distributions or to enforce or preserve any rights that the Pledgor has in the Posted Collateral (VM).

(b) *Eligibility to Hold Posted Collateral (VM); Custodians (VM).*

(i) *General.* Subject to the satisfaction of any conditions specified in Paragraph 13 for holding Posted Collateral (VM), the Secured Party will be entitled to hold Posted Collateral (VM) or to appoint an agent (a *"Custodian (VM)"*) to hold Posted Collateral (VM) for the Secured Party. Upon notice by the Secured Party to the Pledgor of the appointment of a Custodian (VM), the Pledgor's obligations to make any Transfer will be discharged by making the Transfer to that Custodian (VM). The holding of Posted Collateral (VM) by a Custodian (VM) will be deemed to be the holding of that Posted Collateral (VM) by the Secured Party for which the Custodian (VM) is acting.

Paragraph 6(b)(i) provides that a Secured Party may hold the Posted Collateral (VM) itself provided that he meets any eligibility conditions specified in Paragraph 13(h). The Secured Party may also appoint an agent to hold the Posted Collateral (VM). This agent is defined in Paragraph 6(b) as a "Custodian (VM)" and is acting as an agent and taking instructions from the Secured Party. It is not acting as an escrow agent on behalf of both parties nor does it have any fiduciary duties to the Pledgor. If the Pledgor wanted to create such a relationship, the parties would need to create some kind of triparty custodial agreement similar to those sometimes used with repos.

Where a Custodian (VM) is holding Posted Collateral (VM) it is considered equivalent to the Secured Party holding it himself.

(ii) *Failure to Satisfy Conditions*. If the Secured Party or its Custodian (VM) fails to satisfy any conditions for holding Posted Collateral (VM), then upon a demand made by the Pledgor, the Secured Party will, not later than five Local Business Days after the demand, Transfer or cause its Custodian (VM) to Transfer all Posted Collateral (VM) held by it to a Custodian (VM) that satisfies those conditions or to the Secured Party if it satisfies those conditions.

If a Secured Party or its Custodian (VM) does not meet the Paragraph 13(h)(i) eligibility conditions, Paragraph 6(b)(ii) gives a Pledgor the right by demand to require the Secured Party or its Custodian (VM) to transfer the Posted Collateral (VM) (within 5 Local Business Days of demand by the Pledgor) to a custodian who does meet the eligibility tests of Paragraph 13(h)(i) or to the Secured Party itself (if it meets those requirements) and no other qualifying alternative custodian can be found.

(iii) *Liability*. The Secured Party will be liable for the acts or omissions of its Custodian (VM) to the same extent that the Secured Party would be liable hereunder for its own acts or omissions.

Paragraph 6(b)(iii) reflects general agency law in that it requires a party to be liable for the actions of its agent. This provides some comfort to the Pledgor because it will always have recourse against the Secured Party regardless of whether it was the Secured Party or the Custodian (VM) that breached its duties of care in holding the Posted Collateral (VM).

(c) *Use of Posted Collateral (VM)*. Unless otherwise specified in Paragraph 13 and without limiting the rights and obligations of the parties under Paragraphs 3, 4(d)(ii), 5, 6(d) and 8, if the Secured Party is not a Defaulting Party or an Affected Party with respect to a Specified Condition and no Early Termination Date has occurred or been designated as the result of an Event of Default or Specified Condition with respect to the Secured Party, then the Secured Party will, notwithstanding Section 9-207 of the New York Uniform Commercial Code, have the right to:

(i) sell, pledge, rehypothecate, assign, invest, use, commingle or otherwise dispose of, or otherwise use in its business any Posted Collateral (VM) it holds, free from any claim or right of any nature whatsoever of the Pledgor, including any equity or right of redemption by the Pledgor; and
(ii) register any Posted Collateral (VM) in the name of the Secured Party, its Custodian (VM) or a nominee for either.

For purposes of the obligation to Transfer Eligible Credit Support (VM) or Posted Credit Support (VM) pursuant to Paragraphs 3 and 5 and any rights or remedies authorized under this Agreement, the Secured Party will be deemed to continue to hold all Posted Collateral (VM) and to receive Distributions made thereon, regardless of whether the Secured Party has exercised any rights with respect to any Posted Collateral (VM) pursuant to (i) or (ii) above.

Paragraph 6(c) grants the Secured Party "use" or "rehypothecation" rights to the Posted Collateral (VM).

To withdraw these rights, the parties would need to state in Paragraph 13(h) (ii) that Paragraph 6(c) did not apply. The fallback situation if no election is made is for rehypothecation to apply. However, this right of use of collateral does not apply if an Event of Default or Specified Condition has occurred to the Secured Party.

Although it may have reused the Posted Collateral (VM), this sub-paragraph stipulates that the Secured Party is still regarded and remains as the holder of the Posted Collateral (VM) and the recipient of Distributions even if it has used its sale and rehypothecation rights under this sub-paragraph.

(d) *Distributions, Interest Amount (VM) and Interest Payment (VM).*

(i) *Distributions.* Subject to Paragraph 4(a), if the Secured Party receives or is deemed to receive Distributions on a Local Business Day, it will Transfer to the Pledgor not later than the following Local Business Day any Distributions it receives or is deemed to receive to the extent that a Delivery Amount (VM) would not be created or increased by that Transfer, as calculated by the Valuation Agent (and the date of calculation will be deemed to be a Valuation Date for this purpose).

The general rule under Paragraph 6(d) is that Distributions (such as principal or interest payments on Posted Collateral (VM)) are to be passed through to the Pledgor. This rule would generally preserve the rights of the Pledgor, as the owner of the Posted Collateral (VM), to any Distributions made on it. However, such a passthrough of a Distribution does not need to be made to the Pledgor if it would create a Delivery Amount (VM) (i.e. a collateral call). This is because the value of the Posted Collateral (VM) held by the Secured Party would reduce due to the passthrough of the Distribution to the Pledgor. This often happens because when accrued interest on a bond is paid on its due date, the price and hence value of the bond deceases.

In these circumstances the amount of the Distribution is retained and forms part of the collateral balance.

(ii) *Interest Amount (VM) and Interest Payment (VM).* Unless otherwise specified in Paragraph 13 and subject to Paragraph 4(a), in lieu of any interest, dividends or other amounts paid or deemed to have been paid with respect to Posted Collateral (VM) in the form of Cash (all of which may be retained by the Secured Party),

(A) if "Interest Transfer" is specified as applicable in Paragraph 13, the Interest Payer (VM) will Transfer to the Interest Payee (VM), at the times specified in Paragraph 13, the relevant Interest Payment (VM); *provided* that if "Interest Payment Netting" is specified as applicable in Paragraph 13:

(I) if the Interest Payer (VM) is entitled to demand a Delivery Amount (VM) or Return Amount (VM), in respect of the date such Interest Payment (VM) is required to be Transferred:

(a) such Delivery Amount (VM) or Return Amount (VM) will be reduced (but not below zero) by such Interest Payment (VM); *provided* that, in case of such Return Amount (VM), if the amount of Posted Collateral (VM) which is comprised of Cash in the Base Currency is less than such Interest Payment (VM), such reduction will only be to the extent of the amount of such Cash which is Posted Collateral (VM) (the *"Eligible Return Amount (VM)"*); and

(b) the Interest Payer (VM) will Transfer to the Interest Payee (VM) the amount of the excess, if any, of such Interest Payment (VM) over such Delivery Amount (VM) or Eligible Return Amount (VM), as applicable; and

(II) if under Paragraph 6(d)(ii)(A)(I)(a) a Delivery Amount (VM) is reduced (the amount of such reduction, the *"Delivery Amount Reduction (VM)"*) or a Return Amount (VM) is reduced (the amount of such reduction, the *"Return Amount Reduction (VM)"*), then for purposes of determining Posted Collateral (VM), the Secured Party (a) will be deemed to have received an amount in Cash in the Base Currency equal to any Delivery Amount Reduction (VM), and such amount will constitute Posted Collateral (VM) in such Cash and will be subject to the security interest granted under Paragraph 2 or (b) will be deemed to have Transferred an amount in Cash in the Base Currency equal to any Return Amount Reduction (VM), as applicable, in each case on the day on which the relevant Interest Payment (VM) was due to be Transferred, as applicable; and

Paragraph 6(d)(ii) details whether and how the Secured Party will pay interest on Cash that is Posted Collateral (VM).

It is assumed that, as a minimum, the Secured Party will invest the Cash in federal funds or a similar investment during the period that it holds the Cash. Instead of paying over the actual interest earned, the Secured Party will pay the Pledgor a fixed amount based upon an interest rate formula agreed by the parties in Paragraph 13(i).

Similar to the English Law VM CSA, the interest provisions in the New York Law VM CSA have been substantially amended from those in the 1994 New York Law CSA.

New defined terms of "Interest Transfer", "Interest Payment Netting" and "Interest Adjustment" have been introduced.

One of the main reasons for the changes is to address how interest is calculated when negative interest rates apply.

Paragraph 6(d)(ii)(A)(I) outlines the procedure when Interest Transfer applies.

The Interest Payer (VM) will transfer interest to the Interest Payee (VM) on the frequency specified in Paragraph 13(i)(ii). Typically such interest is paid in arrears on the first, second or third Local Business Day of the month depending upon a party's operational capability.

When Interest Transfer applies, the parties will also elect whether Interest Payment Netting is applied.

This is a process whereby the parties net interest payments that are due against any Delivery Amount (VM) or Return Amount (VM) payable on the same day. It is only possible to offset these amounts if:

1. The Interest Payment (VM) is less than the Delivery Amount (VM) or Return Amount (VM); and
2. The Interest Payment (VM) is more than the amount of Cash held as part of the Posted Collateral (VM).

If the value of the Interest Payment (VM) is more, an additional interest amount is still payable.

Paragraph 6(d)(ii)(A)(II) clarifies that while the Delivery Amount (VM) / Return Amount (VM) and Interest Payment (VM) are offset and therefore a single net payment is made, the two payments are deemed to have been made separately for the purposes of calculating the Posted Collateral (VM) and the net payment received will be caught under the security interest granted under Paragraph 2.

Please note that it is not common in the market for parties to apply Interest Payment Netting. Typically interest transfers are handled separately from collateral transfers.

(B) if "Interest Adjustment" is specified as applicable in Paragraph 13, the Posted Collateral (VM) will be adjusted by the Secured Party, at the times specified in Paragraph 13, as follows:

(I) if the Interest Amount (VM) for an Interest Period is a positive number, the Interest Amount (VM) will constitute Posted Collateral (VM) in the form of Cash in the Base Currency and will be subject to the security interest granted under Paragraph 2; and

(II) if the Interest Amount (VM) for an Interest Period is a negative number and any Posted Collateral (VM) is in the form of Cash in the Base Currency, the Interest Amount (VM) will constitute a reduction of Posted Collateral (VM) in the form of such Cash in an amount (such amount, the *"Interest Adjustment Reduction Amount (VM)"*) equal to the absolute value of the Interest Amount (VM); *provided* that if the amount of Posted Collateral (VM) which is comprised of such Cash is less than the Interest Adjustment Reduction Amount (VM), such reduction will only be to the extent of the amount of such Cash which is Posted Collateral (VM) and the Pledgor will

> be obligated to Transfer the remainder of the Interest Adjustment Reduction Amount (VM) to the Secured Party on the day that such reduction occurred.

Paragraph 6(d)(ii)(B) details the process when Interest Adjustment applies. In this case, the Secured Party looks to adjust the Posted Collateral (VM) to factor in any interest rather than transferring it. The provision looks at two scenarios:

(1) the Interest Amount (VM) is positive and therefore added to the Posted Collateral (VM)

(2) the Interest Amount (VM) is negative and therefore a reduction is made to the Posted Collateral (VM). If the Interest Amount (VM) is more that the amount of cash held as part of the Posted Collateral (VM) then only the cash portion can be offset. Any additional Interest Amount (VM) will need to be transferred to the other party.

Paragraph 7. Events of Default

> **Paragraph 7. Events of Default**
>
> For purposes of Section 5(a)(iii)(1) of this Agreement, an Event of Default will exist with respect to a party if:
>
> (i) that party fails (or fails to cause its Custodian (VM)) to make, when due, any Transfer of Eligible Collateral (VM), Posted Collateral (VM) or the Interest Payment (VM), as applicable, required to be made by it and that failure continues for two Local Business Days after notice of that failure is given to that party;
>
> (ii) that party fails to comply with any restriction or prohibition specified in this Annex with respect to any of the rights specified in Paragraph 6(c) and that failure continues for five Local Business Days after notice of that failure is given to that party; or
>
> (iii) that party fails to comply with or perform any agreement or obligation other than those specified in Paragraphs 7(i) and 7(ii) and that failure continues for 30 days after notice of that failure is given to that party.

Section 5(a)(iii)(1) of the ISDA Master Agreement covers Credit Support Default. Paragraph 7 sets forth what constitutes an Event of Default under the New York Law VM CSA for purposes of Section 5(a)(iii)(1).

In particular, it is an Event of Default under the ISDA Master Agreement if a party fails to make a required Transfer of collateral or interest on cash collateral and such failure lasts for two Local Business Days after notice is given. In fact many parties are now demanding that the cure period for the failure to make a Transfer is reduced to one Local Business Day to bring it in line with the standard grace period for Failure to Pay and Deliver under Section 5(a)(i) of the 2002 ISDA Master Agreement.

Paragraph 7(ii) relates to a party's failure to comply with any restrictions on reuse of collateral within five (5) Local Business Days after notice of such failure.

Paragraph 7(iii) deals with any other failure by a party to perform its obligations under the New York Law VM CSA which is not remedied for 30 days after notice. Such a failure could arise from shortcomings in safeguarding Posted Collateral (VM).

Paragraph 8. Certain Rights and Remedies

Paragraph 8. Certain Rights and Remedies

(a) *Secured Party's Rights and Remedies*. If at any time (1) an Event of Default or Specified Condition with respect to the Pledgor has occurred and is continuing or (2) an Early Termination Date has occurred or been designated as the result of an Event of Default or Specified Condition with respect to the Pledgor, then, unless the Pledgor has paid in full all of its Obligations that are then due, the Secured Party may exercise one or more of the following rights and remedies:

(i) all rights and remedies available to a secured party under applicable law with respect to Posted Collateral (VM) held by the Secured Party;

(ii) any other rights and remedies available to the Secured Party under the terms of Other Posted Support (VM), if any;

(iii) the right to Set-off (A) any amounts payable by the Pledgor with respect to any Obligations and (B) any Cash amounts and the Cash equivalent of any non-Cash items posted to the Pledgor by the Secured Party as margin under any Other CSA (other than any Other CSA Excluded Credit Support) the return of which is due to the Secured Party against any Posted Collateral (VM) or the Cash equivalent of any Posted Collateral (VM) held by the Secured Party (or any obligation of the Secured Party to Transfer that Posted Collateral (VM)); and

(iv) the right to liquidate any Posted Collateral (VM) held by the Secured Party through one or more public or private sales or other dispositions with such notice, if any, as may be required under applicable law, free from any claim or right of any nature whatsoever of the Pledgor, including any equity or right of redemption by the Pledgor (with the Secured Party having the right to purchase any or all of the Posted Collateral (VM) to be sold) and to apply the proceeds (or the Cash equivalent thereof) from the liquidation of the Posted Collateral (VM) to (A) any amounts payable by the Pledgor with respect to any Obligations and (B) any Cash amounts and the Cash equivalent of any non-Cash items posted to the Pledgor by the Secured Party as margin under any Other CSA (other than any Other CSA Excluded Credit Support) the return of which is due to the Secured Party in that order as the Secured Party may elect.

Each party acknowledges and agrees that Posted Collateral (VM) in the form of securities may decline speedily in value and is of a type customarily sold on a recognized market, and, accordingly, the Pledgor is not entitled to prior notice of any sale of that Posted Collateral (VM) by the Secured Party, except any notice that is required under applicable law and cannot be waived.

Paragraph 8(a) gives important rights and remedies to the Secured Party. It is first important to note that the Secured Party can exercise its rights and remedies under the New York Law VM CSA (and under applicable law) upon the occurrence of an Event of Default or a Specified Condition (i.e. certain Termination Events stated in Paragraph 13(e)(ii)) whether or not an Early Termination Date has occurred. Please note also that only the occurrence of a Termination Event or the designation of an Early Termination Date under the ISDA Master Agreement for a Termination Event that is identified as a Specified Condition in Paragraph 13(e)(ii) of the New York Law VM CSA are considered in relation to these rights and remedies under the New York Law VM CSA. If the Termination Event is not a Specified Condition then these rights and remedies do not apply. As discussed in Paragraph 4(a), the election of Specified Conditions is made in Paragraph 13(e)(ii) and is usually a selection of the Termination Events or Additional Termination Events which appear in the ISDA Master Agreement Schedule. If a Specified Condition applies to a party he cannot call for collateral, substitute it or receive Distributions or interest on collateral posted by him.

The rights and remedies under Paragraph 8(a) for the Secured Party are:

- Any rights or remedies it has under applicable law in respect of the Posted Collateral (VM). This maximises the possibilities for action by the Secured Party;

- Any rights and remedies under the terms of Other Posted Support (VM) such as a surety bond (which is a relatively uncommon type of collateral;
- The right to set off any amounts payable by the Pledgor under the Master Agreement against any Posted Collateral (VM) held by the Secured Party. This includes any collateral held under Other CSAs (e.g. a 1994 New York Law CSA) provided it is not categorised as Other CSA Excluded Credit Support; and
- The right to liquidate Posted Collateral (VM), for example, through public or private sales or a sale to himself free from any claim from the Pledgor and without any notice unless required by law.

The proceeds of the liquidation of Posted Collateral (VM) will be applied by the Secured Party in any order it sees fit against the Pledgor's Obligations to it under the New York Law VM CSA or under Other CSAs unless this is prohibited as Other CSA Excluded Credit Support.

(b) *Pledgor's Rights and Remedies.* If at any time an Early Termination Date has occurred or been designated as the result of an Event of Default or Specified Condition with respect to the Secured Party, then (except in the case of an Early Termination Date relating to fewer than all Transactions where the Secured Party has paid in full all of its obligations that are then due under Section 6(e) of this Agreement):

(i) the Pledgor may exercise all rights and remedies available to a pledgor under applicable law with respect to Posted Collateral (VM) held by the Secured Party;

(ii) the Pledgor may exercise any other rights and remedies available to the Pledgor under the terms of Other Posted Support (VM), if any;

(iii) the Secured Party will be obligated immediately to Transfer all Posted Collateral (VM) and, if the Secured Party is an Interest Payer (VM), the Interest Payment (VM) to the Pledgor; and

(iv) to the extent that Posted Collateral (VM) or the Interest Payment (VM) is not so Transferred pursuant to (iii) above, the Pledgor may:

(A) Set-off any amounts payable by the Pledgor with respect to any Obligations against any Posted Collateral (VM) or the Cash equivalent of any Posted Collateral (VM) held by the Secured Party (or any obligation of the Secured Party to Transfer that Posted Collateral (VM));

(B) Set-off, net, or apply credit support received under any Other CSA or the proceeds thereof against any Posted Collateral (VM) or the Cash equivalent of any Posted Collateral (VM) held by the Secured Party (or any obligation of the Secured Party to Transfer that Posted Collateral (VM)); and

(C) to the extent that the Pledgor does not Set-off under (iv)(A) or (iv)(B) above, withhold payment of any remaining amounts payable by the Pledgor with respect to any Obligations, up to the Value of any remaining Posted Collateral (VM) held by the Secured Party, until that Posted Collateral (VM) is Transferred to the Pledgor.

Paragraph 8(b) is important to the Pledgor. In contrast with Paragraph 8(a), the Pledgor can only exercise its rights and remedies after an Early Termination Date has been designated for all Transactions.

The rights and remedies under Paragraph 8(b) for the Pledgor are:

- any rights or remedies it has under applicable law in respect of the Posted Collateral (VM);
- any rights and remedies under the terms of Other Posted Support (VM) such as a surety bond (a relatively uncommon type of collateral);
- the right to the return of all Posted Collateral (VM) and interest on cash collateral from the Secured Party (this may be unrealistic to rely upon, however, if the Secured Party itself is in financial trouble);
- if all the Posted Collateral (VM) is not returned, the right to set off any amounts payable by the Pledgor under the Master Agreement against any Posted Collateral (VM) held by the Secured Party and any collateral held under Other CSAs; and
- if the Pledgor does not fully exercise its set off rights, the right to withhold its own residual early termination payments until the Posted Collateral (VM) is returned.

The Pledgor would only be an unsecured creditor with respect to its right to the return of any Posted Collateral (VM) upon the insolvency of a Secured Party because it does not have a "lien" on the Posted Collateral (VM) that it has pledged to the Secured Party. It will normally be easier for it to exercise its set off rights rather than petition the bankruptcy court for the return of its Posted Collateral (VM).

(c) **Deficiencies and Excess Proceeds.** The Secured Party will Transfer to the Pledgor any proceeds and Posted Credit Support (VM) remaining after liquidation, Set-off and/or application under Paragraphs 8(a) and 8(b) after satisfaction in full of all amounts payable by the Pledgor with respect to any Obligations; and the Pledgor in all events will remain liable for any amounts remaining unpaid after any liquidation, Set-off and/or application under Paragraphs 8(a) and 8(b).

Paragraph 8(c) restates a Pledgor's rights to any surplus Posted Credit Support (VM) after the Secured Party has received its full early termination payment. In addition, it restates the Secured Party's right to pursue the Pledgor further for payment if the Posted Collateral (VM) is not sufficient to satisfy all the Pledgor's Obligations to the Secured Party.

(d) **Final Returns.** When no amounts are or thereafter may become payable by the Pledgor with respect to any Obligations (except for any potential liability under Section 2(d) of this Agreement, any obligation to Transfer any Interest Payment (VM) under this Paragraph 8(d) or any obligation to transfer any interest payment under any Other CSA), (i) the Secured Party will Transfer to the Pledgor all Posted Credit Support (VM), and (ii) the Interest Payer (VM) will Transfer to the Interest Payee (VM) any Interest Payment (VM).

Where the Pledgor has satisfied all of its payment obligations to the Secured Party, Paragraph 8(d) requires that the Secured Party returns any Posted Collateral (VM) held as well as any interest that may be payable by the Secured Party on cash collateral. Any potential liability to withholding tax is ignored in these circumstances.

Paragraph 9. Representations

Paragraph 9. Representations

Each party represents to the other party (which representations will be deemed to be repeated as of each date on which it, as the Pledgor, Transfers Eligible Collateral (VM)) that:

(i) it has the power to grant a security interest in and lien on any Eligible Collateral (VM) it Transfers as the Pledgor and has taken all necessary actions to authorize the granting of that security interest and lien;

(ii) it is the sole owner of or otherwise has the right to Transfer all Eligible Collateral (VM) it Transfers to the Secured Party hereunder, free and clear of any security interest, lien, encumbrance or other restrictions other than the security interest and lien granted under Paragraph 2;

(iii) upon the Transfer of any Eligible Collateral (VM) to the Secured Party under the terms of this Annex, the Secured Party will have a valid and perfected first priority security interest therein (assuming that any central clearing corporation or any third-party financial intermediary or other entity not within the control of the Pledgor involved in the Transfer of that Eligible Collateral (VM) gives the notices and takes the action required of it under applicable law for perfection of that interest); and

(iv) the performance by it of its obligations under this Annex will not result in the creation of any security interest, lien or other encumbrance on any Posted Collateral (VM) other than the security interest and lien granted under Paragraph 2.

These representations made by the Pledgor (which could be either party depending on the mark-to-market risk exposure of the deal portfolio at that time) serve the same purpose as the Basic Representations made in Section 3(a) of the Master Agreement. They are deemed repeated each time Eligible Collateral (VM) is Transferred. If there is a breach of any of these representations it would constitute a misrepresentation and therefore result in a Misrepresentation Event of Default under Section 5(a)(iv) of the ISDA Master Agreement. This would allow the Secured Party to terminate all Transactions under it. The representations are fairly straightforward and are very rarely amended by the parties in Paragraph 13.

They are:

(i) The Pledgor has power and is authorised to grant a security interest and lien on its collateral;

(ii) It is sole beneficial owner of the collateral which is free of encumbrances;

(iii) Upon transfer the Secured Party will have a valid and perfected first priority security interest in the collateral even if a third party is involved in giving any necessary notices to perfect that security interest; and

(iv) No competing security interest will be created by the Pledgor on the collateral.

Paragraph 10. Expenses

Paragraph 10. Expenses

(a) *General.* Except as otherwise provided in Paragraphs 10(b) and 10(c), each party will pay its own costs and expenses in connection with performing its obligations under this Annex and neither party will be liable for any costs and expenses incurred by the other party in connection herewith.

Paragraph 10(a) is a simple statement that each party will pay its own expenses relating to its performance of its obligations under the New York Law VM CSA and will not be liable for any costs or expenses incurred by its counterparty.

(b) *Posted Credit Support (VM).* The Pledgor will promptly pay when due all taxes, assessments or charges of any nature that are imposed with respect to Posted Credit Support (VM) held by the Secured Party upon becoming aware of the same, regardless of whether any portion of that Posted Credit Support (VM) is subsequently disposed of under Paragraph 6(c), except for those taxes, assessments and charges that result from the exercise of the Secured Party's rights under Paragraph 6(c).

Paragraph 10(b) makes it clear that that the Pledgor will be responsible for taxes and other assessments in relation to the Posted Collateral (VM) except for those resulting from the Secured Party exercising its rehypothecation rights under Paragraph 6(c).

(c) *Liquidation/Application of Posted Credit Support (VM).* All reasonable costs and expenses incurred by or on behalf of the Secured Party or the Pledgor in connection with the liquidation and/or application of any Posted Credit Support (VM) under Paragraph 8 will be payable, on demand and pursuant to the Expenses Section of this Agreement, by the Defaulting Party or, if there is no Defaulting Party, equally by the parties.

Under Paragraph 10(c) if a Non-defaulting Party exercises its enforcement rights under Paragraph 8 all reasonable costs and expenses are borne by the Defaulting Party, or if there is none, by both parties equally.

Paragraph 11. Miscellaneous

Paragraph 11. Miscellaneous

(a) *Default Interest*. A Secured Party that fails to make, when due, any Transfer of Posted Collateral (VM) will be obligated to pay the Pledgor (to the extent permitted under applicable law) an amount equal to interest at the Default Rate multiplied by the Value of the items of property that were required to be Transferred, from (and including) the date that Posted Collateral (VM) was required to be Transferred to (but excluding) the date of Transfer of that Posted Collateral (VM). This interest will be calculated on the basis of daily compounding and the actual number of days elapsed. An Interest Payer (VM) that fails to make, when due, any Transfer of an Interest Payment (VM) will be obligated to pay the Interest Payee (VM) (to the extent permitted under applicable law) an amount equal to interest at the Default Rate (and for such purposes, if the Default Rate is less than zero, it will be deemed to be zero) multiplied by that Interest Payment (VM), from (and including) the date that Interest Payment (VM) was required to be Transferred to (but excluding) the date of Transfer of that Interest Payment (VM). This interest will be calculated on the basis of daily compounding and the actual number of days elapsed.

In line with with Section 2(e) of the 1992 ISDA Master Agreement and Section 9(h)(i) of the 2002 ISDA Master Agreement, if Posted Collateral (VM) is not transferred on its due date under the New York Law VM CSA then the Secured Party is required to pay interest at the Default Rate (i.e. 1% over the Pledgor's cost of funds) on the value of any Posted Collateral (VM) that is not delivered. The Default Interest accrued is compounded daily from and including the day it was due to but excluding the day the Transfer is actually made.

Similarly if the Interest Payer (VM) (which could be the Secured Party or Pledgor depending on whether interest is positive or negative) has not made an Interest Payment (VM) when due then Default Interest can be applied on a daily compounding basis for the actual number of days involved. However, if the Default Rate is negative, it will be deemed to be zero.

(b) *Further Assurances*. Promptly following a demand made by a party, the other party will execute, deliver, file and record any financing statement, specific assignment or other document and take any other action that may be necessary or desirable and reasonably requested by that party to create, preserve, perfect or validate any security interest or lien granted under Paragraph 2, to enable that party to exercise or enforce its rights under this Annex with respect to Posted Credit Support (VM) or an Interest Payment (VM) or to effect or document a release of a security interest on Posted Collateral (VM) or an Interest Payment (VM).

Firstly, when called upon to do so, the Pledgor is obliged to co-operate with the Secured Party where the Secured Party is having difficulty attaching, perfecting or enforcing its security interest in the Posted Collateral (VM) or Interest Payment (VM). Failure by the Pledgor to co-operate would constitute an Event of Default under Paragraph 7(iii).

The Secured Party is also required upon demand to co-operate with the Pledgor in order to enable the Pledgor to obtain the release of a security interest in the Posted Collateral (VM) or an Interest Payment (VM). The failure of the Secured Party to co-operate would also constitute an Event of Default under Paragraph 7(iii) because the New York Law VM CSA is a Credit Support Document for both for the Secured Party and for the Pledgor.

(c) *Further Protection*. The Pledgor will promptly give notice to the Secured Party of, and defend against, any suit, action, proceeding or lien that involves Posted Credit Support (VM) Transferred by the Pledgor or that could adversely affect the security interest and lien granted by it under Paragraph 2, unless that suit, action, proceeding or lien results from the exercise of the Secured Party's rights under Paragraph 6(c).

Paragraph 11(c) is a useful provision for the Secured Party because it requires the Pledgor to defend any third party claims against the Posted Collateral (VM). Again, it would constitute an Event of Default under Paragraph 7(iii) if the Pledgor fails to assist the Secured Party in such a defence. Please note that where such legal action arises as a result of the Secured Party's reuse of the Posted Collateral (VM) under Paragraph 6(c), the Pledgor has no obligation to assist the Secured Party against such action.

(d) *Good Faith and Commercially Reasonable Manner.* Performance of all obligations under this Annex, including, but not limited to, all calculations, valuations and determinations made by either party, will be made in good faith and in a commercially reasonable manner.

This sub-paragraph emphasises each party's obligations to act in good faith and in a commercially reasonable manner under the New York Law VM CSA.

(e) *Demands and Notices.* All demands and notices made by a party under this Annex will be made as specified in the Notices Section of this Agreement, except as otherwise provided in Paragraph 13.

Although Paragraph 11(e) is rather banal, it is critical that a party understands how to make demands and give notice so as to ensure that it can exercise its rights and remedies under the New York Law VM CSA promptly. This would ensure that notice and cure periods are triggered promptly and effectively under this clause.

(f) *Specifications of Certain Matters.* Anything referred to in this Annex as being specified in Paragraph 13 also may be specified in one or more Confirmations or other documents and this Annex will be construed accordingly.

Paragraph 11(f) highlights that the terms of the New York Law VM CSA can be made through a Confirmation as well as in the New York Law VM CSA itself. However, such a use of a Confirmation in isolation could present an operational challenge for a long dated Transaction because it would be difficult to ensure that an Operations Department could monitor it or pick it up in the first place. If such a course of action is taken, the Confirmation concerned should state that such a provision will survive the maturity of the Transaction covered by it.

(g) *Legally Ineligible Credit Support (VM).* Unless otherwise specified in Paragraph 13, upon delivery of a Legal Ineligibility Notice by a party, each item of Eligible Credit Support (VM) (or a specified amount of such item) identified in such notice (i) will cease to be Eligible Credit Support (VM) for purposes of Transfers to such party as the Secured Party hereunder as of the applicable Transfer Ineligibility Date, (ii) will cease to be Eligible Credit

Support (VM) for the other party as the Pledgor for all purposes hereunder as of the Total Ineligibility Date and (iii) will have a Value of zero on and from the Total Ineligibility Date.

"Legal Ineligibility Notice" means a written notice from the Secured Party to the Pledgor in which the Secured Party (i) represents that the Secured Party has determined that one or more items of Eligible Credit Support (VM) (or a specified amount of any such item) either has ceased to satisfy, or as of a specified date will cease to satisfy, collateral eligibility requirements under law applicable to the Secured Party requiring the collection of variation margin (the *"Legal Eligibility Requirements"*), (ii) lists the item(s) of Eligible Credit Support (VM) (and, if applicable, the specified amount) that have ceased to satisfy, or as of a specified date will cease to satisfy, the Legal Eligibility Requirements, (iii) describes the reason(s) why such item(s) of Eligible Credit Support (VM) (or the specified amount thereof) have ceased to satisfy, or will cease to satisfy, the Legal Eligibility Requirements and (iv) specifies the Total Ineligibility Date and, if different, the Transfer Ineligibility Date.

"Total Ineligibility Date" means the date on which the relevant item of Eligible Credit Support (VM) (or a specified amount of such item) has ceased to satisfy, or will cease to satisfy, the Legal Eligibility Requirements applicable to the Secured Party for all purposes hereunder; *provided* that, unless otherwise specified in Paragraph 13, if such date is earlier than the fifth Local Business Day following the date on which the Legal Ineligibility Notice is delivered, the Total Ineligibility Date will be the fifth Local Business Day following the date of such delivery.

"Transfer Ineligibility Date" means the date on which the relevant item of Eligible Credit Support (VM) (or a specified amount of such item) has ceased to satisfy, or will cease to satisfy, the Legal Eligibility Requirements for purposes of Transfers to the Secured Party hereunder; *provided* that, unless otherwise specified in Paragraph 13, if such date is earlier than the fifth Local Business Day following the date on which the Legal Ineligibility Notice is delivered, the Transfer Ineligibility Date will be the fifth Local Business Day following the date of such delivery.

Paragraphs 11(g)-(j) are new to the New York Law VM CSA.

Similar to the English Law VM CSA, Paragraph 11(g) introduces the concept of Legally Ineligible Credit Support (VM) and how it should be handled.

The types of collateral that are permitted under a VM CSA vary depending upon the regulatory regimes that apply. The general rule is that collateral needs to be high quality and liquid. Sometimes there will be restrictions on certain collateral types. This could be a minimum credit rating or a wrong way risk requirement (e.g. the posting party cannot deliver corporate bonds where they own all or part of the shares in the underlying company).

When collateral becomes ineligible it will cease to be eligible for transfers to the Secured Party as of the applicable Transfer Ineligibility Date. It will also cease being eligible collateral for the Pledgor from the Total Ineligibility Date and will have a value of zero on and from that date. If the Secured Party identifies that the collateral has become legally ineligible, it must notify the Pledgor by sending him a Legal Ineligibility Notice.

This written notice must include the following:

- A representation that one or more types of collateral (in whole or in part) do not or will not on a future specified date meet the collateral eligibility requirements under the relevant uncleared margin rules(s) applicable to the Secured Party;
- A list of the types of collateral that are impacted;
- The reason(s) why such collateral no longer fulfils or will not fulfil the Legal Eligibility Requirements; and
- The date on which the collateral has or will become ineligible.

There are two dates referenced in this provision:

Transfer Ineligibility Date: the date on which certain collateral items no longer meet or will no longer meet the Legal Eligibility Requirements for the purposes of **transfers to the Secured Party** (i.e. no more collateral of this type can be transferred to the Secured Party but collateral of this type that is currently held by the Secured Party is still eligible and valued).

Total Ineligibility Date: the date on which certain collateral items no longer meet or will no longer meet the Legal Eligibility Requirements applicable to the Transferee for **all other purposes** (i.e. all collateral of this type is no longer eligible and is valued at zero).

If the collateral is already ineligible unless Paragraph 13(c)(iii) states otherwise, there is a five Local Business Day grace period where this collateral will still be deemed eligible. This provides the parties some time to arrange for a substitution of collateral.

(h) *Return of Posted Credit Support (VM) with a Value of Zero*. Subject to Paragraph 4(a), the Secured Party will, promptly upon demand (but in no event later than the time at which a Transfer would be due under Paragraph 4(b) with respect to a demand for the Transfer of Eligible Credit Support (VM) or Posted Credit Support (VM)), Transfer to the Pledgor any item of Posted Credit Support (VM) (or the specified amount of such item) that as of the date of such demand has a Value of zero; *provided* that the Secured Party will only be obligated to Transfer any Posted Credit Support (VM) in accordance with this Paragraph 11(h), if, as of the date of Transfer of such item, the Pledgor has satisfied all of its Transfer obligations under this Annex, if any.

(h) Except in the situation where an Event of Default, Potential Event of Default or a Specified Condition has occurred or is continuing or where an Early Termination Date has been designated, if any collateral has a Value of zero (i.e. if it is no longer eligible) then the Secured Party is required to return such collateral upon demand provided that the Pledgor has satisfied all its other collateral transfer obligations under the CSA. It is likely that if an item of Eligible Credit Support (VM) is valued at zero then the Secured Party would be undercollateralised and would need to call for more collateral in a form that is eligible.

(i) *Reinstatement of Credit Support Eligibility*. Upon a reasonable request by the Pledgor, the Secured Party will determine whether an item (or a specified amount of such item) of Eligible Credit Support (VM) that was the subject of a prior Legal Ineligibility Notice would currently satisfy the Legal Eligibility Requirements applicable to the Secured Party. If the Secured Party determines that as of such date of determination such item (or specified amount of such item) satisfies the Legal Eligibility Requirements applicable to the Secured Party, the Secured Party will promptly following such determination rescind the relevant Legal Ineligibility Notice with respect to such item (or specified amount of such item) by written notice to the Pledgor. Upon the delivery of such notice, the relevant item (or specified amount of such item) will constitute Eligible Credit Support (VM) hereunder.

(i) This sub-paragraph deals with the situation where the Pledgor believes that collateral that was previously categorised as legally ineligible in whole or in part has become eligible again. He can request that the Secured Party reviews and determines if it is still ineligible or not. If it is eligible then the Secured Party will promptly provide a written notice withdrawing the relevant Legal Ineligibility Notice and the collateral will become eligible again.

(j) *Credit Support Offsets*. If the parties specify that "Credit Support Offsets" is applicable in Paragraph 13, and on any date:

(i) a Transfer of Eligible Credit Support (VM) is due under this Annex to satisfy a Delivery Amount (VM) or a Return Amount (VM) obligation, and a transfer of credit support (other than any Other CSA Excluded Credit Support) is also due under any Other CSA;

(ii) the parties have notified each other of the credit support that they intend to Transfer under this Annex and transfer under such Other CSA (other than any Other CSA Excluded Credit Support) to satisfy their respective obligations; and

(iii) in respect of Paragraph 11(j)(ii), each party intends to transfer one or more types of credit support that is fully fungible with one or more types of credit support the other party intends to transfer (each such credit support, a *"Fungible Credit Support Type"*),

then, on such date and in respect of each such Fungible Credit Support Type, each party's obligation to make a transfer of any such Fungible Credit Support Type hereunder or under such Other CSA will be automatically satisfied and discharged and, if the aggregate amount that would have otherwise been transferred by one party exceeds the aggregate amount that would have otherwise been transferred by the other party, replaced by an obligation hereunder or under such Other CSA, as applicable, upon the party by which the larger aggregate amount would have been transferred to transfer to the other party the excess of the larger aggregate amount over the smaller aggregate amount. If a party's obligation to make a transfer of credit support under this Annex or an Other CSA is automatically satisfied and discharged pursuant to this Paragraph 11(j), then, for purposes of this Annex or the Other CSA, as applicable, the other party will be deemed to have received credit support of the applicable Fungible Credit Support Type in the amount that would otherwise have been required to be transferred, in each case on the day on which the relevant transfer was due.

(j) Credit Support Offsets provide the parties with an option to offset collateral deliveries between different CSAs they have with each other. It could often be the case that the parties have two CSAs in place – an existing 1994 New York

Law CSA for trades entered into before the relevant regulatory implementation date and a New York Law VM CSA for trades from this date. This effectively means that there are two collateral pools existing at the same time. Depending on market movements, it is possible that one party is required to post collateral under the old CSA and the other party is required to post collateral under the new VM CSA. Rather than two transfers taking place, the parties can agree to offset the amounts due and for only one transfer be made covering the excess. This is only possible if the types of collateral being transferred are fully fungible (e.g. (a) cash or (b) bonds issued by the same issuer, of the same issue and the same nominal value). However, this would not be possible with collateral categorised as Other CSA Excluded Credit Support under an Other CSA.

Therefore Credit Support Offsets allow parties effectively to settlement net transfers of collateral between CSAs provided that the collateral in question is fully fungible and does not need to be segregated.

Most parties would like to implement Credit Support Offsets to reduce operational burdens and risks but currently very few entities have the systems or operational capability do to this.

Paragraph 12. Definitions

Paragraph 12 is the Definitions Paragraph.

Paragraph 12. Definitions

As used in this Annex:—

"Base Currency" means the currency specified as such in Paragraph 13.

"Base Currency Equivalent" means, with respect to an amount on a Valuation Date, in the case of an amount denominated in the Base Currency, such Base Currency amount and, in the case of an amount denominated in a currency other than the Base Currency (the *"Other Currency"*), the amount of Base Currency required to purchase such amount of the Other Currency at the spot exchange rate on such Valuation Date as determined by the Valuation Agent.

"Cash" means, respectively, the Base Currency and each other Eligible Currency.

"Covered Transaction" has the meaning specified in Paragraph 13.

"Credit Support Eligibility Condition (VM)" means, with respect to any item specified for a party as Eligible Collateral (VM) in Paragraph 13, any condition specified for that item in Paragraph 13.

"Custodian (VM)" has the meaning specified in Paragraphs 6(b)(i) and 13.

"Delivery Amount (VM)" has the meaning specified in Paragraph 3(a).

"Delivery Amount Reduction (VM)" has the meaning specified in Paragraph 6(d)(ii)(A)(II).

"Disputing Party" has the meaning specified in Paragraph 5.

"Distributions" means with respect to Posted Collateral (VM) other than Cash, all principal, interest and other payments and distributions of cash or other property with respect thereto, regardless of whether the Secured Party has disposed of that Posted Collateral (VM) under Paragraph 6(c). Distributions will not include any item of property acquired by the Secured Party upon any disposition or liquidation of Posted Collateral (VM) or, with respect to any Posted Collateral (VM) in the form of Cash, any distributions on that collateral, unless otherwise specified herein.

"Eligible Collateral (VM)" has the meaning specified in Paragraph 13.

"Eligible Credit Support (VM)" means Eligible Collateral (VM) and Other Eligible Support (VM).

"Eligible Currency" means each currency specified as such in Paragraph 13, if such currency is freely available.

"Eligible Return Amount (VM)" has the meaning specified in Paragraph 6(d)(ii)(A)(I)(a).

"Exposure" means, unless otherwise specified in Paragraph 13, for any Valuation Date or other date for which Exposure is calculated and subject to Paragraph 5 in the case of a dispute:

(i) if this Agreement is a 1992 ISDA Master Agreement, the amount, if any, that would be payable to a party that is the Secured Party by the other party (expressed as a positive number) or by a party that is the Secured Party to the other party (expressed as a negative number) pursuant to Section 6(e)(ii)(2)

(A) of this Agreement as if all Covered Transactions were being terminated as of the relevant Valuation Time on the basis that the Base Currency is the Termination Currency; *provided* that Market Quotation will be determined by the Valuation Agent on behalf of that party using its estimates at mid-market of the amounts that would be paid for Replacement Transactions (as that term is defined in the definition of "Market Quotation"); and

(ii) if this Agreement is an ISDA 2002 Master Agreement or a 1992 ISDA Master Agreement in which the definition of Loss and/or Market Quotation has been amended (including where such amendment has occurred pursuant to the terms of a separate agreement or protocol) to reflect the definition of Close-out Amount from the pre-printed form of the ISDA 2002 Master Agreement as published by ISDA, the amount, if any, that would be payable to a party that is the Secured Party by the other party (expressed as a positive number) or by a party that is the Secured Party to the other party (expressed as a negative number) pursuant to Section 6(e)(ii)(1) (but without reference to clause (3) of Section 6(e)(ii)) of this Agreement as if all Covered Transactions were being terminated as of the relevant Valuation Time on the basis that the Base Currency is the Termination Currency; *provided* that the Close-out Amount will be determined by the Valuation Agent on behalf of that party using its estimates at mid-market of the amounts that would be paid for transactions providing the economic equivalent of (X) the material terms of the Covered Transactions, including the payments and deliveries by the parties under Section 2(a)(i) in respect of the Covered Transactions that would, but for the occurrence of the relevant Early Termination Date, have been required after that date (assuming satisfaction of the conditions precedent in Section 2(a)(iii)), and (Y) the option rights of the parties in respect of the Covered Transactions.

"Fungible Credit Support Type" has the meaning specified in Paragraph 11(j)(iii).

"FX Haircut Percentage" means, for any item of Eligible Collateral (VM), the percentage specified as such in Paragraph 13.

"Interest Adjustment Reduction Amount (VM)" has the meaning specified in Paragraph 6(d)(ii)(B)(II).

"Interest Amount (VM)" means, with respect to an Interest Period, the aggregate sum of the Base Currency Equivalents of the amounts of interest determined for each relevant currency and calculated for each day in that

Interest Period on any Posted Collateral (VM) in the form of Cash in such currency held by the Secured Party on that day, determined by the Secured Party for each such day as follows:

(i) the amount of Cash in such currency on that day plus, only if "Daily Interest Compounding" is specified as applicable in Paragraph 13, the aggregate of each Interest Amount (VM) in respect of such currency determined for each preceding day, if any, in that Interest Period; multiplied by

(ii) the Interest Rate (VM) in effect for that day; divided by

(iii) 360 (or, in the case of pounds sterling or any other currency specified as an "A/365 Currency" in Paragraph 13, 365);

provided that, unless "Negative Interest" is specified as applicable in Paragraph 13, if the Interest Amount (VM) for an Interest Period would be a negative amount, it will be deemed to be zero.

"Interest Payee (VM)" means, in relation to an Interest Payer (VM), the other party.

"Interest Payer (VM)" means the Secured Party; *provided* that if "Negative Interest" is specified as applicable in Paragraph 13 and an Interest Payment (VM) is determined in respect of a negative Interest Amount (VM), the Interest Payer (VM) in respect of such Interest Payment (VM) will be the Pledgor.

"Interest Payment (VM)" means, with respect to an Interest Period, the Interest Amount (VM) determined in respect of such Interest Period; *provided* that in respect of any negative Interest Amount (VM), the Interest Payment (VM) will be the absolute value of such negative Interest Amount (VM).

"Interest Period" means the period from (and including) the last day on which (i) a party became obligated to Transfer an Interest Payment (VM) or (ii) an Interest Amount (VM) was included or otherwise became constituted as part of Posted Collateral (VM) (or, if no Interest Payment (VM) or Interest Amount (VM) has yet fallen due or been included or otherwise became constituted as a part of Posted Collateral (VM), respectively, the day on which Eligible Credit Support (VM) in the form of Cash was Transferred to or received by the Secured Party) to (but excluding) the day on which (i) a party is obligated to Transfer the current Interest Payment (VM) or (ii) the

current Interest Amount (VM) is included or otherwise becomes constituted as a part of Posted Collateral (VM).

"Interest Rate (VM)" means, with respect to an Eligible Currency, the rate specified in Paragraph 13 for that currency.

"Legal Eligibility Requirements" has the meaning specified in Paragraph 11(g).

"Legal Ineligibility Notice" has the meaning specified in Paragraph 11(g).

"Local Business Day", unless otherwise specified in Paragraph 13, means:

(i) in relation to a Transfer of cash or other property (other than securities) under this Annex, a day on which commercial banks are open for business (including dealings in foreign exchange and foreign currency deposits) in the place where the relevant account is located and, if different, in the principal financial center, if any, of the currency of such payment;

(ii) in relation to a Transfer of securities under this Annex, a day on which the clearance system agreed between the parties for delivery of the securities is open for the acceptance and execution of settlement instructions or, if delivery of the securities is contemplated by other means, a day on which commercial banks are open for business (including dealings in foreign exchange and foreign currency deposits) in the place(s) agreed between the parties for this purpose;

(iii) in relation to the Resolution Time, a day on which commercial banks are open for business (including dealings in foreign exchange and foreign currency deposits) in at least one Valuation Date Location for Party A and at least one Valuation Date Location for Party B; and

(iv) in relation to any notice or other communication under this Annex, a day on which commercial banks are open for business (including dealings in foreign exchange and foreign currency deposits) in the place specified in the address for notice most recently provided by the recipient.

"Minimum Transfer Amount" means, with respect to a party, the amount specified as such for that party in Paragraph 13; if no amount is specified, zero.

"Notification Time" has the meaning specified in Paragraph 13.

"Obligations" means, with respect to a party, all present and future obligations of that party under this Agreement and any additional obligations specified for that party in Paragraph 13.

"Other CSA" means, unless otherwise specified in Paragraph 13, any other credit support annex or credit support deed that is in relation to, or that is a Credit Support Document in relation to, this Agreement.

"Other CSA Excluded Credit Support" means, with respect to an Other CSA, any amounts and items posted as margin under such Other CSA, which, pursuant to the terms of such Other CSA, Party A and Party B have agreed must be segregated in an account maintained by a third-party custodian or for which offsets are prohibited.

"Other Eligible Support (VM)" means, with respect to a party, the items, if any, specified as such for that party in Paragraph 13.

"Other Posted Support (VM)" means all Other Eligible Support (VM) Transferred to the Secured Party that remains in effect for the benefit of that Secured Party.

"Pledgor" means either party, when that party (i) receives a demand for or is required to Transfer Eligible Credit Support (VM) under Paragraph 3(a) or (ii) has Transferred Eligible Credit Support (VM) under Paragraph 3(a).

"Posted Collateral (VM)" means all Eligible Collateral (VM), other property, Distributions, and all proceeds thereof that have been Transferred to or received by the Secured Party under this Annex and not Transferred to the Pledgor pursuant to Paragraph 3(b), 4(d)(ii), 6(d)(i) or 11(h) or released by the Secured Party under Paragraph 8. With respect to any Interest Amount (VM) in respect of any Interest Payment (VM) or relevant part thereof not Transferred pursuant to Paragraph 6(d)(ii)(A) or Paragraph 6(d)(ii)(B), as applicable, if such Interest Amount (VM) is a positive number, such Interest Amount (VM) will constitute Posted Collateral (VM) in the form of Cash in the Base Currency.

"Posted Credit Support (VM)" means Posted Collateral (VM) and Other Posted Support (VM).

"Recalculation Date" means the Valuation Date that gives rise to the dispute under Paragraph 5; *provided*, *however*, that if a subsequent Valuation Date occurs under Paragraph 3 prior to the resolution of the dispute, then the "Recalculation Date" means the most recent Valuation Date under Paragraph 3.

"Regular Settlement Day," means, unless otherwise specified in Paragraph 13, the same Local Business Day on which a demand for the Transfer of Eligible Credit Support (VM) or Posted Credit Support (VM) is made.

"Resolution Time" has the meaning specified in Paragraph 13.

"Return Amount (VM)" has the meaning specified in Paragraph 3(b).

"Return Amount Reduction (VM)" has the meaning specified in Paragraph 6(d)(ii)(A)(II).

"Secured Party" means either party, when that party (i) makes a demand for or is entitled to receive Eligible Credit Support (VM) under Paragraph 3(a) or (ii) holds or is deemed to hold Posted Credit Support (VM).

"Set-off" means set-off, offset, combination of accounts, right of retention or withholding or similar right or requirement (whether arising under this Agreement, another contract, applicable law or otherwise) and, when used as a verb, the exercise of any such right or the imposition of any such requirement.

"Specified Condition" means, with respect to a party, any event specified as such for that party in Paragraph 13.

"Substitute Credit Support (VM)" has the meaning specified in Paragraph 4(d)(i).

"Substitution Date" has the meaning specified in Paragraph 4(d)(ii).

"Total Ineligibility Date" has the meaning specified in Paragraph 11(g) unless otherwise specified in Paragraph 13.

"Transfer" means, with respect to any Eligible Credit Support (VM), Posted Credit Support (VM) or Interest Payment (VM), and in accordance with the instructions of the Secured Party, Pledgor or Custodian (VM), as applicable:

(i) in the case of Cash, payment or delivery by wire transfer into one or more bank accounts specified by the recipient;

(ii) in the case of certificated securities that cannot be paid or delivered by book-entry, payment or delivery in appropriate physical form to the recipient or its account accompanied by any duly executed instruments of transfer, assignments in blank, transfer tax stamps and any other documents necessary to constitute a legally valid transfer to the recipient;

(iii) in the case of securities that can be paid or delivered by book-entry, causing the relevant depository institution(s) or other securities intermediaries to make changes to their books and records sufficient to result in a legally effective transfer of the relevant interest to the recipient or its agent; and

(iv) in the case of Other Eligible Support (VM) or Other Posted Support (VM), as specified in Paragraph 13.

"Transfer Ineligibility Date" has the meaning specified in Paragraph 11(g) unless otherwise specified in Paragraph 13.

"Valuation Agent" has the meaning specified in Paragraph 13.

"Valuation Date" means, unless otherwise specified in Paragraph 13, each day from, and including, the date of this Annex, that is a day on which commercial banks are open for business (including dealings in foreign exchange and foreign currency deposits) in at least one Valuation Date Location for Party A and at least one Valuation Date Location for Party B.

"Valuation Date Location" has the meaning specified in Paragraph 13.

"Valuation Percentage" means, for any item of Eligible Collateral (VM), the percentage specified as such in Paragraph 13.

"Valuation Time" means, unless otherwise specified in Paragraph 13, the time as of which the Valuation Agent computes its end of day valuations of derivatives transactions in the ordinary course of its business (or such other commercially reasonable convenient time on the relevant day as the Valuation Agent may determine).

"Value" means for any Valuation Date or other date for which Value is calculated and subject to Paragraph 5 in the case of a dispute, with respect to:

(i) Eligible Collateral (VM) or Posted Collateral (VM) that is:

(A) an amount of Cash, the Base Currency Equivalent of such amount multiplied by $(VP - H_{FX})$; and
(B) a security, the Base Currency Equivalent of the bid price obtained by the Valuation Agent multiplied by $(VP - H_{FX})$, where:

VP equals the applicable Valuation Percentage; and

H_{FX} equals the applicable FX Haircut Percentage;

(ii) Posted Collateral (VM) that consists of items that are not Eligible Collateral (VM) (including any item or any portion of any item that fails to satisfy any (A) Credit Support Eligibility Condition (VM) applicable to it or (B) applicable Legal Eligibility Requirements), zero; and

(iii) Other Eligible Support (VM) and Other Posted Support (VM), as specified in Paragraph 13.

Glossary of terms in Paragraph 12

The following is a simplified glossary of all terms in the New York Law VM CSA.

Base Currency	The currency into which risk exposure and collateral is converted to calculate if a collateral call needs to be made.
Base Currency Equivalent	If collateral is denominated in another currency, the amount in the Base Currency needed to buy the other currency at the spot rate of exchange so as to convert it into the Base Currency.
Cash	Cash in the Base Currency and any other Eligible Currency.
Covered Transaction	The OTC derivative trades covered in Paragraph 13(b) of the New York Law VM CSA.
Credit Support Eligibility Condition (VM)	Any restrictions or conditions applied to collateral that must be considered when assessing whether it is eligible or not under the New York Law VM CSA.

Custodian (VM)	A third party appointed by a party to care for cash and securities collateral.
Delivery Amount (VM)	The amount of collateral the collateral giver (the Pledgor) needs to deliver if he agrees a collateral call from the collateral taker (the Secured Party).
Delivery Amount Reduction (VM)	The amount by which a Delivery Amount (VM) is reduced by an offsetting interest payment where the parties have agreed that Interest Transfer and Interest Payment Netting apply.
Disputing Party	A party who disputes the Valuation Agent's calculations of Covered Transaction values in determining risk exposure and/or the value of any collateral held or to be returned.
Distributions	Distributions include any transfers of principal, interest or any other distributions made with respect to Posted Collateral (VM) except for interest on cash collateral.
Eligible Collateral (VM)	The types of collateral and their maturities that can be pledged by the Pledgor under Paragraph 13(c)(ii) of the New York Law VM CSA.
Eligible Credit Support (VM)	The aggregate of Eligible Collateral (VM) and any other credit support agreed by the parties.
Eligible Currency	The agreed currency or currencies for cash collateral transferred under the New York Law VM CSA and which are freely available.
Eligible Return Amount (VM)	The amount of cash collateral held which is taken into consideration when calculating whether an interest payment can be offset and if so, how much can be offset.
Exposure	The estimated termination value of all Covered Transactions so as to calculate risk exposure. The calculation is made as if the Covered Transactions were being closed out as of the Valuation Time.
Fungible Credit Support Type	Collateral of the same type (e.g. (a) cash or (b) bonds issued by the same issuer, of the same issue and the same nominal value).
FX Haircut Percentage	An additional haircut (typically 8%) which may be applied to collateral if certain conditions apply under the relevant uncleared margin regulation applicable to the party concerned.
Interest Adjustment Reduction Amount (VM)	The amount by which cash collateral held is reduced by offsetting interest (which may be at a negative rate) where the parties have agreed that Interest Adjustment applies.

Interest Amount (VM)	The aggregate sum of interest due on Cash collateral.
Interest Payee (VM)	The party due to receive an interest payment.
Interest Payer (VM)	The party required to make an interest payment.
Interest Payment (VM)	The amount of interest that has accrued during an Interest Period.
Interest Period	The period from the date when interest on Cash collateral was last paid or adjusted to the date on which it is next due to be paid or adjusted.
Interest Rate (VM)	The particular benchmark interest rate (e.g. Federal Funds (Effective)) stated in Paragraph 13(i) of the New York Law VM CSA. In agreements involving U.S. parties, it is typically based on Federal Funds (Effective). It may also include a spread.
Legal Eligibility Requirements	The minimum eligibility requirements under the law applicable to the Secured Party that must be applied to collateral.
Legal Ineligibility Notice	A written notice from the Secured Party to the Pledgor providing details of why one or more types of Eligible Credit Support (VM) are no longer eligible.
Local Business Day	A normal business day for commercial banks in the location required for the valuation of Covered Transactions and collateral under the New York Law VM CSA. With securities transfers it is a normal business day when securities clearance systems are open.
Minimum Transfer Amount	The minimum amount that the Delivery Amount (VM) or Return Amount (VM) must reach before a party can be called to deliver or return collateral. If no Minimum Transfer Amount is specified it is zero.
Notification Time	The agreed deadline for making a collateral call in order to receive a Transfer by the deadline specified in the New York Law VM CSA.
Obligations	The present and future obligations of a party under the ISDA Master Agreement. The extent of these obligations may be expanded in Paragraph 13.
Other CSA	Any other credit support annex or credit support deed linked to the same ISDA Master Agreement.

Other CSA Excluded Credit Support	Any amounts of collateral posted under an Other CSA which must be kept segregated or which cannot be offset.
Other Eligible Support (VM)	This constitutes other credit support that the parties may agree to such as surety bonds.
Other Posted Support (VM)	Other Eligible Support (VM) that is actually provided by the Pledgor to the Secured Party.
Pledgor	The party that receives a demand requiring it to post collateral or the party who currently has pledged collateral i.e. the collateral giver.
Posted Collateral (VM)	All collateral that has been pledged to and is currently held by the Secured Party.
Posted Credit Support (VM)	The aggregate of Posted Collateral (VM) and any Other Posted Support (VM).
Recalculation Date	The Valuation Date that gave rise to a dispute.
Regular Settlement Day	The day on which collateral must be provided following a collateral call. This is the same Local Business Day as the demand unless amended in Paragraph 13.
Resolution Time	The deadline for resolving disputes i.e. one Local Business Day after the date on which a party receives a notice that it disputes.
Return Amount (VM)	The collateral amount to be returned by the collateral taker to the collateral giver because it is surplus to the collateral taker's risk exposure on the collateral giver.
Return Amount Reduction (VM)	The amount by which a Return Amount (VM) is reduced by an offsetting interest payment where the parties have agreed that Interest Transfer and Interest Payment Netting apply.
Secured Party	The party making a demand to receive collateral or the party holding Posted Collateral (VM) i.e. the collateral taker.
Set-off	The right to offset amounts due to each party under different contractual agreements between them.
Specified Condition	A Termination Event such as Illegality or Credit Event Upon Merger designated by the parties in Paragraph 13(e)(ii) as a Specified Condition.
Substitute Credit Support (VM)	Collateral transferred to the Secured Party in substitution for previously pledged collateral.

Substitution Date	The date the Secured Party transfers back part or all of the original Posted Credit Support (VM) to the Pledgor after receiving the Substitute Credit Support (VM).
Total Ineligibility Date	Following the delivery of a Legal Ineligibility Notice, the date upon which collateral that is held will be deemed ineligible and of zero value.
Transfer	A Transfer occurs when collateral delivered to a Secured Party is deemed to be received by it or its custodian. For example, a Transfer of Cash occurs when the Cash is delivered to the Secured Party's bank account.
Transfer Ineligibility Date	The date upon which collateral in the form specified in a Legal Ineligibility Notice will no longer be accepted. Collateral of this type that is already held will still be considered eligible and will continue to be valued until the Total Ineligibility Date.
Valuation Agent	The Valuation Agent is the party calculating Exposure and the value of Posted Collateral (VM). It is also the party that makes a request for collateral to be transferred.
Valuation Date	The date upon which risk exposure calculations and collateral valuations are made (based upon those amounts as of the Valuation Time) to determine if a collateral delivery or return is needed. This is each day on which commercial banks are open for business in at least one Valuation Date Location for each party.
Valuation Date Location	The location(s) specified in Paragraph 13 for each party which must be open in order for a Valuation Date to be valid.
Valuation Percentage	The remaining value of collateral expressed in percentage terms after the agreed haircut has been deducted.
Valuation Time	The reference time at which calculations for collateral calls are made. This is the time when the Valuation Agent normally calculates its end of day valuations for OTC derivative trades.
Value	The agreed valuation bases for Cash and securities collateral taking into consideration any FX Haircut Percentage.

Paragraph 13. Elections and Variables

Paragraph 13 is the Elections and Variables Paragraph where the parties complete necessary information and make choices and amendments to the standard form of the New York Law VM CSA. It is the CSA equivalent of the ISDA Master Agreement Schedule. It is important for the parties to consider and complete it very carefully.

Paragraph 13. Elections and Variables

(a) *Base Currency and Eligible Currency.*

(i) *"Base Currency"* means United States Dollars, unless otherwise specified here: ....

....

(ii) *"Eligible Currency"* means the Base Currency and each other currency specified here: ....

....

....

....

(a) The New York Law VM CSA now includes an option to select a Base Currency as well as Eligible Currencies. The 1994 New York Law CSA did not include these defined terms and all calculations and amounts were denominated in U.S. dollars.

(b) *Covered Transactions; Security Interest for Obligations; Exposure.*

(i) The term *"Covered Transactions"* as used in this Annex includes any Transaction specified below that is entered into on or after [........................ ......]*, except as otherwise provided in the Confirmation of such Transaction:

(A) For purposes of the foregoing, the term *"Covered Transactions"* includes: [Any Transaction [that is any of the following] [Swap], [Security-Based Swap], [OTC Derivative], [Physically Settled FX Forward] or [Physically Settled FX Swap]] [and is not any of the following: [Swap], [Security-Based Swap], [OTC Derivative], [Physically Settled FX Forward], or [Physically Settled FX Swap].................................]**

As used above:

[*"OTC Derivative"* means an "OTC derivative" or "OTC derivative contract" as defined in Article 2(7) of Regulation (EU) No 648/2012 of the European Parliament and of the Council of 4 July 2012 on OTC derivatives,

---

central counterparties and trade repositories (*"EMIR"*) other than one which constitutes (i) a "foreign exchange forward" as defined in Article 7(1)(a) of the final draft regulatory technical standards on risk-mitigation techniques for OTC-derivative contracts not cleared by a CCP under Article 11(15) of EMIR dated March 8, 2016 (the *"EMIR RTS"*) for so long as such transactions are subject to the transitional exemption from the variation margin requirements under Article 39(6) of the EMIR RTS and (ii) a single stock equity option or index option transaction as referred to in Article 39(7) of the EMIR RTS for so long as such transactions are subject to the transitional exemption from the variation margin requirements under Article 39(7) of the EMIR RTS.]

[*"Physically Settled FX Forward"* means [................................]]

[*"Physically Settled FX Swap"* means [................................]]

[*"Security-Based Swap"* means a "security-based swap" as defined in Section 3(a)(68) of the U.S. Securities Exchange Act of 1934, as amended (*"SEA"*), and the rules adopted thereunder. For the avoidance of doubt, the term "Security-Based Swap" does not include a security-based swap that has been cleared by a "clearing agency," as such term is defined in Section 3(a)(23) of the SEA and the rules adopted thereunder.]

[*"Swap"* means a "swap" as defined in Section 1a(47) of the U.S. Commodity Exchange Act, as amended (*"CEA"*), and the regulations adopted thereunder. For the avoidance of doubt, the term "Swap" does not include a swap that has been cleared by a "derivatives clearing organization," as such term is defined in Section 1a(15) of the CEA and the regulations adopted thereunder.]

[For the purposes of the foregoing, a Transaction will be deemed to be entered into on or after the date specified in this Paragraph 13(b)(i) if an amendment, novation or other lifecycle event with respect to such Transaction would cause such Transaction to be entered into after such date under law applicable to either party requiring the collection or delivery of variation margin.][**]

Footnote:
[*] Insert the relevant date.
[**] Parties may retain, delete or revise any of these definitions or add any additional definitions, as applicable.

*** Parties may retain, delete or revise the bracketed language, as applicable.

The parties specify here which trades are included under the New York Law VM CSA. There are typically two choices made.

The first is the types of trades. This is often all OTC derivative trades other than spot FX.

The second is the date from which trades are collateralised under the New York Law VM CSA. This is generally either (1) the date of the ISDA Master Agreement meaning that all trades are collateralised or (2) the relevant regulatory implementation date (e.g. 1st March 2017) meaning that any existing trades executed before that date will not be captured under the New York Law VM CSA. These trades will typically be covered by an existing CSA or perhaps even remain uncollateralised.

If the relevant regulatory implementation date is selected then all new OTC derivative trades included in the Covered Transactions definition will be captured under the New York Law VM CSA. In addition, any trades that are amended by lifecycle events (e.g. novations) after the relevant regulatory implementation date will also be covered under the New York Law VM CSA.

Covered Transactions under the New York Law VM CSA are specifically excluded when calculating risk exposure under any Other CSA.

> (ii) The term *"Obligations"* as used in this Annex includes the following additional obligations:
> With respect to Party A: ....
> With respect to Party B: ....

Paragraph 13(b)(ii) provides parties with the option to expand the definition of "Obligations" to include other obligations of their counterparty that are outside of the ISDA Master Agreement.

Generally parties do not extend this definition.

> (iii) *"Exposure"* has the meaning specified in Paragraph 12, unless otherwise specified here:...

There is also in Paragraph 13(b)(iii) scope to redefine Exposure if necessary. Following the expanded Exposure definition in the New York Law VM CSA covering termination payment measures in both the 1992 and 2002 versions of the ISDA Master Agreement and also the introduction of the Covered Transaction definition in Paragraph 13(b)(i), this is rarely amended.

(c) *Credit Support Obligations.*

(i) *Delivery Amount (VM) and Return Amount (VM).*

(A) *"Delivery Amount (VM)"* has the meaning specified in Paragraph 3(a), unless otherwise specified here: ....
....

(B) *"Return Amount (VM)"* has the meaning specified in Paragraph 3(b), unless otherwise specified here: ....
....

Paragraph 13(c)(i) typically provides that the standard definitions of Delivery Amount (VM) and Return Amount (VM) apply.

If you change the definition of either of these you should change the other because they are mirror images of each other.

As previously mentioned, when the 2016 ISDA Credit Support Annexes For Variation Margin were published, revisions were made to the Annexes to remove Independent Amount (non-regulatory initial margin) terms. While variation margin is calculated on a net basis, regulatory driven initial margin would need to be handled on a gross basis and therefore the English Law and New York Law VM CSAs are not appropriate for this purpose.

However, non-regulatory Independent Amounts could be posted net or gross. A non-regulatory Independent Amount may be required from a business perspective depending on either the types of trades the parties are entering into (e.g. if highly structured then daily valuations may be insufficient/inaccurate when there is a market disruption) or from a credit perspective when considering the creditworthiness of your counterparty.

Where non-regulatory Independent Amount is agreed, the Credit Support Obligations section would need to be updated. ISDA has published language which can be used for this purpose. It introduces "Credit Support Amount (VM/IA)" (similar to that in the 1994 New York Law CSA) which incorporates Independent Amount into the calculations used to determine Delivery Amounts (VM) and Return Amounts (VM). The relevant Independent Amount would also be included under Paragraph 13(c)(i).

An Independent Amount could be a fixed monetary sum or a percentage of the notional amount of one or more Transactions. Independent Amounts based on the value at risk (VAR) for the entire trade portfolio or for all trades of the same product type (e.g. all interest rate swaps) are also often seen in the market.

(ii) *Eligible Collateral (VM).* Subject to Paragraph 11(g), if applicable, and each Credit Support Eligibility Condition (VM) applicable to it specified in Paragraph 13, if any, the following items will qualify as *"Eligible Collateral (VM)"* for the party specified (as the Pledgor):

	Party A	Valuation Percentage	Party B	Valuation Percentage
(A) cash in an Eligible Currency	[ ]	[ ]%	[ ]	[ ]%
(B) other:	[ ]	[ ]%	[ ]	[ ]%

The parties state in Paragraph 13(c)(ii) the types of Eligible Collateral (VM) that each party, when acting as Pledgor, is permitted to deliver. This is typically cash and/or securities that are eligible under the relevant uncleared margin regulations.

(iii) *Legally Ineligible Credit Support (VM).* The provisions of Paragraph 11(g) will not apply to the [party/parties] specified here (as the Secured Party):**

[ ] Party A
[ ] Party B

(A) *"Total Ineligibility Date"* has the meaning specified in Paragraph 11(g), unless otherwise specified here : ....
....

(B) *"Transfer Ineligibility Date"* has the meaning specified in Paragraph 11(g), unless otherwise specified here: ....
....

Footnote:

** Parties should leave the relevant box below unmarked unless they agree to disapply Paragraph 11(g) with respect to a party as the Secured Party.

You state if the Legally Ineligible Credit Support (VM) provisions apply in Paragraph 13(c)(iii). In most cases the parties will apply this to both parties when they are acting as the Secured Party unless the only Eligible Collateral (VM) is cash in which case the provisions are not applied. This is because the market generally agrees that cash will not become legally ineligible. As outlined in the footnote, if no election is made these provisions are deemed to apply.

It is also possible to amend the definitions of Total Ineligibility Date and Transfer Ineligibility Date here but these are very rarely amended.

(iv) *Credit Support Eligibility Conditions (VM)*. The following conditions will each be a "Credit Support Eligibility Condition (VM)" for the party specified. Any item will not qualify as Eligible Collateral (VM) for a party (as the Pledgor) if such item does not satisfy each Credit Support Eligibility Condition (VM) applicable to it.

[....]
[....]

In Paragraph 13(c)(iv) the parties have the option to include Credit Support Eligibility Conditions (VM). In order for collateral to be eligible under the New York Law VM CSA it must meet all conditions specified here (if any).

Where only cash collateral is included as Eligible Collateral (VM), no Credit Support Eligibility Conditions (VM) are normally specified.

For non-cash collateral, the parties may wish to include minimum credit rating requirements or conditions on the currency of the securities. Under uncleared margin regulations in different jurisdictions there is often an FX Haircut Percentage of 8% on non-cash collateral denominated in a currency that is not an Eligible Currency (under EMIR) or a Major Currency (under PR or CFTC rules).

(v) *"Valuation Percentage"; "FX Haircut Percentage"*

(A) *"Valuation Percentage"* means, with respect to each party (as the Pledgor) and item of Eligible Collateral (VM), the percentage (expressed as a decimal) specified in Paragraph 13(c)(ii); *provided* that if nothing is specified in Paragraph 13(c)(ii), the Valuation Percentage will be 100% unless otherwise specified below. The Valuation Percentage for either party and any item of Eligible Collateral (VM) will further be subject to the terms and conditions, if any, specified below as applicable to such party and item:

....

[If at any time the Valuation Percentage assigned to an item of Eligible Collateral (VM) with respect to a party (as the Pledgor) under this Annex is greater than the maximum permitted valuation percentage (prescribed or implied) for such item of collateral under any law requiring the collection of variation margin applicable to the other party (as the Secured Party), then the Valuation Percentage with respect to such item of Eligible Collateral (VM) and such party will be such maximum permitted valuation percentage.]*

Footnote:
* Parties may retain, delete or revise the bracketed language, as applicable.

Sub-paragraph (v) addresses various Valuation Percentage matters.

Firstly, there is a provision that makes it clear that the Valuation Percentage stated in any Eligible Collateral (VM) table will apply but if no percentage is shown there then the default Valuation Percentage is 100%. Ideally, parties should ensure that the Valuation Percentages are referenced in the Eligible Collateral (VM) table because it may not be regulatory compliant to accept this 100% Valuation Percentage fallback.

There is then a useful optional provision stating that if the Valuation Percentage specified for any item of Eligible Collateral (VM) is greater than the maximum valuation percentage permitted by law or regulation then the Valuation Percentage is automatically amended to the maximum percentage permitted.

While this additional clause can be useful to limit the requirement to update documentation if there is a regulatory breach or change in regulation, care should be taken to ensure that you can operationally support it and reference this automatic amendment in the appropriate system.

(B) *"FX Haircut Percentage"* means, with respect to each party (as the Pledgor) and item of Eligible Collateral (VM), [[8]%, unless the Eligible Collateral (VM) or Posted Collateral (VM) is in the form of cash [in a Major Currency] or is denominated in a currency that matches [an Eligible Currency], in which case the FX Haircut Percentage will be 0%.]

[As used above, *"Major Currency"* means any of: (1) United States Dollar; (2) Canadian Dollar; (3) Euro; (4) United Kingdom Pound; (5) Japanese Yen; (6) Swiss Franc; (7) New Zealand Dollar; (8) Australian Dollar; (9)

Swedish Kronor; (10) Danish Kroner; (11) Norwegian Krone or any other currency specified below:

[...

..................]]**

Footnote:
** Parties may revise the bracketed language and the related definitions, as applicable.

Here there is an option to specify an FX Haircut Percentage. An 8% haircut is required under most uncleared margin regulation but there are exceptions. Under EMIR the haircut does not apply to any cash collateral or non-cash collateral denominated in an Eligible Currency. Under PR and CFTC rules the same applies if the currency is a Major Currency which can be one or more of the eleven currencies stated in Paragraph 13.

(vi) *Other Eligible Support (VM)*. The following items will qualify as "*Other Eligible Support (VM)*" for the party specified (as the Pledgor):

		Party A	Party B
(A)	....	[ ]	[ ]
(B)	....	[ ]	[ ]

With Paragraph 13(c)(vi) you occasionally see general wording for other "Other Eligible Support (VM)". It is highly unusual, however, that Other Eligible Support (VM) (such as a surety bond) would ever actually be taken and so this sub-paragraph is usually disapplied.

(vii) *Minimum Transfer Amount.*

(A) "*Minimum Transfer Amount*" means with respect to Party A: $ ....

"*Minimum Transfer Amount*" means with respect to Party B: $ ....

Minimum Transfer Amounts are designed to prevent costly transfers of small amounts of collateral. Before a Delivery Amount (VM) or Return Amount (VM) is required to be made under Paragraph 3, the amount concerned must exceed the Minimum Transfer Amount for the relevant party.

Usually the Minimum Transfer Amount is expressed in a fixed monetary sum (e.g. USD 100,000). There are limits to how high the Minimum Transfer Amount can be under uncleared margin regulations. Where EMIR applies this is EUR 500,000 and under CFTC or PR rules USD 500,000.

This limit is set at a counterparty level across documentation for both variation margin and initial margin. Therefore if your counterparty is a fund which has appointed multiple investment managers to act on their behalf under separate CSAs then the aggregate of all the Minimum Transfer Amounts under the CSAs cannot exceed the caps above.

It is common for an additional clause to be included in the Minimum Transfer Amount definition resulting in the Minimum Transfer Amount being reduced to zero if a party suffers an Event of Default.

Generally, it is now a requirement for parties subject to uncleared margin rules to have a zero Threshold under their CSAs. In fact, the definition of Threshold has been completely removed from the New York Law VM CSA.

Some parties view the Minimum Transfer Amount as a form of unsecured credit which could be argued to act in the same way as a Threshold. A party is therefore provided an unsecured amount of credit until the Minimum Transfer Amount is exceeded. However, at this point, the Pledgor is then required to make a Delivery Amount (VM) of the entire Exposure. This is different from how a Threshold would work because a Threshold applies a permanent amount that remains unsecured.

This is one of the reasons why regulators introduced a cap on the maximum level of Minimum Transfer Amount that can apply.

> (B) **Rounding**. The Delivery Amount (VM) and the Return Amount (VM) will be rounded up and down respectively to the nearest integral multiple of $ ....

The Minimum Transfer Amount only establishes a floor for transfers and does not avoid transfers of uneven amounts of collateral. Applying a rounding convention overcomes that.

The Delivery Amount (VM) is rounded up and the Return Amount (VM) is rounded down to the nearest integral multiple specified.

If no rounding convention is stated, then the Delivery Amount (VM) and the Return Amount (VM) will not be rounded.

There is no regulatory cap on the value of Rounding. Typically this value is kept low (e.g. USD 10,000) to reduce the amount that needs to be transferred since the Delivery Amount (VM) is rounded up and therefore additional collateral is payable and the Return Amount (VM) is rounded down meaning that less collateral needs to be returned.

> (viii) *Transfer Timing*. *"Regular Settlement Day"* has the meaning specified in Paragraph 12, unless otherwise specified here: ....
> ....

The standard position under the New York Law VM CSA is for same business day settlement to apply to collateral calls. This is required where PR or CFTC rules apply.

Under EMIR it is possible for a longer time period to be agreed provided that the transfer is initiated on the same business day as the call.

Sub-paragraph 13(c)(viii) provides parties with the option to amend the definition of Regular Settlement Day in order to extend the settlement period. Care should be taken to ensure that this does not breach any regulation applicable to either party.

> (d) *Valuation and Timing*.
>
> (i) *"Valuation Agent"* means, for purposes of Paragraphs 3 and 5, the party making the demand under Paragraph 3, and, for purposes of Paragraph 6(d), the Secured Party, as applicable, unless otherwise specified here: ....
> ....

The Valuation Agent is responsible for calculating the Delivery Amount (VM) and the Return Amount (VM) and reporting these calculations to its counterparty (or to both the Pledgor and Secured Party where a third party is Valuation Agent) so than they can fulfil their obligations under the New York Law VM CSA.

As described in Paragraph 13(d)(i), the party calling for the collateral is the Valuation Agent. In the case of a Delivery Amount (VM) this would be the Secured Party and for a Return Amount (VM) the Pledgor is the Valuation Agent. This approach is sensible because the party making the demand knows the amount required by it.

The Secured Party is also the Valuation Agent for Distributions or Interest Payments (VM) under Paragraph 6(d).

The standard wording is most commonly used.

On occasion, one party will request that the other party act as the Valuation Agent for all purposes. This could occur if one party did not have the operational capability or sophistication to make the necessary calculations itself. Many US dealers resist acting as Valuation Agent over concerns that they may be regarded as a fiduciary of the other party. They may also be concerned about being liable for errors in making the required calculations.

Some parties seek to include additional wording stating that if an Event of Default, Potential Event of Default or Specified Condition occurs with respect to a party then the other party will act as Valuation Agent. Most institutions will have a policy on whether any or all of these additional events should be incorporated.

While it is also possible to appoint a third party to act as Valuation Agent, it is very rarely done in the market due to the fees a Valuation Agent would charge and possible operational and back office headaches that would occur when using a third party.

(ii) *"Valuation Date"* has the meaning specified in Paragraph 12, unless otherwise specified here: ....
....

For purposes of determining the Valuation Date and clause (iii) of the definition of "Local Business Day" in Paragraph 12, *"Valuation Date Location"** means, with respect to each party, each city, region, or country specified below:

Party A: ....
Party B: ....

* If applicable, a party can specify more than one Valuation Date Location.

Valuation Date states the frequency at which Exposure is calculated and collateral is revalued under the New York Law VM CSA. Under regulation this is required on every business day.

On each Valuation Date the Valuation Agent calculates the Exposure, the Value of the Pledgor's Posted Collateral (VM) (if any) and the Delivery Amount (VM) or Return Amount (VM) (if any) as of the Valuation Time and advises the other party of its calculations.

Under the New York Law VM CSA each party specifies one or more Valuation Date Locations. In order for a day to be a valid Valuation Date it must be a day on which commercial banks are open in at least one location for each party. If a party seeks to include more than one Valuation Date Location and requires that all locations must be open then an amendment would be needed to the Valuation Date definition and can be specified here.

> (iii) *"Valuation Time"* has the meaning specified in Paragraph 12, unless otherwise specified here: ....
> ....

The Valuation Time is the time at which the Valuation Agent calculates Exposure and the value of collateral held to determine if a Delivery Amount (VM) or Return Amount (VM) call should be made. The Valuation Agent will also factor in any Distributions or Interest Payments (VM) due at the Valuation Time.

Valuation Time is now defined in Paragraph 12 of the New York Law VM CSA but the parties may choose another means for deciding the Valuation Time by amending this sub-paragraph. However, most parties use the standard definition.

> (iv) *"Notification Time"* means 10:00 a.m., New York time, on a Local Business Day, unless otherwise specified here: ....
> ....

This is the time by which, among other things, the Valuation Agent must notify its counterparty or both parties of its calculations. It is also the time by which a party must make a demand for a transfer or return of collateral so that the other party can make the appropriate transfer not later than the close of business on the Regular Settlement Day (i.e. on the same Local Business Day). If a demand for a transfer is made after the Notification Time then it does not have to be made until the close of business on the next Regular Settlement Day. Transfers are contingent on there being no dispute and no condition precedent is unfulfilled in Section 2(a) (iii) of the ISDA Master Agreement.

The Notification Time is stated to mean 10:00 a.m. New York time on the appropriate Local Business Day unless the parties agree otherwise. The Notification Time stated in the pre-printed version of the New York Law VM CSA has been moved from 1.00 p.m. in in the pre-printed version of the 1994 New York Law CSA to earlier in the day at 10.00 a.m. to facilitate same day settlement of collateral.

(e) *Conditions Precedent and Secured Party's Rights and Remedies.*
(i) The provisions of Paragraph 4(a) will apply, unless otherwise specified here: ....
....

First the parties will specify whether Paragraph 4(a) is applicable or not.

Paragraph 4(a) outlines that each Transfer obligation is subject to the condition precedent that no Event of Default, Potential Event or Default or Specified Condition has occurred and continues and no Early Termination Date has been designated as a result of an Event of Default or Specified Condition.

If the parties do not state whether Paragraph 4(a) applies or not then the fallback position is that Paragraph 4(a) applies.

If Paragraph 4(a) applies then the parties will choose which Termination Events under the ISDA Master Agreement will be Specified Conditions under the New York Law VM CSA.

(ii) If the provisions of Paragraph 4(a) are applicable, the following Termination Event(s) will be a *"Specified Condition"* for the party specified (that party being the Affected Party if the Termination Event occurs with respect to that party):

	Party A	Party B
Illegality	[ ]	[ ]
Force Majeure Event**	[ ]	[ ]
Tax Event	[ ]	[ ]
Tax Event Upon Merger	[ ]	[ ]
Credit Event Upon Merger	[ ]	[ ]
Additional Termination Event(s):	[ ]	[ ]

Footnote:** Include if the relevant ISDA Master Agreement is an ISDA 2002 Master Agreement.

By designating a Specified Condition, the parties agree that when it occurs:

- if the Affected Party (i.e. the condition has occurred to that party) is the Pledgor, the Secured Party's obligations to transfer collateral and interest payments to the Pledgor under Paragraphs 3, 4(d)(ii) and 6(d) are suspended and the Secured Party may exercise its rights and remedies under Paragraph 8(a);

- if the Affected Party is the Secured Party, the Pledgor's obligations to transfer collateral under Paragraphs 3 and 5 and 6(d) are suspended and the Pledgor may exercise its rights and remedies under Paragraph 8(b).

The most common Specified Conditions that are selected are Illegality and Credit Event Upon Merger.

Many parties are concerned about posting collateral to a party that is impacted by an Illegality because the Secured Party may not be able to return the pledged collateral because it would be unlawful.

In addition, parties also would not want to pledge collateral to a party whose creditworthiness has become materially weaker due to a merger. They would be concerned that their counterparty might fall into bankruptcy due to the merger and that any pledged collateral might be trapped in an insolvency proceeding. Some parties also view the occurrence of a Credit Event Upon Merger as the fault of the Affected Party and therefore think it should be treated in a similar way to an Event of Default for the purposes of the New York Law VM CSA.

That said, some dealers are reluctant to agree to the inclusion of any Specified Conditions (expect perhaps Illegality). Such dealers are concerned about the situation where a Specified Condition has occurred to it at the same time as it is the Secured Party. If the dealer has risk exposure on its counterparty, it does not want the Pledgor's obligation to pledge collateral to be suspended because a Specified Condition has occurred to it (i.e. the dealer).

(f) *Substitution*.

(i) *"Substitution Date"* has the meaning specified in Paragraph 4(d)(ii), unless otherwise specified here: ....
....

The ability to substitute collateral is an important right for Pledgors. A Pledgor may require the return of a particular security that he previously pledged to the Secured Party e.g. the collateral may actually have been repledged by the Pledgor to the Secured Party and he may then need to return that same security to its original pledgor.

Often Secured Parties will insist that they have the right to consent to a substitution. Even though the Secured Party will be receiving Substitute Credit Support (VM), the substitution process can be time consuming and use up the normally limited back office resources of the Secured Party. By having the right to consent, a Secured Party hopes to limit the number of substitutions that it could be required to perform by the Pledgor.

(ii) *Consent.* If specified here as applicable, then the Pledgor must obtain the Secured Party's consent for any substitution pursuant to Paragraph 4(d): [applicable/inapplicable]***

*** Parties should consider selecting "applicable" where substitution without consent could give rise to a registration requirement to perfect properly the security interest in Posted Collateral (*e.g.*, where a party to the Annex is the New York branch of an English bank).

This is where parties can choose whether consent to substitutions is required under their New York Law VM CSA.

A compromise here could be to require consent but to state that it shall not be unreasonably withheld.

(g) *Dispute Resolution.*

(i) *"Resolution Time"* means 1:00 p.m., New York time, on the Local Business Day following the date on which the notice is given that gives rise to a dispute under Paragraph 5, unless otherwise specified here: ....
....

The Resolution Time is the deadline for the parties to resolve their dispute under Paragraph 5. If they fail the Valuation Agent makes certain recalculations under Paragraph 5(iv)(A) and (B).

The fallback dispute Resolution Time is 1:00 p.m. New York time on the Local Business Day after the date notice is given that gives rise to a dispute under Paragraph 5.

(ii) *Value.* For the purpose of Paragraphs 5(iv)(A)(3) and 5(iv)(B), the Value of Posted Credit Support (VM) will be calculated as follows: ....
....

Paragraph 5(iv) requires the parties to agree to a procedure to value Posted Collateral (VM) where there is a dispute.

Many U.S. counterparties prefer to require the parties to look to published quotations for valuing Posted Collateral (VM) rather than seeking quotations from dealers that trade in the disputed type of collateral.

Alternatively the parties can outline a process whereby the parties try to obtain a fixed number of quotations from market delears (e.g. three bid quotations) and if this is not possible to use fewer quotations or the Valuation Agent's original calculations if no prices are available.

(iii) *Alternative*. The provisions of Paragraph 5 will apply, unless an alternative dispute resolution procedure is specified here: ....
....

This provision enables the parties to adopt a different dispute resolution procedure to that contained in Paragraph 5. Normally parties adopt Paragraph 5. Alternative dispute resolutions have in the past included splitting the difference between the amounts calculated by each party or by allowing a financial tolerance level (e.g. up to USD 1 million). Such tolerances are very rarely used in the current market and if agreed, it is important that, as a minimum the undisputed amount is transferred in full.

(h) *Holding and Using Posted Collateral (VM)*.

(i) *Eligibility to Hold Posted Collateral (VM); Custodians (VM)*. Party A and its Custodian (VM) will be entitled to hold Posted Collateral (VM) pursuant to Paragraph 6(b); *provided* that the following conditions applicable to it are satisfied:

(1) Party A is not a Defaulting Party.
(2) ....

Initially, the *Custodian (VM)* for Party A is ....
....

Party B and its Custodian (VM) will be entitled to hold Posted Collateral (VM) pursuant to Paragraph 6(b); *provided* that the following conditions applicable to it are satisfied:

(1) Party B is not a Defaulting Party.
(2) ....

> Initially, the *Custodian (VM)* for Party B is ....
> ....

Sub-paragraph (h)(i) allows the entities to apply conditions which a party or its Custodian (VM) must meet in order to hold Posted Collateral (VM) transferred by the other party.

Parties often worry about the sophistication and credit quality of a Secured Party holding the Posted Collateral (VM).

However, if the Secured Party itself is to hold the Posted Collateral (VM), it must not be a Defaulting Party and must often have a high credit rating. Typically parties will request that a party or its Custodian (VM) have a credit rating of at least BBB+ from S&P and Baa1 from Moody's and hold either a certain amount of assets (e.g. USD 10 billion) or have a high net worth.

A Pledgor would be seriously concerned if there was a risk that its Secured Party were to become insolvent. Then it may be difficult for the Pledgor to obtain the return of the Posted Collateral (VM). This is because it would probably only rank as an unsecured creditor with only a contractual claim to the return of the collateral that it had pledged to the Secured Party.

As explained in Paragraph 6(b), a custodian selected by the Secured Party is defined as an agent of that Secured Party and is not intended to have any fiduciary duties to the Pledgor. If the Pledgor wanted to have this the parties would need the custodian to enter into a triparty custodial agreement with both the Pledgor and the Secured Party.

> (ii) *Use of Posted Collateral (VM)*. The provisions of Paragraph 6(c) will not apply to the [party/parties*] specified here:
>
> [ ] Party A
> [ ] Party B
>
> and [that party/those parties*] will not be permitted to: ....
> ....
>
> Footnote:
> * Delete as applicable.

Paragraph 6(c) assumes that the parties permit "rehypothecation" or use rights in the collateral unless otherwise stated here in Paragraph 13.

The following provision provides additional protection for a Pledgor if it grants the Secured Party rehypothecation rights:

(ii) *Use of Posted Collateral (VM)*. The provisions of Paragraph 6(c) will apply to both parties, and in addition to the other conditions set forth in Paragraph 6(c), the Secured Party's rights under Paragraph 6(c) are subject to the condition precedent that each of the conditions set forth in Paragraph 13(h)(i) is satisfied with respect to it.

It provides that a party must stop using the collateral if it no longer meets the eligibility requirements. Some parties also request the inclusion of a ratings trigger that would require the Secured Party to stop rehypothecating collateral in the event that its credit rating fell below a particular level.

(i) *Distributions and Interest Payment (VM)*.

(i) *Interest Rate (VM)*. The *"Interest Rate (VM)"* in relation to each Eligible Currency specified below will be:

Eligible Currency	Interest Rate (VM)	A/365 Currency
....	....	....
....	....	....
....	....	....

The Interest Rate is the interest which will be paid by the Interest Payer (VM) on the cash collateral. If cash is Eligible Collateral (VM) this section must be completed as there is no ISDA fallback.

The Interest Rate for USD is almost always based on the Federal Funds (Effective) rate. This represents the interest rate traditionally used when banks lend money on the interbank market overnight between themselves. Because this represents the rate of return anticipated by most banks on their overnight cash balances, they are generally reluctant to agree to other interest rates. In general, the market standard for interest rates in VM CSAs is the relevant OIS (overnight index swap) rate for the currency concerned. For USD this would be the Federal Funds (Effective) rate, for GBP it is SONIA and for EUR it is EONIA.

The parties will also specify whether an Eligible Currency is an A/365 Currency or not. If no choice is made, the fallback for all currencies other than Pounds Sterling is that it is not an A/365 Currency. Typically GBP, JPY, AUD, NZD and CAD all use the A/365 day count fraction and this should be reflected here when one or more of these currencies is agreed in the New York Law VM CSA.

(ii) *Transfer of Interest Payment (VM) or application of Interest Amount (VM).*

Interest Transfer: [Applicable/Not Applicable]
Interest Payment Netting: [Applicable/Not Applicable]

[The Transfer of an Interest Payment (VM) by the Interest Payer (VM) will be made on [the last Local Business Day of each calendar month] [and on any Local Business Day that a Return Amount (VM) consisting wholly or partly of cash is Transferred to the Pledgor pursuant to Paragraph 3(b)]. The Transfer of an Interest Payment (VM) by the Interest Payer (VM) will be made on [the last Local Business Day of each calendar month] [and on any Local Business Day that a Delivery Amount (VM) consisting wholly or partly of cash is Transferred to the Secured Party pursuant to Paragraph 3(a)].]

Interest Adjustment: [Applicable/Not Applicable]

[The Posted Collateral (VM) will be adjusted by the Secured Party on [the last Local Business Day of each calendar month][each day].]

Here the parties can elect whether Interest Transfer or Interest Adjustment applies. You should only select one.

If Interest Transfer applies then the parties also need to decide if Interest Payment Netting is to apply too.

Most parties are only able operationally to support Interest Transfer. Interest Payment Netting is normally not applicable.

The parties also specify the frequency that the transfer or adjustment will take place. Paragraph 13(i)(ii) proposes that this is on the last Local Business Day of each month. Whether this payment structure is acceptable will depend upon the parties' operational systems. Many parties prefer such interest transfers to take place on the second or third Local Business Day of the following calendar month because they can spend the first Local Business Day of that month checking calculations and preparing the necessary electronic transfers.

(iii) *Other Interest Elections.*

Negative Interest: [Applicable/Not Applicable]

Daily Interest Compounding: [Applicable/Not Applicable]

The parties can make their choices in relation to Negative Interest and Daily Interest Compounding here.

> (iv) *Alternative to Interest Amount (VM) and Interest Payment (VM).* The provisions of Paragraph 6(d)(ii) will apply, unless otherwise specified here:
> ....
> ....

Finally, there is an option to agree an alternative to Interest Amount. This could be an investment in zero coupon bonds. This provision is very rarely used.

> (j) *Credit Support Offsets.*
>
> If specified here as applicable, then the *"Credit Support Offsets"* provisions in Paragraph 11(j) of this Annex will apply: [applicable/inapplicable].

The parties can state if Credit Support Offsets will apply. Most institutions are not currently operationally able to support this and so it is normally marked inapplicable.

> (k) *Additional Representation(s).*
>
> [Party A/Party B] represents to the other party (which representation(s) will be deemed to be repeated as of each date on which it, as the Pledgor, Transfers Eligible Collateral (VM)) that:
>
> (i) ....
> (ii) ....

Parties have the opportunity to add any additional representations to the New York Law VM CSA here but this is rarely done.

> (l) *Other Eligible Support (VM) and Other Posted Support (VM).*
>
> (i) *"Value"* with respect to Other Eligible Support (VM) and Other Posted Support (VM) means: ....
> ....

This provision is also rarely used unless the parties have agreed to include Other Posted Support (VM) and Other Eligible Support (VM). If Other Posted Support (VM) is pledged to the Secured Party, the parties might want to consider adding special provisions as to how to value it.

> (ii) *"Transfer"* with respect to Other Eligible Support (VM) and Other Posted Support (VM) means: ....
> ....

Where Other Eligible Support (VM) and Other Posted Support (VM) are relevant, if there are any conditions necessary for it to make transfers successfully, these would be stated here. This provision is rarely used.

> (m) *Demands and Notices.*
>
> All demands, specifications and notices under this Annex will be made pursuant to the Notices Section of this Agreement, unless otherwise specified here:
>
> Party A: ....
> ....
>
> Party B: ....
> ....

In large institutions, the collateral management unit may be completely separate from the OTC derivatives desk or legal department. Therefore, a party may want to state additional addresses for notification where collateral is managed by its Operations Department.

> (n) *Addresses for Transfers.*
>
> Party A: ....
> ....
>
> Party B: ....
> ....

This sub-paragraph must be completed if collateral transfers and interest payments and Distributions are to be correctly routed to the recipient. Sometimes these details are spelt out by currency for cash and securities. However, often collateral management units will have standard settlement instructions ("SSIs") for Cash and securities and may not want to include these in the New York Law VM CSA itself but instead make reference to the latest SSIs that are available.

(o) *"Other CSA"* has the meaning specified in Paragraph 12, unless otherwise specified here: ....

Normally the standard Paragraph 12 definition applies. If the parties look to apply Credit Support Offset then they may decide to amend this by identifying the Other CSA(s) here in more detail.

(p) *Other Provisions.*

Paragraph 13(p) is similar to Part 5 of the ISDA Master Agreement Schedule. It is where additional provisions may be inserted. There is no general market practice as to what should be inserted in Paragraph 13(p).

There are, however provisions that some parties will ask to be added. Because these provisions are not often market standard, they can be difficult and time consuming to negotiate.

ISDA Elections and Fallbacks

At this point it might be useful to summarise the ISDA fallbacks for Paragraph 13 and the provisions which must be completed for the New York Law VM CSA to work properly.

If no choice is made the following apply by default:

Alternative: Paragraph 5 dispute resolution procedures apply.
Consent for Substitution: No consent required.
Eligibility to Hold Posted Collateral (VM): Secured Party cannot be a Defaulting Party.
Minimum Transfer Amount: Zero
Notification Time: 10:00am New York time.
Notices: Pursuant to Notices Section of ISDA Master Agreement.
Resolution Time: 1:00pm New York time.

Rounding: No rounding.

Specified Condition: No Specified Conditions apply.

Substitution Date: Local Business Day following receipt of Substitute Credit Support (VM).

Transfer of Interest Payment (VM) (if applicable): Last Local Business Day of a calendar month and any Local Business Day when a cash Return Amount (VM) is due to the Pledgor.

Use or Rehypothecation of Posted Collateral: Use or rehypothecation permitted.

Valuation Agent: The Secured Party for purposes of Paragraph 3(a) and Paragraph 6(d). The Pledgor for purposes of Paragraph 3(b).

Provisions which must be completed as there is no fallback:

- Addresses for Transfers
- Eligible Collateral (VM)
- Interest Rate (VM)
- Other Eligible Support (VM) and Other Posted Support (VM)
- Value

Chapter 4

Important developments since the global financial crisis

ISDA Margin Survey 2017

On 18th September 2017 ISDA published its latest Margin Survey (the previous one was in August 2015). The Survey shows significant growth in cleared derivatives due to the implementation of new margin regulations since the last Survey. It divides margin into initial margin ("IM") and variation margin ("VM") and reports figures for both of them as at 31st March 2017.

Based upon replies from 18 of the top 20 dealers, collateral received for uncleared OTC derivatives totalled an estimated USD 977.5 billion.

From publicly available information from two US CCPs and three European and two Asian ones, collateral for cleared interest rate swaps and credit default swaps totalled USD 434 billion.

This made a total of posted collateral of USD 1.41 trillion as at 31st March 2017.

It should be noted that IM is divided into regulatory IM and bilaterally negotiated IM not required for regulatory purposes (the latter normally at the behest of credit officers).

As regards collateral types, the Survey estimates that as at 31st March 2017, 70.9% of collateral posted was cash, 20.7% government securities, 8.3% other securities and presumably 0.1% other forms of collateral. Typically government securities are used as IM because uncleared margin regulations require IM to be bankruptcy remote and securities are deemed to meet this requirement better than cash. Collateral for VM is usually cash.

This is only a short summary of the ISDA Margin Survey 2017 which contains more detailed information than that summarised above.

Collateral squeeze risk

Regulators' demands for new and higher quality collateral for VM is becoming a concern. VM calls are mostly covered by cash and/or government bonds. Equities and corporate bonds are largely out of scope. In addition, the range of acceptable government bonds has narrowed because credit departments often exclude countries like Italy, Spain and Portugal.

While cash is a natural fallback, it only attracts very low interest rate returns in the current environment.

The potential collateral squeeze envisaged here would cover all collateralised products as the supply of high quality and liquid collateral is finite. The cost of trading collateralised products will increase and firms who cannot find alternatives may have to leave the market. We shall see.

Too big to fail

One of the iconic phrases of the global financial crisis was "too big to fail", referring to large banks which got themselves in trouble. Of course, Lehman Brothers and Bear Stearns were not too big to fail but the irony was that the big banks which took them over in whole or in part or those which bought smaller banks in trouble at least theoretically increased the problem by getting bigger themselves.

Of course, the core problem was too much indiscriminate lending on insufficient capital.

One of the measures introduced to combat this was the Basel III Capital Accord.

Basel III

Basel III (or the Third Basel Accord) is a global regulatory framework covering bank capital adequacy, stress testing and financial market liquidity. It was formulated in response to the 2007–2009 global financial crisis with the aims of boosting bank capital requirements and reducing bank leverage and contagion from the banking sector into the real economy. This was to be achieved through the combination of four ratios viz:

- Capital Ratio
- Liquidity Cover Ratio
- Leverage Ratio
- Net Stable Funding Ratio

Basel III is being implemented in stages between 1st January 2014 and 1st January 2019, although national regulators can accelerate this process. Indeed on 26th October 2016 the European Commission announced it planned to do this. Under the Basel III timetable both the Leverage Ratio and the Net Stable Funding Ratio ("NSFR") were to be fully implemented by 1st January 2018.

On 7th December 2017 final Basel III rules were published. Jurisdictions are now free to apply the revised definition of exposure method for the Leverage Ratio before 1st January 2022.

As far as OTC derivatives liabilities are concerned, the NSFR was proposed on 7th December 2017 by the European Council to be set at 5% which was favourably greeted by the derivatives market.

Under the Leverage Ratio banks are expected to maintain liquid cover of a minimum of 3% of their on and off balance sheet risk exposures. In the US this has been taken a stage further with a requirement that the most systemically important US bank holding companies have capital coverage for a 5% leverage ratio rising to 6% for any federally insured depository institution which is a subsidiary of these bank holding companies.

This means that this ratio requires banks to hold additional capital for all assets regardless of their riskiness.

This has arisen because capital ratios that weigh assets according to their riskiness can invite manipulation by banks. So regulators have turned their attention to simple leverage ratios which measure the level of tier 1 capital (that is, equity and retained earnings) against total assets without taking the riskiness of those assets into account.

While the Liquidity Cover Ratio requires a bank to hold enough high quality liquid assets to cover its total net cash outflows over a 30 day stress period, the NSFR requires an amount of stable funding to be set aside to cover a one-year period of stress where banks are trading with non-banks.

Europe and the United States have disagreed over the extent to which banks can use their own risk models to calculate their capital requirements.

The Basel III regulators tried to set an "output floor" that would limit the extent to which a bank's capital requirements based its own risk model can diverge from how they would be calculated under a more conservative standardised model set by regulators.

On 7th December 2017 this output floor was agreed at 72.5%. This means it limits the gain a bank can achieve from using its internal models to 27.5%.

However, this requirement comes with a lengthy phase-in starting on 1st January 2022 at 50% and reaching 72.5% on 1st January 2027, meaning it could be up to 10 years before it is fully implemented.

Of course, the Basel III Accord has over the past few years resulted in banks increasing their capital bases significantly. In a speech to the Banking Standards Board on 21st March 2017, Bank of England governor Mark Carney estimated that since the global financial crisis banks had increased their capital by USD 1.5 trillion (USD 1500 billion).

Also thanks in part to the Dodd-Frank Act, US banks are far safer than they were. The ratio of the six largest banks' Tier 1 capital (chiefly equity) to risk-weighted assets, the main gauge of their strength, was a low 8-9% before the crisis. Now it is 12-14%. In addition Dodd-Frank also introduced stiff stress tests for the most important banks' ability to withstand further storms; obliged them to draw up "living wills" to prepare for bankruptcy should calamity strike; and banned them from trading in securities for their own profit, under the Volcker Rule.

Living wills for banks

As a result of the 2008 financial crisis, regulators around the world have been demanding so-called living wills to be drawn up by banks and financial institutions. A living will for a bank or other financial institution is a contingency plan that is on the shelf in case that entity becomes insolvent and needs to be closed, broken up or sold.

One of the frequently discussed features of living wills is that it would be very difficult and time consuming to close down complex major multinational financial institutions. Therefore restructuring financial institutions to implement living wills would very likely seriously reduce their profitability, their ability to offer credit and perhaps also reduce their financial strength.

Another ironic twist is that credit ratings agencies have begun to indicate that the existence of a detailed living will may force a downgrade in a bank's credit rating. This is because with a living will, it may be easier for regulators to let an institution fail if it runs into severe financial difficulties.

Indeed, much of the rationale for living wills is once again to reduce the incidence of financial companies that are "too big to fail."

The Dodd-Frank Act mandates that bank holding companies with over USD 50 billion in assets must prepare living wills and file them with financial regulators.

The plans must be updated annually and regulators can demand more frequent revisions.

Troubled banks can be forced to raise more capital or to restrict growth.

The Federal Deposit Insurance Corporation in consultation with the Federal Reserve Bank can break up a troubled bank.

EU Bank Recovery and Resolution Directive ("BRRD")

The BRRD is the EU's response to global initiatives led by the Financial Stability Board to end the so-called "too big to fail" problem.

Recital (1) of the BRRD states that it aims to "prevent insolvency or, when insolvency occurs, to minimise negative repercussions by preserving systemically important functions of the institution concerned" and to minimise the cost for taxpayers.

As an EU directive, the BRRD was required to be implemented into the national law of each EU member state by 1 January 2015 other than the "bail-in" tool which was required to be implemented by 1 January 2016.

So while it is important to note that the BRRD is required to be implemented into the national law of each EU member state, the resolution regime in each EU member state may not be the same.

The BRRD will not only affect parties directly within its scope. It will also impact any entity that transacts with such parties.

If a party meets the criteria for a resolution then resolution authorities may use various "resolution tools". OTC derivatives contracts may therefore (i) be transferred to a new counterparty; (ii) be "bailed-in" – i.e. written down (but only to the extent they are unsecured) or converted into equity (but only the unsecured portion), or (iii) remain with the party under resolution.

The resolution tool "bail-in" forces bank creditors and depositors to bear some of the burden by taking a loss on their holdings. A bail-in is the opposite of a bail-out which involves the rescue of a financial institution by external parties, typically governments using taxpayers' money.

Typically, bail-outs have been far more common than bail-ins but in recent years after massive bail-outs some governments now require that investors and depositors in a bank take a loss before taxpayers become involved. Typically bail-ins are resorted to in cases where a government bail-out is unlikely because either (a) the financial institution's collapse is not likely to pose a systemic risk because it does not fall into the "too big to fail" category; or (b) the government lacks the financial resources necessary for a bail-out because it is itself heavily indebted.

In a resolution OTC derivatives would be terminated and valued by resolution authorities for the purposes of bail-in in accordance with the procedure set out in the BRRD. However, this only applies to the net close-out amount of OTC derivatives.

Resolution authorities have wide ranging powers in respect of the liabilities of a party undergoing resolution. Contractual termination and other rights may be temporarily suspended and/or permanently overridden. Payment and delivery obligations may also be temporarily suspended and contractual terms may be modified or cancelled. These powers may be used in respect of OTC derivatives liabilities.

However, the BRRD provides for safeguards to ensure the protection of netting, set-off, security and collateral (including title transfer collateral) arrangements in resolution. The safeguards also include the prevention of a transfer of only part of the rights and liabilities under a protected arrangement (to avoid "cherry-picking" by resolution authorities).

A final safeguard is also included so that creditors are not worse off in a bail-in or partial property transfer than they would have been if normal insolvency proceedings had been commenced.

Cross-border recognition of resolution action is a major concern and as a result:

- Contractual recognition of bail-in for certain derivatives liabilities governed by non-EU law is required by the BRRD. ISDA has assisted this with protocols referred to below.
- Regulators requested ISDA Resolution Stay Protocols to be produced as a contractual solution to ensure that stays and overrides on termination and that other rights in resolution will be respected in third country jurisdictions. Statutory stay rules are also being developed in certain jurisdictions.

Therefore, counterparties may be required contractually to agree to bail-ins and the imposition of resolution stays in their contracts with in-scope parties if they wish to continue to trade with them.

On 2nd November 2017 concern was raised by systematically important banks about a proposed revision to the BRRD by the European Commission. This is to extend the close-out stays on swap contracts from the current two working days to a period between 5-12 working days. The systematically important banks question whether it will be applied to them. Those in Europe believe that it will increase capital and margin requirements and may threaten their global competitiveness.

This matter was raised in a paper published by ISDA on 28th September 2017 entitled *Proposed Moratoria Under the BRRD: A Step Backwards in Efforts to End 'Too Big to Fail'*.

ISDA initiatives

In recent years ISDA has actively worked on various legal and regulatory matters in respect of bank recovery and resolution.

It uses a number of resources viz:

The **BRRD Implementation Monitor** is a resource launched by ISDA to keep track of the status of implementation of the BRRD.

The **ISDA Bank Recovery and Resolution Summary and FAQs** is a resource which sets out the key impacts on OTC derivatives under the BRRD and addresses frequently asked questions on it and related ISDA documentation initiatives, including protocols.

The **ISDA Bank Resolution Stay Matrix** sets out information on several key developments in a number of jurisdictions related to the resolution of financial institutions and includes links to relevant legislation and related ISDA documentation initiatives, again including protocols.

ISDA has developed numerous documentation and technology solutions to ease compliance with regulatory requirements for bank recovery and resolution.

It has also issued a number of Resolution Stay Protocols and Bail-In Protocols.

Legal opinions

As part of the annual update process for the legal opinions on the enforceability of the netting and collateral provisions of ISDA documentation which ISDA commissions on behalf of its members, ISDA also expects the relevant local counsel to include an outline of the key features of bank resolution in the relevant jurisdiction from an OTC derivatives perspective.

US Federal Reserve Bank Rules to help unwind big banks

On 1st September 2017 the Federal Reserve Bank issued a new rule which should ease winding down systematically important US banks by creating a safe harbour for financial contracts after a bank defaults.

The decision once again forms part of global post-crisis efforts to end 'too big to fail' institutions that are so large and complex that they could endanger the entire US financial system if they became insolvent.

The rule requires global systematically important banks ("G-SIBs") to amend the language in common financial contracts so they cannot be immediately cancelled if one of these banks enters bankruptcy.

By imposing new legal protections, regulators aim to prevent a run on a G-SIB's subsidiaries that could be triggered if a large number of counterparties rush to terminate their contracts as occurred in the case of Lehman Brothers in 2008.

The Financial Stability Board working in consultation with the Basel Committee on Banking Supervision and national authorities publish a list of G-SIBs on an annual basis in November each year. There are currently 30 G-SIBS of which eight are incorporated in the US.

The new rules would apply to the eight US G-SIBs i.e. Bank of America, Bank of New York Mellon, Citigroup, Goldman Sachs, JPMorgan Chase, Morgan Stanley, State Street Corporation and Wells Fargo. As G-SIBs transact a huge number of deals, typically worth hundreds of billions of dollars, a market panic to terminate deals could potentially drag down other institutions.

This requirement will help manage the risk to the US financial system when a G-SIB fails.

The rule applies to a range of products, including OTC derivatives, securities lending deals and short-term funding agreements that are privately negotiated rather than processed through a central clearing house.

The Fed first proposed the rule in May 2016, and finalised it on 1st September 2017.

This final rule also gives banks more time to comply.

UK Independent Banking Commission report and ringfencing

In September 2011 The Independent Commission on Banking published its Final Report, part of which recommended the ringfencing of large banks' riskier investment banking businesses from their deposit taking activities by January 2019. This was another approach to resolving the "too big to fail" problem and to prevent taxpayer bailouts of such banks that risk customer deposits when bets by their investment banking units go wrong.

A ringfenced bank must be a separate legal entity with its own board and there will be limits on how much capital retail and investment banking entities can share. Ringfencing will apply to all UK banks with more than GBP 25 billion in deposits.

High Court hearings are taking place between autumn 2017 and spring 2018 with a High Court judge ruling on the suitability of each bank's plans to transfer large parts of its business to a new legal entity in order to comply with ringfencing legislation. The banks' ringfenced entities are expected to be up-and-running from the middle of 2018, well before the January 2019 deadline. This staggered approach is by design to give the UK Prudential Regulation Authority ("PRA") and the banks the chance to test out their systems one at a time to minimise chances of a mass breakdown at the point of transfer. However, the advent of such ringfencing near the scheduled time of Brexit is not ideal for the banks concerned.

It is also uncertain whether the UK will retain the ability to "passport" financial services across the EU after Brexit. Losing this right would have a wide-reaching impact on London-based banks that are currently using branches to passport their services across the EU.

The cost of this ringfencing exercise is estimated to be GBP 500 million.

Currently regulators at the PRA are getting ready to authorise the creation of the 5 largest new banks to come into existence in the UK – the new ringfenced legal entities of HSBC, Barclays, Lloyds Banking Group, RBS Group and Santander UK.

In the market it was reported on 3rd October 2017 that UK banks are offering discounts of up to 25% on legacy swaps before ringfencing which in itself is expected significantly to increase funding costs for riskier OTC derivatives trades.

On 24th October 2017 the European Commission announced that it had abandoned its idea of requiring EU banks to separate their retail and investment banking businesses. The European Commission believes that other regulatory measures such as those governing the resolution of failed banks are sufficient.

Central clearing counterparties ("CCPs")

With global regulators wanting to process as many standardised OTC derivatives as possible through clearing houses or CCPs, the question has arisen as to whether these could also become "too big to fail". In August 2016 the Financial Stability Board published draft guidance on regulations it wanted in place by the end of

2017. In November 2016 the European Commission also published proposals. On 28th September 2017 the European Parliament ("EP") also weighed in with a draft report on this issue.

CCPs are important because when OTC derivatives are processed through them they sit between each counterparty and ensure that trades are completed even if one side defaults on payment.

The EP's draft report proposes tougher measures than the Financial Stability Board or the European Commission.

The EP wants to give regulators more power over CCPs to ensure that the institutions and the banks that use them shoulder the financial burden if they run into trouble. It proposes that a failing CCP would first have to raise its reserve financial buffers and then force customers to raise emergency cash if needed. Losses should be borne by the CCP itself to the fullest extent possible, with CCPs' own resources heading the queue, those of clearing members second and those of clients third in order to protect and lessen recourse to taxpayers.

The EP's draft report supports a prescriptive approach which gives institutions little scope to deviate in a crisis. The EP, European Commission and national governments will in early 2018 begin discussing proposals to allow regulators and central banks to wind down CCPs safely. However, the two MEPs who co-authored the draft report disagree on several issues relating to CCPs. These include whether to create a single European authority to oversee how to handle the failure of a CCP and the establishment of a further reserve fund that would be held by the CCP and used for emergency funds in stressed markets. This latter issue is likely to be unpopular with CCP members who are mostly banks and who already have to pay into their own resolution funds.

Alongside the ideas of a CCP raising its financial buffers and users contributing emergency funds, a proposed third layer of defence would allow authorities to seize the margin that asset managers and other customers use to back their OTC derivatives deals. After the publication of the EP draft report, the *Financial Times* reported that some of the biggest clients of CCPs, such as JPMorgan Chase, have pushed back and want CCPs to raise their financial buffers before any losses are passed on to their users.

On 17th October 2017 the CFTC announced that CME Clearing, ICE Clear US and LCH had passed a stress test to show they could generate enough liquidity to withstand a major market disruption where two major CCP members defaulted at the same time.

On 18th September 2017 ISDA published a paper entitled *Safeguarding Clearing: The Need for a Comprehensive CCP Recovery and Resolution Framework*. In its press release ISDA states that the paper sets out steps for "implementing robust, unambiguous and predictable recovery and resolution mechanisms". At the same time ISDA acknowledges that its recommendations need to be adapted by jurisdiction and CCP due to different structures and existing legal regimes.

ISDA notes that CCPs reduce systemic risk in the markets they serve but they could accumulate risks which if not properly managed in stressed markets could financially damage their members, trading platforms and other market players.

ISDA believes that regulators should focus upon:

- Evaluating CCP resilience in periods of market stress;
- The establishment of robust recovery and risk management frameworks for CCPs; and
- What to do when a CCP recovery does not succeed and may cause substantial financial instability.

ISDA's recommendations are:

- Maximum transparency and predictable information on the key elements of and triggers for a CCP resolution.
- A resolution regime which clearly indicates when a CCP resolution could commence but with flexibility for recovery to continue beyond that time.
- Subject to safeguards, the potential use of variation margin gains haircutting ("VMGH") to allocate losses at the very end of a CCP's default waterfall. VMGH is a comprehensive loss allocation tool which addresses CCP losses without requiring any taxpayer money.
- Initial margin haircutting never to be allowed. ISDA considers that CCP members would not want to bid on positions which would increase their initial margin requirements if a haircut was applied to them.
- Subject to safeguards, the use of Partial Tear-Ups ("PTUs") if an auction or similar voluntary mechanism fails to rebalance a CCP's books. Because it stands between buyers and sellers and vice versa, a CCP cannot be viable without a balanced book. PTUs are, however, a last resort tool in these circumstances.
- CCP assessments on clearing members must be capped in aggregate across recovery and resolution.
- Clearing members suffering losses beyond a certain point in a CCP recovery or resolution must receive claims that make them senior to existing CCP equity holders.
- Forced allocation of positions to non-defaulting clearing members should never be permitted. This is because forced allocation could require non-defaulting clearing members to take on positions where they may not be able to manage the risks in extreme market conditions.
- While it is appropriate for clearing members to bear some non-default losses, CCPs and their equity holders must bear the risks of non-default losses which are exclusively under their control. *See three paragraphs below on non-default losses on page 185.*

- Access to liquidity from central banks on standard market terms (including the provision of high quality central bank eligible collateral) is necessary to support CCP recovery and resolution.

CCP recovery measures aim to ensure that a CCP continues to be viable in extremely stressed market conditions. CCP resolution refers to the measures a resolution authority (e.g. a regulator) takes under law to resolve a CCP if recovery measures do not succeed.

Problems could arise for a CCP from an accumulation of either default losses or non-default losses or both. Default losses occur when clearing members default on their obligations to the CCP. CCP rule books contain default waterfalls which set out the order in which CCPs and their members must contribute to cover default losses.

Non-default losses can arise from settlement risks, operational risks, custodial risks, legal risks, cyber risks and fraud.

So while detailed measures exist within CCPs, it is clear to ISDA that more work is needed to provide a comprehensive recovery and resolution regime for CCPs.

However, one important recent move occurred in the October 2017 US Treasury Report (see pp. 187–189) which recommended that the Federal Deposit Insurance Corporation acts as receiver for a troubled systemically important US CCP to assist its recovery.

MiFID 2

The original Markets in Financial Instruments Directive which we will call MiFID 1 came into force in the EU in 2007. It concentrated on providing a robust, regulatory structure to protect EU investors trading in shares. Elements of this structure were pre and post trade pricing transparency and best conduct practices for financial firms. MiFID 1 also provided a passport for UK firms to trade in the EU and vice versa. MiFID 1 succeeded in breaking the monopoly of national stock exchanges by encouraging the growth of new share trading platforms which drove down share trading costs. However, it also fostered the growth of "dark pools" – private trading fora run by investment banks possibly currently responsible for 10% of European share trading.

Of course, when MiFID 1 started in 2007 it was the start of the global financial crisis and it became clear that some changes would be necessary. One of these was the regulatory approach to third country firms. This was left up to each EU member state and gave competitive advantage and possible regulatory arbitrage opportunities to firms in third countries which had lighter regulation compared to MiFID 1.

This particular issue was addressed in MiFID 2 when it came into force in the EU on 3rd January 2018.

MiFID 2 will harmonise the rules for all firms trading with EU clients.

The Markets in Financial Instruments Regulation ("MiFIR") also came into force on 3rd January 2018. It will work alongside MiFID 2 and being a regulation does not need to be voted on and implemented by EU member states. It has direct validity throughout the EU and a focus on extending codes of conduct beyond shares to bonds, derivatives and structured finance products.

Key features of MiFID 2 are:

- Trading in bonds and OTC derivatives will be pushed towards electronic trading platforms which will offer greater price transparency to investors. This will become compulsory for interest rate swaps which are standard and not structured deals.
- Trading in dark pools will be restricted. Investment banks will not be allowed to line up buyers and sellers directly and there will be a cap on trading levels.
- Full pre and post trade pricing transparency continues to be required by regulators.
- Full reporting of every trade will be required by regulators to avoid market abuse.
- Asset managers must have "best execution" policies to prove they are trading assets at the best possible prices.
- Fund managers will have to pay separately for investment bank research notes rather than rolling them up in their fees and commissions to clients. This might lead to analyst job losses if fund managers cut back on research.

MiFID 2 has had a long gestation period and its implementation has already been postponed for a year. Despite the above summary, aspects of it are complex and its implementation has proved difficult.

Some EU countries have not finalised their interpretation of its rules. However, more worrying are cross border clashes. The most important of these has been with the USA where EU rules have clashed with US ones which forbid charging institutional clients for research.

However, on 19th October 2017 the SEC announced that it would allow US firms to break out research costs for European clients without them having to register as investment managers.

Another issue is investor protection for some derivatives transactions notably with commodity firms.

Even more important is a MiFID 2 requirement for EU regulators to declare foreign trading platforms as "equivalent" so that European firms can continue to trade on them. This is a long standing and vexed issue because such recognition needs to be mutual.

Fortunately there was a step forward on this on 13th October 2017 when EU and US negotiators were reported as having come to an agreement on recognising each other's trading rules and this is referred to more fully in Chapter 1 on page 40.

On 24th October 2017 the UK government told representatives of the UK financial services industry that no changes are planned to MiFID 2 after the UK leaves the EU.

Finally it is useful to note that the effectiveness of MiFID 2 will be reviewed by the European Commission in 2020.

US Treasury Report: Core Principles for Regulating the United States Financial System

This comprehensive 232 page report in response to President Trump's Executive Order 13772 of 3rd February 2017 was published by the US Treasury in October 2017. It covers the US banking market, capital markets, clearing houses and regulatory agencies and contains just over 100 recommendations to enhance the current US financial system.

Some of the report's Core Principles are:

- To prevent taxpayer funded bailouts;
- To foster vibrant financial markets through more rigorous regulatory impact analysis which addresses systemic risk and market failures;
- To advance US interests in international financial regulatory negotiations;
- To make regulation efficient, effective and appropriately tailored; and
- To restore public accountability within Federal financial regulatory agencies and to rationalise the Federal regulatory framework.

The following summary only focuses on matters relevant to this book.

Recalibration of derivatives regulation

To promote market efficiency and effective risk mitigation, the US Treasury recommends greater harmonisation between the CFTC and SEC to minimise duplications in regulations and inconsistent compliance burdens on market players. The SEC should also finalise its rules under the Dodd-Frank Act. In addition, the US Congress should consider further action to harmonise the regulation of swaps and security based swaps.

Margin requirements for uncleared swaps

Here the US Treasury recommends that:

- US regulators take steps to harmonise their uncleared swap margin requirements domestically and also internationally where non-US jurisdictions have implemented the BCBS/IOSCO regulatory framework.
- The US banking agencies should consider providing an exemption from the initial margin requirements for uncleared swaps for transactions between affiliates of a bank or of a bank holding company in line with the CFTC's margin requirements in this respect.
- US regulators should work with international regulators to amend the uncleared swap margin framework so as to align it more closely to relevant risks. This might include lowering the margin requirement for uncleared swaps and extending the margin delivery timeline. It seems that many US firms have represented to the US Treasury that they struggle to meet the T+1 settlement requirements especially with international transactions.
- The CFTC and US banking regulators should reconsider the one-size-fits-all treatment of financial end users in respect of the uncleared swap margin requirements in order to focus upon the most significant sources of risk.

Cross border Application and Scope

Here the US Treasury recommends that the CFTC and SEC provide clarity on the cross border scope of their regulations and make their rules compatible with non-US jurisdictions, where possible, to avoid market fragmentation, complexity, conflicts of law and regulatory arbitrage.

However, another recommendation revives an old bugbear.

It suggests reconsideration of whether swap counterparties, trading platforms and CCPs in jurisdictions which comply with international standards should be required to register with the CFTC or SEC when doing business with a US firm's foreign branch or affiliate.

Additionally the US Treasury suggests that reconsideration should be given as to whether US swap dealer registration should apply to a US firm's non-US affiliate when trading with non-US counterparties if that affiliate is effectively regulated under its foreign jurisdiction's own regulatory regime or complies with the Basel III capital requirements.

These two recommendations would, in the authors' opinions, revive extraterritoriality issues raised in Chapter 1.

Substituted Compliance

The US Treasury's tone changes here where it recommends that effective cross-border co-operation includes meaningful substituted compliance programmes to minimise conflicts.

Points raised are that:

- The CFTC and SEC should be judicious when applying their swaps rules to activities outside the USA and should permit entities, as far as possible, to comply with comparable non-U.S. derivatives regulations instead of or as well as complying with U.S. regulations.
- The CFTC and the SEC should adopt substituted compliance regimes that consider the rules of other jurisdictions in an outcomes-based approach in their entirety rather than focusing on rule-by-rule analysis. They should also work toward achieving timely recognition of their regimes by non-U.S. regulatory authorities.
- The CFTC should undertake truly outcomes-based comparability determinations, using either a category-by-category comparison or a comparison of the CFTC regime to the foreign regime as a whole.
- Meaningful substituted compliance could also include consideration of recognition regimes for non-U.S. CCPs clearing derivatives for certain U.S. persons and for non-U.S. platforms for swaps trading.

The first three bullet points referred to above mirror the approach ISDA recommended in its 18ᵗʰ September 2017 white paper entitled *Safeguarding Clearing: The Need for a Comprehensive CCP Recovery and Resolution Framework* (see pp. 183–185 above).

Swap Dealer De Minimis Threshold

The US Treasury recommends that the CFTC maintains this registration threshold at USD 8 billion but that any future change to it will be subject to formal rulemaking and a public comment process.

Support of Central Clearing

The US Treasury recommends that regulators properly balance the goal of moving more OTC derivatives into central clearing with appropriately tailored and targeted capital requirements because of the critical role CCPs play in the US financial system.

EMIR Review

In November 2016 the European Commission issued a report to the European Parliament and European Council outlining the areas where updates could be made to EMIR to provide a more proportionate, effective and efficient implementation of the rules. This report considered feedback provided in earlier consultations as well as specific input from various authorities. In May 2017, the European Commission published its legislative proposal for the review of EMIR.

The proposal primarily outlines possible adjustments impacting central counterparties and trade repositories.

In summary the key proposed changes recommended by the European Commission are:

- Changes to the classifications of entities
- New responsibilities for clearing firms that offer clearing services to clients
- Removal of frontloading obligations for cleared OTC trades
- Extension of the current clearing exemption for pension schemes
- Updates to reporting requirements including whether to continue with each party reporting trades or just one of them doing so
- Expansion of supervisory processes relating to approval of IM models for uncleared OTC derivative trades.

The following commentary focuses on matters relevant to this book.

One area of interest is the potential introduction of a new counterparty classification. Currently entities are classified as financial counterparties (FCs), non-financial counterparties above the clearing threshold (NFC+s), non-financial counterparties below the clearing threshold (NFC-s) and third country entities (TCEs).

It is proposed that a new classification of "small financial counterparties" (SFCs) is introduced. This is effectively a financial counterparty that would not be subject to clearing requirements because it is not economically practicable for such entities to clear trades due to their low trading activity and they are not considered to pose a systemic risk to the market as a whole.

In addition, it is proposed that the financial counterparty category is expanded to cover:

- All alternative investment funds rather than only covering those that are managed by a manager authorised or registered under the Alternative Investment Fund.
- "Securitisation Special Purpose Entities".

This would lead to entities that were previously categorised as NFC entities (generally expected to be below the clearing threshold) being reclassified as FCs.

The changes to classifications under EMIR could lead to a change in the population of entities being subject to clearing obligations as well as uncleared margin requirements under EMIR.

It is expected that the review and approval process by the European Parliament and European Council will be completed in the second half of 2018. There are different implementation dates proposed for the various changes.

On 18th July 2017 ISDA provided commentary to the European Commission on its proposed changes on behalf of its members. Among other things, it highlights that many proposed amendments would come into force 20 calendar days after the regulation is published in the Official Journal and urges the European Commission to extend the implementation date in many cases to allow a six month period for compliance.

A further review of EMIR would be expected three years after the revised regulation comes into force.

Brexit

Until 8th December 2017 major uncertainties swirled around Brexit (the UK's withdrawal from the European Union).

On that morning after a night of intensive negotiations, Donald Tusk, the President of the European Council, announced that the UK's offer on withdrawal terms was satisfactory and that sufficient progress had been made to move on to Phase 2 of the Brexit negotiations.

On 15th December 2017 the European Council comprising EU heads of state endorsed this recommendation.

The European Council also authorised the opening of Phase 2 negotiations in January 2018 on the framework of the UK's future relationship with the EU. This will include the negotiation of a transitional period between the official 29th March 2019 date for the UK's departure and the final agreement on the future of the UK/EU relationship especially in relation to trade terms.

Of course more work needs to be done on each of the Phase 1 issues (i.e. the Ireland/Northern Ireland border issue; the UK's financial settlement with the EU; and the resident rights of UK and EU citizens post Brexit).

European Union (Withdrawal) Bill

This bill will repeal the 1972 European Communities Act which took Britain into the EU and meant that European law took precedence over laws passed in the UK Parliament. It will also end the jurisdiction of the European Court of Justice.

All existing EU legislation will be copied across into domestic UK law to ensure a smooth transition on the day after Brexit.

There are believed to be 12,000 EU regulations in force, while the UK Parliament has passed 7,900 statutory instruments implementing EU legislation and 186 acts which incorporate some EU influence.

Of course, new EU legislation is being created all the time and will continue to apply to the UK until it leaves the EU.

Different types of EU legislation work in different ways and will be treated differently by the bill. Therefore regulations which apply automatically in the UK will be converted into UK law.

However, directives require a new UK law to come into force and this type of legislation will be preserved by the bill.

The UK Parliament can then "amend, repeal and improve" the laws as necessary.

Ensuring the continuity of EU rules and regulations is hoped will aid trade negotiations with the EU because the UK will already meet all of its product standards.

The repeal bill will need to be in its final form on the day the UK leaves.

The UK government plans to enact its amendments to UK law using what are known as Henry VIII powers after the Statute of Proclamations 1539 which gave Henry VIII the power to legislate by proclamation or decree.

Given that this will not involve the usual Parliamentary scrutiny process, opposition parties have protested.

Government ministers have attempted to reassure critics by saying such measures will be time limited and not used to make policy changes.

In total, the UK government estimates that 800 to 1,000 measures called statutory instruments will be required to make sure the bill functions properly.

It continues to pass through the UK Parliament. The bill was considered and amended in a committee of the whole House of Commons which completed its work on 20th December 2017.

Members of the UK Parliament will next consider the bill at its Third Reading and Report Stage which is due to take place on 16th-17th January 2018.

Bank of England concerns over Brexit and derivatives

At its Financial Policy Committee meeting on 20th September 2017, the Bank of England expressed concern that Brexit could disrupt the UK-EU derivatives market with potentially GBP 20 trillion of cross-border contracts facing legal uncertainty and possibly needing renegotiation. The Bank of England's concern applies to uncleared OTC derivatives contracts involving tens of thousands of counterparties. This could arise from the loss of the UK's MiFID financial passporting arrangements in the EU after Brexit which could also spill over into cross border banking, central clearing and asset management services.

Currently it is estimated that the UK handles 39% of the global interest rate swap market while the EU handles 9%. So this problem is bigger for the UK than the EU if UK companies and institutions lose the right to enter into new OTC derivatives contracts with EU counterparties. This could be avoided if the EU granted equivalence to UK derivatives regulation after Brexit.

Another solution suggested is to novate existing contracts to a legal entity established in the EU with the necessary regulatory permissions. However, this is a logistical nightmare with tens of thousands of counterparties needing to provide consent in each case for each contract from three parties - the two existing ones and the EU entity concerned. Moreover, in six large EU member states novations and even compressions are regarded as regulated activities normally covered under EMIR.

A more streamlined solution would be for a new law to be passed in both the UK and the EU to grandfather existing OTC derivatives contracts or for this to be covered in the Brexit agreement. The Bank of England called for this as their preferred solution to this problem in an announcement made on this issue on 1st November 2017.

The Bank of England is therefore urging UK and EU regulators to focus on a solution to this legal invalidity risk as a priority.

In an analysis published by ISDA in November 2017 they stated that after Brexit existing cross-border OTC derivatives contracts between counterparties in the UK and the other 27 EU states would not suddenly become invalid.

Parties should be able to continue to perform their contractual obligations such as payments, settlements and collateral transfers as before.

However, as mentioned before, lifecycle activities in OTC derivatives might be affected. These include novations, some sorts of portfolio compression, the rolling of open positions (e.g. extending the maturity of a trade) and material amendments which could each be categorised as an EU regulated activity needing local permissions.

Assuming that (a) financial passporting between the UK and the EU 27 is no longer available after Brexit and (b) market players lack local permissions, then it could be more challenging to trade with counterparties in those EU states. Unless there is an exemption for the UK or an equivalence determination covering it, this might lead to market players having to transfer existing deals to a locally authorised subsidiary in the relevant EU country or seek a banking licence there for trading activities to continue uninterrupted.

It should be noted that the European Banking Authority has stated that such locally authorised subsidiaries in the EU would need to be sufficiently capitalised.

In the wider world many UK banks and companies are more confident now that Brexit negotiators for the UK and EU can move on to Phase 2 of the negotiations. For now they can defer decisions about how much of their business they will need to relocate in the EU and when. However, if Phase 2 negotiations falter, these plans would probably be urgently revived.

ISDA Master Agreement and collateral issues

At this stage one can only largely discuss the following issues theoretically until we know the final shape of a Brexit deal.

However, Sterling cash and UK securities are regularly used as collateral for OTC derivatives contracts. Fluctuations and volatility in the OTC derivatives and FX markets might create or increase mark-to-market risk exposures under OTC derivatives contracts. In turn this would trigger calls to post more collateral.

This could also arise if companies had significant exposure to the UK economy.

They might find that their credit rating or their counterparties' view of their creditworthiness is adversely affected by Brexit. However, if a company has a credit rating Additional Termination Event in its ISDA Schedules then if its credit rating falls below the stated level this could expose it to possible termination of all its Transactions under these Agreements.

ISDA itself has published a number of useful Brexit briefings with Frequently Answered Questions.

The authors consider the following to be of particular interest to readers of this book.

Impossibility under the 1992 ISDA Master Agreement and Force Majeure Event under the 2002 ISDA Master Agreement

Impossibility and Force Majeure Events both need a practical impediment to payment/delivery which seems unlikely even if the UK were to lose its MiFID passporting rights for financial services in the UK. However, a broadly drafted Material Adverse Change clause or Additional Termination Event in a Master Agreement could be more problematical.

Illegality Termination Event under the ISDA Master Agreements

This is theoretically possible if Brexit resulted in a total loss of access for UK financial services companies to the EU financial markets and led to performance of Transactions becoming illegal in an EU member state because regulatory approval for such deals was absent post Brexit. This is why the Bank of England is seeking the continued recognition of the legal validity of pre-existing contracts.

Collateral

The European Directive on Collateral Financial Arrangements (2002) was enacted in the UK in the UK Financial Collateral Regulations (No.2) Regulations in 2003 and provided significant legal protection for the enforcement of collateral arrangements including where certain security interests were not registered. Without such protection those security interests would risk legal invalidity.

The UK's track record in EU derivatives regulation and its possible influence for equivalence recognition

Because the UK has been in the forefront of EU regulatory developments in the past 15 years (e.g. the EU Collateral Directive, MiFID 1 and 2 and EMIR) much of which it wants to preserve and in view of its intention to write much EU legislation via the European Union (Withdrawal) Bill (and then Act) into English law, it is hoped that this will result in a "soft" Brexit rather than a more perilous hard one.

In addition, maintaining equivalent rules may help the UK in establishing that if it satisfies equivalent EU standards, it may apply to retain cross border access.

Without EU membership, the UK would be regarded as a third country under EMIR and would need the European Commission to adopt an equivalent act under EMIR for the UK. However, this would be simplified if the UK adopts EMIR requirements without amendment. However, the EU has no time limit or deadline to make an equivalence decision of this nature.

Only if future UK regulatory rules on OTC derivatives diverge significantly from EU ones could parties with cross-border operations and transactions be faced with a dual compliance burden in order to continue to trade with the EU.

Bibliography

Allen & Overy: *Brexit-legal consequences for commercial parties: Derivatives-possible implications* (April 2016).

The Balance: *What caused the 2008 Financial Crisis: 4 Underlying Causes* (Updated 17th June 2017).

The Balance: *The 2008 Financial Crisis* (Updated 1st July 2017).

The Balance: *Learning About Living Wills for Banks* (Updated 10th August 2017).

Bank of England: *Financial Policy Statement from its meeting of 20th September 2017.*

Basel Committee on Banking Supervision and Board of IOSCO: *Margin requirements for non-centrally cleared derivatives* (March 2015).

Basel Committee on Banking Supervision: *High-level summary of Basel III reforms* (December 2017)

The Bank for International Settlements: *Statistical release: OTC derivatives statistics at end – June 2017* (November 2017).

BBC News: *The EU Withdrawal Bill: A guide to the Brexit legislation* (October 2017).

Arthur Cox: *EMIR-Margin Rules for Uncleared Transactions* (November 2016).

Commodity Futures Trading Commission: *Federal Register – Vol. 81, No. 3 Part III - 17 CFR Parts 23 and 140 - Margin Requirements for Uncleared Swaps for Swap Dealers and Major Swap Participants; Final Rule (6 January 2016)* Available on website http://www.cftc.gov/idc/groups/public/@lrfederalregister/documents/file/2015-32320a.pdf

The Economist: *Crash course: the 2008 Financial Crisis* (series in 2013).

The Economist: *American financial regulation: shearing and shaving* (11th February 2017).

The Economist: *The Federal Reserve: Switching to autopilot* (16th September 2017).

The Economist: *Europe's capital markets face a big shake up and are not ready* (30th September 2017).

The Economist: *Day of the MiFID: A new law heralds a new era for Europe's financial markets* (30th September 2017).

The Economist: *Brexit will give the derivatives market a nasty headache* (4th October 2017).

European Central Bank: *Monetary policy decisions* (26th October 2017).

European Securities and Markets Authority: *Commission Delegated Regulation (EU) 2016/2251 of 4 October 2016 supplementing Regulation (EU) No 648/2012 of the European Parliament and of the Council on OTC derivatives, central counterparties and trade repositories with regard to regulatory technical standards for risk-mitigation techniques for OTC derivative contracts not cleared by a central counterparty*. Available on website http://eur-lex. europa.eu/legal-content/EN/TXT/?uri=uriserv:OJ.L_.2016.340.01.0009.01. ENG&toc=OJ:L:2016:340:TOC

European Supervisory Authorities: *Variation margin exchange for physically-settled FX forwards under EMIR announcement* (24th November 2017).

European Supervisory Authorities: *Draft regulatory technical standards on amending Delegated Regulation (EU) 2016/2251 supplementing Regulation (EU) No 648/2012 of the European Parliament and of the Council with regard to regulatory technical standards on risk-mitigation techniques for OTC derivative contracts not cleared by a CCP under Article 11(15) of Regulation (EU) No 648/2012 with regard to physically settled foreign exchange forwards* (18th December 2017)

Financial Conduct Authority: *Variation margin requirements under EMIR for physically settled FX forwards statement* (7th December 2017).

Financial Times: *Cross-border chaos dogs derivatives rules* (5th December 2013).

Financial Times: *Lessons from the credit crunch* (6th August 2017).

Financial Times: *Regulators get ready to authorise "ringfenced" UK banks* (19th August 2017).

Financial Times: *ECB begins discussions on tapering QE despite strong euro* (7th September 2017).

Financial Times: *European Parliament seeks to toughen clearing house rules* (28th September 2017).

Financial Times: *Clock ticks down on EU's Mifid reform* (9th October 2017).

Financial Times: *Bank of England calls for clarity over derivatives post-Brexit* (1st November 2017).

Fieldfisher: *Uncleared Margin Rules in EU and US – Summary and Comparison* (Updated 27 January 2017).

G20 – *Leaders' Statement The Pittsburgh Summit September 24-25 2009.*

Paul C. Harding and Christian A. Johnson: Mastering ISDA ®Collateral Documents, 2nd edition (Pearson Education 2012).

Herbert Smith Freehills: *No Margin for Error: The Upcoming EMIR Margin Rules* (January 2017).

Hogan Lovells: *EU regulatory changes affecting derivatives: what's already in force and what's to come* (December 2016).

International Financial Law Review: *Why Dodd-Frank extraterritoriality is fundamentally flawed* (4th September 2012).

International Swaps and Derivatives Association, Inc.: Comments on the "EMIR Refit" proposal (18th July 2017).

International Swaps and Derivatives Association, Inc.: *ISDA Bank Recovery and Resolution Summary and FAQ.*(ISDA website).

International Swaps and Derivatives Association, Inc.: *ISDA Brexit Briefings* (latest October 2017).

International Swaps and Derivatives Association, Inc.: *White paper on Cross-Border Harmonization of Derivatives Regulatory Framework* (September 2017).

International Swaps and Derivatives Association, Inc.: *ISDA Margin Survey 2017* (September 2017).

International Swaps and Derivatives Association, Inc.: *Safeguarding Clearing: The Need for a Comprehensive CCP Recovery and Resolution Framework.* (September 2017).

International Swaps and Derivatives Association, Inc.: *Proposed Moratoria Under the BRRD: A Step Backwards in Efforts to End 'To Big to Fail'.* (September 2017).

International Swaps and Derivatives Association, Inc.: *Brexit and Contracts* (Quarterly Review, November 2017).

Kramer Levin Naftalis & Frankel LLP: *Implementing impending margin Regulations- Industry Initiatives: ISDA 2016 Variation Margin Protocol and Regulatory Self-Disclosure Letter* (November 2016).

Latham & Watkins: *CFTC Uncleared Swap Margin Rules to Take Effect in September* (February 2016).

Latham & Watkins: *US vs EU Margin Rules: A Comparative Summary* (January 2017).

Lombard Risk: *Latest Dodd-Frank ruling on final entity definitions* (August 2012).

McCann Fitzgerald: New *EMIR Margin Requirements for Uncleared OTC Derivatives* (February 2017).

The OTC Space: *Uncleared Margin Rules-how was the challenge met?* (April 2017).

The OTC Space: *EMIR under review: a quick fix or a structural improvement?* (October 2017).

Regtek: *Margin requirements for uncleared derivatives* (5th July 2017).

Reuters: *Federal Reserve finalizes rules to help unwind big banks* (1st September 2017).

Risk Magazine: *A rule by any other name* (January 2014).

Skadden Arps Slate Meagher & Flom: *Non-Cleared Swap Variation Margin Requirements To Spark Credit Support Annex Amendments For Financial End Users* (December 2016).

Skadden Arps Slate Meagher & Flom: *CFTC and European Commission Make Progress on Cross-Border Agreements* (18th October 2017).

Sunday Times: *Ten years on from the crisis, are we falling into a new trap?* (6th August 2017).

The Telegraph: *Trillions of pounds at risk without Brexit deal on derivatives, warns Bank of England* (25th September 2017).

The Trade News: *Banks could unwind non-compliant derivatives contracts* (21st August 2017).

US Practical Law: *The 2016 ISDA Credit Support Annexes and Global Margin Compliance for Uncleared Swaps* (November 2016).

US Treasury Department: *Core Principles for Regulating the United States Financial System* (October 2017).

White & Case: *European Margin Rules for Non-Cleared OTC Derivatives – The Margin Big Bang* (January 2017).

EMIR Margin Rules for Uncleared OTC Derivatives Implementation and Proposed Implementation

Date	EMIR Margin Rules for Uncleared OTC Derivatives Implementation and Proposed Implementation
15 December 2016	EMIR regulatory technical standard for risk-mitigation techniques for OTC derivative contracts not cleared by a central counterparty ("EMIR Uncleared Margin RTS") published in the Official Journal of the European Union
4 January 2017	EMIR Uncleared Margin RTS came into force
4 February 2017	**Phase 1**: VM and IM obligations started for parties whose group average aggregate notional amount ("AANA") exceeds EUR 3 trillion of uncleared OTC derivatives
1 March 2017	**Phase 2 VM**: VM obligations started for all other in-scope entities trading uncleared OTC derivatives
4 July 2017	IM and VM obligations started for intragroup uncleared OTC derivative transactions
1 September 2017	**Phase 2 IM**: IM obligations started for parties whose group AANA exceeds EUR 2.25 trillion of uncleared OTC derivatives
3 January 2018	Physically settled FX forwards in scope for VM obligations (temporary exemption expires). This is currently under review at the time of writing (January 2018) and is expected to be revised.
1 September 2018	**Phase 3 IM**: IM obligations start for parties whose group AANA exceeds EUR 1.5 trillion of uncleared OTC derivatives

1 September 2019	**Phase 4 IM**: IM obligations start for parties whose group AANA exceeds EUR 0.75 trillion of uncleared OTC derivatives
4 January 2020	Single stock equity options and index options in scope for VM and IM obligations (temporary exemption expires)
1 September 2020	**Phase 5 IM**: IM obligations start for parties whose group AANA exceeds EUR 8 billion of uncleared OTC derivatives

2016 ISDA® Credit Support Annex For Variation Margin under English Law

ISDA Sate, Efficient Markets

International Swaps and Derivatives Association, Inc.

2016 CREDIT SUPPORT ANNEX FOR VARIATION MARGIN (VM)

dated as of   ....

to the Schedule to the

ISDA Master Agreement

dated as of ....

between

.... and ....
         ("Party A")   ("Party B")

This Annex supplements, forms part of, and is subject to, the ISDA Master Agreement referred to above and is part of its Schedule. For the purposes of this Agreement, including, without limitation, Sections 1(c), 2(a), 5 and 6, the credit support arrangements set out in this Annex constitute a Transaction (for which this Annex constitutes the Confirmation).

Paragraph 1. Interpretation

(a)   ***Definitions and Inconsistency.*** Capitalised terms not otherwise defined in this Annex or elsewhere in this Agreement have the meanings specified pursuant to Paragraph 10, and all references in this Annex to Paragraphs are to Paragraphs of this Annex. In the event of any inconsistency between this Annex and the other provisions of this Schedule, this Annex will prevail, and in the event of any inconsistency between Paragraph 11 and the other provisions of this Annex, Paragraph 11 will

---

[1] This document is not intended to create a charge or other security interest over the assets transferred under its terms. Persons intending to establish a collateral arrangement based on the creation of a charge or other security interest should consider using the ISDA Credit Support Deed (English law) or the ISDA Credit Support Annex (New York law), as appropriate.

[2] This Credit Support Annex has been prepared for use with ISDA Master Agreements subject to English law. Users should consult their legal advisers as to the proper use and effect of this form and the arrangements it contemplates. In particular, users should consult their legal advisers if they wish to have the Credit Support Annex made subject to a governing law other than English law or to have the Credit Support Annex subject to a different governing law than that governing the rest of the ISDA Master Agreement (e.g., English law for the Credit Support Annex and New York law for the rest of the ISDA Master Agreement).

prevail. For the avoidance of doubt, references to "transfer" in this Annex mean, in relation to cash, payment and, in relation to other assets, delivery.

(b) **Scope of this Annex and the Other CSA.** The only Transactions which will be relevant for the purposes of determining "Exposure" under this Annex will be the Covered Transactions specified in Paragraph 11. Each Other CSA, if any, is hereby amended such that the Transactions that will be relevant for purposes of determining "Exposure" thereunder, if any, will exclude the Covered Transactions and the Transaction constituted by this Annex. Except as provided in Paragraph 9(h), nothing in this Annex will affect the rights and obligations, if any, of either party with respect to "independent amounts" or initial margin under each Other CSA, if any, with respect to Transactions that are Covered Transactions.

Paragraph 2. Credit Support Obligations

(a) **Delivery Amount (VM).** Subject to Paragraphs 3 and 4, upon a demand made by the Transferee on or promptly following a Valuation Date, if the Delivery Amount (VM) for that Valuation Date equals or exceeds the Transferor's Minimum Transfer Amount, then the Transferor will transfer to the Transferee Eligible Credit Support (VM) having a Value as of the date of transfer at least equal to the applicable Delivery Amount (VM) (rounded pursuant to Paragraph 11(c)(vi)(B)). Unless otherwise specified in Paragraph 11(c), the **"Delivery Amount (VM)"** applicable to the Transferor for any Valuation Date will equal the amount by which:

  (i) the Transferee's Exposure

exceeds

  (ii) the Value as of that Valuation Date of the Transferor's Credit Support Balance (VM) (adjusted to include any prior Delivery Amount (VM) and to exclude any prior Return Amount (VM) , the transfer of which, in either case, has not yet been completed and for which the relevant Regular Settlement Day falls on or after such Valuation Date).

(b) **Return Amount (VM).** Subject to Paragraphs 3 and 4, upon a demand made by the Transferor on or promptly following a Valuation Date, if the Return Amount (VM) for that Valuation Date equals or exceeds the Transferee's Minimum Transfer Amount, then the Transferee will transfer to the Transferor Equivalent Credit Support (VM) specified by the Transferor in that demand having a Value as of the date of transfer as close as practicable to the applicable Return Amount (VM) (rounded pursuant to Paragraph 11(c)(vi)(B)) and the Credit Support Balance (VM) will, upon such transfer, be reduced accordingly. Unless otherwise specified in Paragraph 11(c)(i)(B), the **"Return Amount (VM)"** applicable to the Transferee for any Valuation Date will equal the amount by which:

  (i) the Value as of that Valuation Date of the Transferor's Credit Support Balance (VM) (adjusted to include any prior Delivery Amount (VM) and to exclude any prior Return Amount (VM), the transfer of which, in either case, has not yet been completed and for which the relevant Regular Settlement Day falls on or after such Valuation Date)

exceeds

  (ii) the Transferee's Exposure.

2

Paragraph 3. Transfers, Calculations and Exchanges

(a)   *Transfers.* All transfers under this Annex of any Eligible Credit Support (VM), Equivalent Credit Support (VM), Interest Payment (VM) or Equivalent Distributions will be made in accordance with the instructions of the Transferee or Transferor, as applicable, and will be made:

      (i)   in the case of cash, by transfer into one or more bank accounts specified by the recipient;

      (ii)   in the case of certificated securities which cannot or which the parties have agreed will not be delivered by book-entry, by delivery in appropriate physical form to the recipient or its account accompanied by any duly executed instruments of transfer, transfer tax stamps and any other documents necessary to constitute a legally valid transfer of the transferring party's legal and beneficial title to the recipient; and

      (iii)   in the case of securities which the parties have agreed will be delivered by book-entry, by causing the relevant depository institution(s) or other securities intermediaries to make changes to their books and records sufficient to result in a legally effective transfer of the transferring party's legal and beneficial title to the recipient or its agent.

Subject to Paragraph 4, and unless otherwise specified in Paragraph 11, if a demand for the transfer of Eligible Credit Support (VM) or Equivalent Credit Support (VM) is received by the Notification Time, then the relevant transfer will be made not later than the close of business on the Regular Settlement Day relating to the date such demand is received; if a demand is received after the Notification Time, then the relevant transfer will be made not later than the close of business on the Regular Settlement Day relating to the day after the date such demand is received.

(b)   *Calculations.* All calculations of Value and Exposure for purposes of Paragraph 2 and Paragraph 4(a) will be made by the relevant Valuation Agent as of the relevant Valuation Time, *provided* that, the Valuation Agent may use, in the case of any calculation of (i) Value, Values most recently reasonably available for close of business in the relevant market for the relevant Eligible Credit Support (VM) as of the Valuation Time and (ii) Exposure, relevant information or data most recently reasonably available for close of business in the relevant market(s) as of the Valuation Time. The Valuation Agent will notify each party (or the other party, if the Valuation Agent is a party) of its calculations not later than the Notification Time on the Local Business Day following the applicable Valuation Date (or, in the case of Paragraph 4(a), following the date of calculation).

(c)   *Exchanges.*

      (i)   Unless otherwise specified in Paragraph 11, the Transferor may on any Local Business Day by notice inform the Transferee that it wishes to transfer to the Transferee Eligible Credit Support (VM) specified in that notice (the *"New Credit Support (VM)"*) in exchange for certain Eligible Credit Support (VM) (the *"Original Credit Support (VM)"*) specified in that notice comprised in the Transferor's Credit Support Balance (VM).

      (ii)   If the Transferee notifies the Transferor that it has consented to the proposed exchange, (A) the Transferor will be obliged to transfer the New Credit Support (VM) to the Transferee on the first Settlement Day following the date on which it receives notice (which may be oral telephonic notice) from the Transferee of its consent and (B) the Transferee will be obliged to transfer to the Transferor Equivalent Credit Support (VM) in respect of the Original Credit Support (VM) not later than the Settlement Day following the date on which the Transferee receives the New Credit Support (VM), unless otherwise specified in Paragraph 11(e) (the *"Exchange Date"*); *provided* that the Transferee will only be obliged to transfer Equivalent Credit Support (VM) with a Value as of the date of transfer as close as practicable to, but in any event not more than, the Value of the New Credit Support (VM) as of that date.

3

Paragraph 4. Dispute Resolution

(a)   ***Disputed Calculations or Valuations***. If a party (a ***"Disputing Party"***) reasonably disputes (I) the Valuation Agent's calculation of a Delivery Amount (VM) or a Return Amount (VM) or (II) the Value of any transfer of Eligible Credit Support (VM) or Equivalent Credit Support (VM), then:

> (1)   the Disputing Party will notify the other party and the Valuation Agent (if the Valuation Agent is not the other party) not later than the close of business on the date that the transfer is due in respect of such Delivery Amount (VM) or Return Amount (VM) in the case of (I) above, or, in the case of (II) above, the Local Business Day following the date of transfer;

> (2)   in the case of (I) above, the appropriate party will transfer the undisputed amount to the other party not later than the close of business on the date that the transfer is due in respect of such Delivery Amount (VM) or Return Amount (VM);

> (3)   the parties will consult with each other in an attempt to resolve the dispute; and

> (4)   if they fail to resolve the dispute by the Resolution Time, then:

>> (i)   in the case of a dispute involving a Delivery Amount (VM) or Return Amount (VM), unless otherwise specified in Paragraph 11, the Valuation Agent will recalculate the Exposure and the Value as of the Recalculation Date by:

>>> (A)   utilising any calculations of that part of the Exposure attributable to the Covered Transactions that the parties have agreed are not in dispute;

>>> (B)   (I) if this Agreement is a 1992 ISDA Master Agreement, calculating the Exposure for the Covered Transactions in dispute by seeking four actual quotations at midmarket from Reference Market-makers for purposes of calculating Market Quotation, and taking the arithmetic average of those obtained, or (II) if this Agreement is an ISDA 2002 Master Agreement or a 1992 ISDA Master Agreement in which the definition of Loss and/or Market Quotation has been amended (including where such amendment has occurred pursuant to the terms of a separate agreement or protocol) to reflect the definition of Close-out Amount from the pre-printed form of the ISDA 2002 Master Agreement as published by ISDA, calculating that part of the Exposure attributable to the Covered Transactions in dispute by seeking four actual quotations at mid-market from third parties for purposes of calculating the relevant Close-out Amount, and taking the arithmetic average of those obtained; *provided* that, in either case, if four quotations are not available for a particular Covered Transaction, then fewer than four quotations may be used for that Covered Transaction, and if no quotations are available for a particular Covered Transaction, then the Valuation Agent's original calculations will be used for the Covered Transaction; and

>>> (C)   utilising the procedures specified in Paragraph 11(f)(ii) for calculating the Value, if disputed, of the outstanding Credit Support Balance (VM);

>> (ii)   in the case of a dispute involving the Value of any transfer of Eligible Credit Support (VM) or Equivalent Credit Support (VM), the Valuation Agent will recalculate the Value as of the date of transfer pursuant to Paragraph 11(f)(ii).

Following a recalculation pursuant to this Paragraph, the Valuation Agent will notify each party (or the other party, if the Valuation Agent is a party) as soon as possible but in any event not later than the Notification Time on the Local Business Day following the Resolution Time. The appropriate party will, upon demand following such notice given by the Valuation Agent or a resolution pursuant to (3) above and subject to Paragraph 3(a), make the appropriate transfer.

(b)   ***No Event of Default.*** The failure by a party to make a transfer of any amount which is the subject of a dispute to which Paragraph 4(a) applies will not constitute an Event of Default for as long as the procedures set out in this Paragraph 4 are being carried out. For the avoidance of doubt, upon completion of those procedures, Section 5(a)(i) of this Agreement will apply to any failure by a party to make a transfer required under the final sentence of Paragraph 4(a) on the relevant due date.

Paragraph 5. Transfer of Title, No Security Interest, Distributions and Interest Amount (VM)

(a) *Transfer of Title.* Each party agrees that all right, title and interest in and to any Eligible Credit Support (VM), Equivalent Credit Support (VM), Equivalent Distributions or Interest Payment (VM) which it transfers to the other party under the terms of this Annex will vest in the recipient free and clear of any liens, claims, charges or encumbrances or any other interest of the transferring party or of any third person (other than a lien routinely imposed on all securities in a relevant clearance system).

(b) *No Security Interest.* Nothing in this Annex is intended to create or does create in favour of either party any mortgage, charge, lien, pledge, encumbrance or other security interest in any cash or other property transferred by one party to the other party under the terms of this Annex.

(c) *Distributions and Interest Amount.*

   (i) *Distributions*. The Transferee will transfer to the Transferor not later than the Settlement Day following each Distributions Date cash, securities or other property of the same type, nominal value, description and amount as the relevant Distributions (*"Equivalent Distributions"*) to the extent that a Delivery Amount (VM) would not be created or increased by the transfer, as calculated by the Valuation Agent (and the date of calculation will be deemed a Valuation Date for this purpose).

   (ii) *Interest Payment (VM)*. Unless otherwise specified in Paragraph 11(g)(iv):

   (A) if "Interest Transfer" is specified as applicable in Paragraph 11(g)(ii), the Interest Payer (VM) will transfer to the Interest Payee (VM), at the times specified in Paragraph 11(g)(ii) and on any Early Termination Date referred to in Paragraph 6, the relevant Interest Payment (VM), *provided* that if "Interest Payment Netting" is specified as applicable in Paragraph 11(g)(ii):

   (I) if the Interest Payer (VM) is entitled to demand a Delivery Amount (VM) or Return Amount (VM) in respect of the date such Interest Payment (VM) is required to be transferred:

   (a) such Delivery Amount (VM) or Return Amount (VM) will be reduced (but not below zero) by the Interest Payment (VM), *provided* that, in case of such Return Amount (VM), if the amount in the Credit Support Balance (VM) which is comprised of cash in the Base Currency is less than such Interest Payment (VM), such reduction will only be to the extent of the amount of such cash comprised in the Credit Support Balance (VM) (the *"Eligible Return Amount (VM)"*); and

   (b) the Interest Payer (VM) will transfer to the Interest Payee (VM) the amount of the excess, if any, of such Interest Payment (VM) over such Delivery Amount (VM) or Eligible Return Amount (VM), as applicable;

   (II) if under Paragraph 5(c)(ii)(A)(I)(a) a Delivery Amount (VM) is reduced (the amount of such reduction, the "*Delivery Amount Reduction (VM)*") or a Return

5

Amount (VM) is reduced (the amount of such reduction, the "***Return Amount Reduction (VM)***"), then for purposes of calculating the Credit Support Balance (VM) only, the Transferee will be deemed to have received an amount in cash in the Base Currency equal to any Delivery Amount Reduction (VM) and will be deemed to have transferred an amount in cash in the Base Currency equal to any Return Amount Reduction (VM), as applicable, in each case on the day on which the relevant Interest Payment (VM) was due to be transferred; and

(B) if "Interest Adjustment" is specified as applicable in Paragraph 11(g)(ii), the Credit Support Balance (VM) will be adjusted by the Transferee, at the times specified in Paragraph 11(g)(ii) and on any Early Termination Date referred to in Paragraph 6 as follows:

(I)   if the Interest Amount (VM) for an Interest Period is a positive number, the Interest Amount (VM) will constitute an addition of an amount of cash in the Base Currency comprised in the Credit Support Balance (VM); and

(II)   if the Interest Amount (VM) for an Interest Period is a negative number, the Interest Amount (VM) will constitute a reduction to the amount of cash in the Base Currency comprised in the Credit Support Balance (VM) in an amount (such amount, the ***"Interest Adjustment Reduction Amount (VM)"***) equal to the absolute value of the Interest Amount (VM); *provided* that if the amount in the Credit Support Balance (VM) which is comprised of cash in the Base Currency is less than the Interest Adjustment Reduction Amount (VM), such reduction will only be to the extent of the amount of such cash comprised in the Credit Support Balance (VM) and the Transferor will be obliged to transfer the remainder of the Interest Adjustment Reduction Amount (VM) to the Transferee on the day that such reduction occurred.

Paragraph 6. Default

If an Early Termination Date is designated or deemed to occur as a result of an Event of Default in relation to a party, an amount equal to the Value of the Credit Support Balance (VM), determined as though the Early Termination Date were a Valuation Date, will be deemed to be an Unpaid Amount due to the Transferor (which may or may not be the Defaulting Party) for purposes of Section 6(e). For the avoidance of doubt (a) any Market Quotation determined under Section 6(e) in relation to the Transaction constituted by this Annex will be deemed to be zero, (b) any Loss determined under Section 6(e) in relation to the Transaction constituted by this Annex will be limited to the Unpaid Amount representing the Value of the relevant Credit Support Balance (VM) and any unsatisfied obligations with respect to the transfer of an Interest Payment (VM); (c) any Close-out Amount determined under Section 6(e) in relation to the Transaction constituted by this Annex will be deemed to be zero; and (d) no Unpaid Amount will be determined with respect to an unsatisfied obligation under Paragraph 2 and Paragraph 3(c).

Paragraph 7. Representation

Each party represents to the other party (which representation will be deemed to be repeated as of each date on which it transfers Eligible Credit Support (VM), Equivalent Credit Support (VM) or Equivalent Distributions) that it is the sole owner of or otherwise has the right to transfer all Eligible Credit Support (VM), Equivalent Credit Support (VM) or Equivalent Distributions it transfers to the other party under this Annex, free and clear of any security interest, lien, encumbrance or other restriction (other than a lien routinely imposed on all securities in a relevant clearance system).

Paragraph 8. Expenses

Each party will pay its own costs and expenses (including any stamp, transfer or similar transaction tax or duty payable on any transfer it is required to make under this Annex) in connection with performing its obligations under this Annex, and neither party will be liable for any such costs and expenses incurred by the other party.

Paragraph 9. Miscellaneous

(a)   ***Default Interest.***   Other than in the case of an amount which is the subject of a dispute under Paragraph 4, if a Transferee fails to make, when due, any transfer of Equivalent Credit Support (VM) or Equivalent Distributions, it will be obliged to pay the Transferor (to the extent permitted under applicable law) an amount equal to interest at the Default Rate multiplied by the Value on the relevant Valuation Date of the items of property that were required to be transferred, from (and including) the date that the Equivalent Credit Support (VM) or Equivalent Distributions were required to be transferred to (but excluding) the date of transfer of the Equivalent Credit Support (VM) or Equivalent Distributions. This interest will be calculated on the basis of daily compounding and the actual number of days elapsed. Other than in the case of an amount which is the subject of a dispute under Paragraph 4, if an Interest Payer (VM) fails to make, when due, any transfer of an Interest Payment (VM), it will be obliged to pay the Interest Payee (VM) (to the extent permitted under applicable law) an amount equal to interest at the Default Rate (and for such purposes, if the Default Rate is less than zero, it will be deemed to be zero) multiplied by that Interest Payment (VM), from (and including) the date that Interest Payment (VM) was required to be transferred to (but excluding) the date of transfer of that Interest Payment (VM). This interest will be calculated on the basis of daily compounding and the actual number of days elapsed.

(b)   ***Good Faith and Commercially Reasonable Manner.***   Performance of all obligations under this Annex, including, but not limited to, all calculations, valuations and determinations made by either party, will be made in good faith and in a commercially reasonable manner.

(c)   ***Demands and Notices.***   All demands and notices given by a party under this Annex will be given as specified in Section 12 of this Agreement.

(d)   ***Specifications of Certain Matters.***   Anything referred to in this Annex as being specified in Paragraph 11 also may be specified in one or more Confirmations or other documents and this Annex will be construed accordingly.

(e)   ***Legally Ineligible Credit Support (VM).***

Unless otherwise specified in Paragraph 11, upon delivery of a Legal Ineligibility Notice by a party, each item of Eligible Credit Support (VM) (or a specified amount of such item) identified in such notice (i) will cease to be Eligible Credit Support (VM) for purposes of transfers to such party as the Transferee hereunder as of the applicable Transfer Ineligibility Date, (ii) will cease to be Eligible Credit Support (VM) for the other party as the Transferor for all purposes hereunder (other than for the purposes of the definitions of Credit Support Balance (VM) and Equivalent Credit Support (VM)) as of the Total Ineligibility Date and (iii) will have a Value of zero on and from the Total Ineligibility Date, other than for the purposes of Paragraph 6.

"Legal Ineligibility Notice" means a written notice from the Transferee to the Transferor in which the Transferee (i) represents that the Transferee has determined that one or more items of Eligible Credit Support (VM) (or a specified amount of any such item) either has ceased to satisfy, or as of a specified date will cease to satisfy, collateral eligibility requirements under law applicable to the Transferee requiring the collection of variation margin (the ***"Legal Eligibility Requirements"***), (ii) lists the item(s) of Eligible Credit Support (VM) (and, if applicable, the specified amount of such

ISDA®2016

item) that have ceased to satisfy, or as of a specified date will cease to satisfy, the Legal Eligibility Requirements, (iii) describes the reason(s) why such item(s) of Eligible Credit Support (VM) (or the specified amount thereof) have ceased to satisfy, or will cease to satisfy, the Legal Eligibility Requirements and (iv) specifies the Total Ineligibility Date and, if different, the Transfer Ineligibility Date.

"Total Ineligibility Date" means the date on which the relevant item of Eligible Credit Support (VM) (or a specified amount of such item) has ceased to satisfy, or will cease to satisfy, the Legal Eligibility Requirements applicable to the Transferee for all purposes hereunder, *provided* that, unless otherwise specified in Paragraph 11, if such date is earlier than the fifth Local Business Day following the date on which the Legal Ineligibility Notice is delivered, the Total Ineligibility Date will be the fifth Local Business Day following the date of such delivery.

"Transfer Ineligibility Date" means the date on which the relevant item of Eligible Credit Support (VM) (or a specified amount of such item) has ceased to satisfy, or will cease to satisfy, the Legal Eligibility Requirements for purposes of transfers to the Transferee hereunder, *provided* that, unless otherwise specified in Paragraph 11, if such date is earlier than the fifth Local Business Day following the date on which the Legal Ineligibility Notice is delivered, the Transfer Ineligibility Date will be the fifth Local Business Day following the date of such delivery.

(f)   *Return of Equivalent Credit Support (VM).* The Transferee will, promptly upon demand (but in no event later than the time at which a transfer would be due under Paragraph 3(a) with respect to a demand for the transfer of Eligible Credit Support (VM) or Equivalent Credit Support (VM)), transfer to the Transferor Equivalent Credit Support (VM) in respect of any item comprised in the Credit Support Balance (VM) (or the specified amount of such item) that as of the date of such demand has a Value of zero; *provided* that the Transferee will only be obligated to transfer any Equivalent Credit Support (VM) in accordance with this Paragraph 9(f), if, as of the date of transfer of such item, the Transferor has satisfied all of its transfer obligations under this Annex, if any.

(g)   *Reinstatement of Credit Support Eligibility* . Upon a reasonable request by the Transferor, the Transferee will determine whether an item (or a specified amount of such item) of Eligible Credit Support (VM) that was the subject of a prior Legal Ineligibility Notice would currently satisfy the Legal Eligibility Requirements applicable to the Transferee. If the Transferee determines that as of such date of determination such item (or specified amount of such item) satisfies the Legal Eligibility Requirements applicable to the Transferee, the Transferee will promptly following such determination rescind the relevant Legal Ineligibility Notice with respect to such item (or specified amount of such item) by written notice to the Transferor. Upon the delivery of such notice, the relevant item (or specified amount of such item) will constitute Eligible Credit Support (VM) hereunder.

(h)   *Credit Support Offsets.* If the parties specify that "Credit Support Offsets" is applicable in Paragraph 11 and on any date:

(i)   a transfer of Eligible Credit Support (VM) or Equivalent Credit Support (VM) is due under this Annex to satisfy a Delivery Amount (VM) or a Return Amount (VM) obligation, and a transfer of credit support (other than any Other CSA Excluded Credit Support) is also due under any Other CSA;

(ii)   the parties have notified each other of the credit support that they intend to transfer under this Annex and transfer under such Other CSA (other than any Other CSA Excluded Credit Support) to satisfy their respective obligations; and

8

(iii)   in respect of Paragraph 9(h)(ii), each party intends to transfer one or more types of credit support that is fully fungible with one or more types of credit support the other party intends to transfer (each such credit support, a "*Fungible Credit Support Type*"),

then, on such date and in respect of each such Fungible Credit Support Type, each party's obligation to make a transfer of any such Fungible Credit Support Type hereunder or under such Other CSA will be automatically satisfied and discharged and, if the aggregate amount that would have otherwise been transferred by one party exceeds the aggregate amount that would have otherwise been transferred by the other party, replaced by an obligation hereunder or under such Other CSA, as applicable, upon the party by which the larger aggregate amount would have been transferred to transfer to the other party the excess of the larger aggregate amount over the smaller aggregate amount. If a party's obligation to make a transfer of credit support under this Annex or an Other CSA is automatically satisfied and discharged pursuant to this Paragraph 9(h), then for purposes of this Annex or the Other CSA, as applicable, the other party will be deemed to have received credit support of the applicable Fungible Credit Support Type in the amount that would otherwise have been required to be transferred, in each case on the day on which the relevant transfer was due.

Paragraph 10. Definitions

As used in this Annex:

"Base Currency" means the currency specified as such in Paragraph 11(a)(i).

"Base Currency Equivalent" means, with respect to an amount on a Valuation Date, in the case of an amount denominated in the Base Currency, such Base Currency amount and, in the case of an amount denominated in a currency other than the Base Currency (the *"Other Currency"*), the amount of Base Currency required to purchase such amount of the Other Currency at the spot exchange rate on such Valuation Date as determined by the Valuation Agent.

"Covered Transaction" has the meaning specified in Paragraph 11(b).

"Credit Support Balance (VM)" means, with respect to a Transferor on a Valuation Date, the aggregate of all Eligible Credit Support (VM) that has been transferred to or received by the Transferee under this Annex, together with any Distributions and all proceeds of any such Eligible Credit Support (VM) or Distributions, as reduced pursuant to Paragraph 2(b), 3(c)(ii) or 6 and as adjusted pursuant to Paragraph 5(c)(ii). Any Equivalent Distributions (or portion thereof) not transferred pursuant to Paragraph 5(c)(i) will form part of the Credit Support Balance (VM).

"Credit Support Eligibility Condition (VM)" means, with respect to any item specified for a party as Eligible Credit Support (VM) in Paragraph 11(c)(ii), any condition specified for that item in Paragraph 11(c)(iv).

"Delivery Amount (VM)" has the meaning specified in Paragraph 2(a).

"Delivery Amount Reduction (VM)" has the meaning specified in Paragraph 5(c)(ii)(A)(II).

"Disputing Party" has the meaning specified in Paragraph 4.

"Distributions" means, with respect to any Eligible Credit Support (VM) comprised in the Credit Support Balance (VM) consisting of securities, all principal, interest and other payments and distributions of cash or other property to which a holder of securities of the same type, nominal value, description and amount as such Eligible Credit Support (VM) would be entitled from time to time.

"Distributions Date" means, with respect to any Eligible Credit Support (VM) comprised in the Credit Support Balance (VM) other than cash, each date on which a holder of such Eligible Credit Support (VM) is entitled to receive Distributions or, if that date is not a Local Business Day, the next following Local Business Day.

"Eligible Credit Support (VM)" means, with respect to a party, the items, if any, specified as such for that party in Paragraph 11(c)(ii) including, in relation to any securities, if applicable, the proceeds of any redemption in whole or in part of such securities by the relevant issuer.

"Eligible Currency" means each currency specified as such in Paragraph 11(a)(ii), if such currency is freely available.

"Eligible Return Amount (VM)" has the meaning specified in Paragraph 5(c)(ii)(A)(I)(a).

"Equivalent Credit Support (VM)" means, in relation to any Eligible Credit Support (VM) comprised in the Credit Support Balance (VM), Eligible Credit Support (VM) of the same type, nominal value, description and amount as that Eligible Credit Support (VM).

"Equivalent Distributions" has the meaning specified in Paragraph 5(c)(i).

"Exchange Date" has the meaning specified in Paragraph 11(e).

"Exposure" means , unless otherwise specified in Paragraph 11 for any Valuation Date or other date for which Exposure is calculated and subject to Paragraph 4 in the case of a dispute:

> (i)   if this Agreement is a 1992 ISDA Master Agreement, the amount, if any, that would be payable to that party by the other party (expressed as a positive number) or by that party to the other party (expressed as a negative number) pursuant to Section 6(e)(ii)(1) of this Agreement if all Covered Transactions (other than the Transaction constituted by this Annex) were being terminated as of the relevant Valuation Time on the basis that (A) that party is not the Affected Party and (B) the Base Currency is the Termination Currency; *provided* that Market Quotations will be determined by the Valuation Agent on behalf of that party using its estimates at mid-market of the amounts that would be paid for Replacement Transactions (as that term is defined in the definition of "Market Quotation"); and

> (ii)   if this Agreement is an ISDA 2002 Master Agreement or a 1992 ISDA Master Agreement in which the definition of Loss and/or Market Quotation has been amended (including where such amendment has occurred pursuant to the terms of a separate agreement or protocol) to reflect the definition of Close-out Amount from the pre-printed form of the ISDA 2002 Master Agreement as published by ISDA, the amount, if any, that would be payable to that party by the other party (expressed as a positive number) or by that party to the other party (expressed as a negative number) pursuant to Section 6(e)(ii)(1) (but without reference to clause (3) of Section 6(e)(ii)) of this Agreement as if all Covered Transactions (other than the Transactions constituted by this Annex) were being terminated as of the relevant Valuation Time on the basis that (A) that party is not the Affected Party and (B) the Base Currency is the Termination Currency; *provided* that the Close-out Amount will be determined by the Valuation Agent on behalf of that party using its estimates at mid-market of the amounts that would be paid for transactions providing the economic equivalent of (X) the material terms of the Covered Transactions, including the payments and deliveries by the parties under Section 2(a)(i) in respect of the Covered Transactions that would, but for the occurrence of the relevant Early Termination Date, have been required after that date (assuming satisfaction of the conditions precedent in Section 2(a)(iii) of this Agreement); and (Y) the option rights of the parties in respect of the Covered Transactions.

"Fungible Credit Support Type" has the meaning specified in Paragraph 9(h)(iii).

"FX Haircut Percentage" means, for any item of Eligible Credit Support (VM), the percentage specified as such in Paragraph 11(c)(v).

"Interest Adjustment Reduction Amount (VM)" has the meaning specified in Paragraph 5(c)(ii)(B)(II).

"Interest Amount (VM)" means with respect to an Interest Period, the aggregate sum of the Base Currency Equivalents of the amounts of interest determined for each relevant currency and calculated for each day in that Interest Period on the portion of the Credit Support Balance (VM) comprised of cash in such currency, determined by the Valuation Agent for each such day as follows:

(i)   the amount of cash in such currency on that day plus, only if "Daily Interest Compounding" is specified as applicable in Paragraph 11(g)(iii), the aggregate of each Interest Amount (VM) determined for each preceding day, if any, in that Interest Period; multiplied by

(ii)   the relevant Interest Rate (VM) in effect for that day; divided by

(iii)   360 (or, in the case of pounds sterling or any other currency specified as an "A/365 Currency" in Paragraph 11(g)(i), 365),

provided that, unless "Negative Interest" is specified as applicable in Paragraph 11(g)(iii), if the Interest Amount (VM) for an Interest Period would be a negative amount, it will be deemed to be zero.

"Interest Payee (VM)" means, in relation to an Interest Payer (VM), the other party.

"Interest Payer (VM)" means the Transferee, *provided* that if "Negative Interest" is specified as applicable in Paragraph 11(g)(iii) and an Interest Payment (VM) is determined in respect of a negative Interest Amount (VM), the Interest Payer (VM) in respect of such Interest Payment (VM) will be the Transferor.

"Interest Payment (VM)" means, with respect to an Interest Period, the Interest Amount (VM) determined in respect of such Interest Period, *provided* that in respect of any negative Interest Amount (VM), the Interest Payment (VM) will be the absolute value of such negative Interest Amount (VM).

"Interest Period" means the period from (and including) the last day on which (i) a party became obliged to transfer an Interest Payment (VM) or (ii) an Interest Amount (VM) was added to the Credit Support Balance (VM) (or, if no Interest Payment (VM) or Interest Amount (VM) has yet fallen due or been added to the Credit Support Balance (VM), respectively, the day on which Eligible Credit Support (VM) or Equivalent Credit Support (VM) in the form of cash was transferred to or received by the Transferee) to (but excluding) the day on which (i) a party is obliged to transfer the current Interest Payment (VM) or (ii) the current Interest Amount (VM) is added to the Credit Support Balance (VM).

"Interest Rate (VM)" means, with respect to an Eligible Currency, the rate specified in Paragraph 11(g)(i) for that currency.

"Legal Eligibility Requirements" has the meaning specified in Paragraph 9(e).

"Legal Ineligibility Notice" has the meaning specified in Paragraph 9(e).

"Local Business Day", unless otherwise specified in Paragraph 11(k), means:

(i)   in relation to a transfer of cash or other property (other than securities) under this Annex, a day on which commercial banks are open for business (including dealings in foreign exchange and foreign currency deposits) in the place where the relevant account is located and, if different, in the principal financial centre, if any, of the currency of such payment;

11

(ii)   in relation to a transfer of securities under this Annex, a day on which the clearance system agreed between the parties for delivery of the securities is open for the acceptance and execution of settlement instructions or, if delivery of the securities is contemplated by other means, a day on which commercial banks are open for business (including dealings in foreign exchange and foreign currency deposits) in the place(s) agreed between the parties for this purpose;

(iii)   in relation to the Resolution Time, a day on which commercial banks are open for business (including dealings in foreign exchange and foreign currency deposits) in at least one Valuation Date Location for Party A and at least one Valuation Date Location for Party B; and

(iv)   in relation to any notice or other communication under this Annex, a day on which commercial banks are open for business (including dealings in foreign exchange and foreign currency deposits) in the place specified in the address for notice most recently provided by the recipient.

"Minimum Transfer Amount" means, with respect to a party, the amount specified as such for that party in Paragraph 11(c)(vi)(A) or if no amount is specified, zero.

"New Credit Support (VM)" has the meaning specified in Paragraph 3(c)(i).

"Notification Time" has the meaning specified in Paragraph 11(d)(iv).

"Original Credit Support (VM)" has the meaning specified in Paragraph 3(c)(i).

"Other CSA" means, unless otherwise specified in Paragraph 11, any other credit support annex or credit support deed that is in relation to, or that is a Credit Support Document in relation to, this Agreement.

"Other CSA Excluded Credit Support" means, with respect to an Other CSA, any amounts and items transferred as credit support under such Other CSA, which, pursuant to the terms of such Other CSA, Party A and Party B have agreed must be segregated in an account maintained by a third-party custodian or for which offsets are prohibited.

"Recalculation Date" means the Valuation Date that gives rise to the dispute under Paragraph 4; *provided, however,* that if a subsequent Valuation Date occurs under Paragraph 2 prior to the resolution of the dispute, then the *"Recalculation Date"* means the most recent Valuation Date under Paragraph 2.

"Regular Settlement Day" means, unless otherwise specified in Paragraph 11, the same Local Business Day on which a demand for the transfer of Eligible Credit Support (VM) or Equivalent Credit Support (VM) is made.

"Resolution Time" has the meaning specified in Paragraph 11(f)(i).

"Return Amount (VM)" has the meaning specified in Paragraph 2(b).

"Return Amount Reduction (VM)" has the meaning specified in Paragraph 5(c)(ii)(A)(II).

"Settlement Day" means, in relation to a date, (i) with respect to a transfer of cash or other property (other than securities), the next Local Business Day and (ii) with respect to a transfer of securities, the first Local Business Day after such date on which settlement of a trade in the relevant securities, if effected on such date, would have been settled in accordance with customary practice when settling through the clearance system agreed between the parties for delivery of such securities or, otherwise, on the market in which such securities are principally traded (or, in either case, if there is no such customary practice, on the first Local Business Day after such date on which it is reasonably practicable to deliver such securities).

"Total Ineligibility Date" has the meaning specified in Paragraph 9(e), unless otherwise specified in Paragraph 11.

"Transferee" means, in relation to each Valuation Date, the party in respect of which Exposure is a positive number and, in relation to a Credit Support Balance (VM), the party which, subject to this Annex, owes such Credit Support Balance (VM) or, as the case may be, the Value of such Credit Support Balance (VM) to the other party.

"Transferor" means, in relation to a Transferee, the other party.

"Transfer Ineligibility Date" has the meaning specified in Paragraph 9(e), unless otherwise specified in Paragraph 11.

"Valuation Agent" has the meaning specified in Paragraph 11(d)(i).

"Valuation Date" means, unless otherwise specified in Paragraph 11, each day from, and including, the date of this Annex, that is a day on which commercial banks are open for business (including dealings in foreign exchange and foreign currency deposits) in at least one Valuation Date Location for Party A and at least one Valuation Date Location for Party B.

"Valuation Date Location" has the meaning specified in Paragraph 11(d)(ii).

"Valuation Percentage" means, for any item of Eligible Credit Support (VM), the percentage specified as such in Paragraph 11(c)(v).

"Valuation Time" means, unless otherwise specified in Paragraph 11, the time as of which the Valuation Agent computes its end of day valuations of derivatives transactions in the ordinary course of its business (or such other commercially reasonable convenient time on the relevant day as the Valuation Agent may determine).

"Value" means, for any Valuation Date or other date for which Value is calculated, and subject to Paragraph 4 in the case of a dispute, with respect to:

    (i)   Eligible Credit Support (VM) comprised in a Credit Support Balance (VM) or Equivalent Credit Support (VM) that is:

         (A)   an amount of cash, the Base Currency Equivalent of such amount multiplied by $(VP - H_{FX})$, *provided* that, in the case of a determination of a Value for the purposes of Paragraph 6, the Value will be the Base Currency Equivalent of such amount; and

         (B)   a security, the Base Currency Equivalent of the bid price obtained by the Valuation Agent multiplied by $(VP - H_{FX})$, where:

             VP equals the applicable Valuation Percentage; and

             H_{FX} equals the applicable FX Haircut Percentage,

         provided that, in the case of a determination of a Value for the purposes of Paragraph 6, the Value will be the Base Currency Equivalent of the bid price obtained by the Valuation Agent; and

    (ii)   items that are comprised in a Credit Support Balance (VM) and are not Eligible Credit Support (VM) (including any item or any portion of any item that fails to satisfy any (A) Credit Support Eligibility Conditions (VM) applicable to it or (B) applicable Legal Eligibility Requirements), zero *provided* that any items that are comprised in a Credit Support Balance (VM) that are not Eligible

Credit Support (VM) will, in the case of a determination of a Value for the purposes of Paragraph 6, have a Value determined in accordance with (i) above as if they were Eligible Credit Support (VM).

Paragraph 11. Elections and Variables

(a)   *Base Currency and Eligible Currency.*

      (i)   *"Base Currency"* means [●] unless otherwise specified here:

           ....

      (ii)   *"Eligible Currency"* means the Base Currency and each other currency specified here:

           ....

           ....

(b)   *"Covered Transactions"; "Exposure"*

      (i)   The term *"Covered Transactions"* as used in this Annex includes any Transaction specified below that is entered into on or after [...................][3], except as otherwise provided in the Confirmation of such Transaction:

      For purposes of the foregoing, the term *"Covered Transactions"* includes: [Any Transaction [that is any of the following] [Swap], [Security-Based Swap], [OTC Derivative], [Physically Settled FX Forward] or [Physically Settled FX Swap]] [and is not any of the following: [Swap], [Security-Based Swap], [OTC Derivative], [Physically Settled FX Forward] or [Physically Settled FX Swap]][4] ....]

      As used above:

      [*"OTC Derivative"* means an "OTC derivative" or "OTC derivative contract" as defined in Article 2(7) of Regulation (EU) No 648/2012 of the European Parliament and of the Council of 4 July 2012 on OTC derivatives, central counterparties and trade repositories (*"EMIR"*) other than one which constitutes (i) a "foreign exchange forward" as defined in Article 7(1)(a) of the final draft regulatory technical standards on risk-mitigation techniques for OTC-derivative contracts not cleared by a CCP under Article 11(15) of EMIR dated March 8, 2016 (the *"EMIR RTS"*) for so long as such transactions are subject to the transitional exemption from the variation margin requirements under Article 39(6) of the EMIR RTS or (ii) a single stock equity option or index option transaction as referred to in Article 39(7) of the EMIR RTS for so long as such transactions are subject to the transitional exemption from the variation margin requirements under Article 39(7) of the EMIR RTS.]

      ["*Physically Settled FX Forward*" means [...............................]]

      ["*Physically Settled FX Swap*" means [...............................]]

      [*"Security-Based Swap"* means a "security-based swap" as defined in Section 3(a)(68) of the U.S. Securities Exchange Act of 1934, as amended (*"SEA"*), and the rules adopted thereunder. For the avoidance of doubt, the term "Security-Based Swap" does not include a security-based swap that has been cleared by a "clearing agency" as such term is defined in Section 3(a)(23) of the SEA and the rules adopted thereunder.]

---

[3]   Insert the relevant date.

[4]   Parties may retain, delete or revise any of these definitions or add any additional definitions as applicable.

ISDA®2016

[*"Swap"* means a "swap" as defined in Section 1a(47) of the U.S. Commodity Exchange Act, as amended (*"CEA"*), and the regulations adopted thereunder. For the avoidance of doubt, the term "Swap" does not include a swap that has been cleared by a "derivatives clearing organization" as such term is defined in Section 1a(15) of the CEA and the regulations adopted thereunder.]

[For the purposes of the foregoing, a Transaction will be deemed to be entered into on or after the date specified in this Paragraph 11(b)(i) if an amendment, novation or other lifecycle event with respect to such Transaction would cause such Transaction to be entered into after such date under law applicable to either party requiring the collection or delivery of variation margin.][5]

(ii)   "*Exposure*" has the meaning specified in Paragraph 10, unless otherwise specified here: ....

(c)   *Credit Support Obligations.*

(i)   *Delivery Amount (VM) and Return Amount (VM).*

(A)   *"Delivery Amount (VM)"* has the meaning specified in Paragraph 2(a), unless otherwise specified here:

....

(B)   *"Return Amount (VM)"* has the meaning specified in Paragraph 2(b), unless otherwise specified here:

....

(ii)   *Eligible Credit Support (VM).*   Subject to Paragraph 9(e), if applicable, and each Credit Support Eligibility Condition (VM) applicable to it specified in Paragraph 11, if any, the following items will qualify as *"Eligible Credit Support (VM)"* for the party specified (as the Transferor):

	Party A	Valuation Percentage	Party B	Valuation Percentage
(A) cash in an Eligible Currency	[ ]	[ ]%	[ ]	[ ]%
(B) other:	[ ]	[ ]%	[ ]	[ ]%

(iii)   *Legally Ineligible Credit Support (VM).* The provisions of Paragraph 9(e) will not apply to the [party/parties] specified here (as the Transferee):[6]

[ ] Party A

[ ] Party B

---

[5] Parties may retain, delete or revise the bracketed language, as applicable.

[6] Parties should leave the relevant box below unmarked unless they agree to disapply Paragraph 9(e) with respect to a party as the Transferee.

ISDA®2016

(A) "**_Total Ineligibility Date_**" has the meaning specified in Paragraph 9(e), unless otherwise specified here:

....

(B) "**_Transfer Ineligibility Date_**" has the meaning specified in Paragraph 9(e), unless otherwise specified here:

....

(iv) **_Credit Support Eligibility Conditions (VM)._** The following conditions will each be a **_"Credit Support Eligibility Condition (VM)"_** for the party specified. Any item will not qualify as Eligible Credit Support (VM) if such item does not satisfy each Credit Support Eligibility Condition (VM) applicable to it.

[..]

[..]

(v) **_"Valuation Percentage"; "FX Haircut Percentage"_**

(A) **_"Valuation Percentage"_** means, with respect to each party (as the Transferor) and item of Eligible Credit Support (VM), the percentage (expressed as a decimal) specified in Paragraph 11(c)(ii), *provided* that if nothing is specified in Paragraph 11(c)(ii), the Valuation Percentage will be 100% unless otherwise specified below. The Valuation Percentage for either party and any item of Eligible Credit Support (VM) will further be subject to the terms and conditions, if any, specified below as applicable to such party and item:

....

[If at any time the Valuation Percentage assigned to an item of Eligible Credit Support (VM) with respect to a party (as the Transferor) under this Annex is greater than the maximum permitted valuation percentage (prescribed or implied) for such item of collateral under any law requiring the collection of variation margin applicable to the other party (as the Transferee), then the Valuation Percentage with respect to such item of Eligible Credit Support (VM) and such party will be such maximum permitted valuation percentage.][7]

(B) **_"FX Haircut Percentage"_** means, with respect to each party (as the Transferor) and item of Eligible Credit Support (VM), [[8%], unless the Eligible Credit Support (VM) or Equivalent Credit Support (VM) is in the form of cash [in a Major Currency] or is denominated in a currency that matches [an Eligible Currency], in which case the FX Haircut Percentage will be 0%.]

[As used above, "**_Major Currency_**" means any of: (1) United States Dollar; (2) Canadian Dollar; (3) Euro; (4) United Kingdom Pound; (5) Japanese Yen; (6) Swiss Franc; (7) New Zealand Dollar; (8) Australian Dollar; (9) Swedish Kronor; (10) Danish Kroner; (11) Norwegian Krone or any other currency specified below:

---

[7] Parties may retain, delete or revise the bracketed language, as applicable.

[..]]^8

 (vi) ***Thresholds.***

  (A) ***"Minimum Transfer Amount"*** means with respect to Party A:
   ....

   "Minimum Transfer Amount" means with respect to Party B:
   ....

  (B) ***Rounding.*** The Delivery Amount (VM) and the Return Amount (VM) will be rounded up and down respectively to the nearest integral multiple of ....

 (vii) ***Transfers.*** *"Regular Settlement Day"* has the meaning specified in Paragraph 10, unless otherwise specified here:

  ....

(d) ***Valuation and Timing.***

 (i) *"Valuation Agent"* means, for purposes of Paragraphs 2 and 4, the party making the demand under Paragraph 2, and, for purposes of Paragraph 5(c), the Transferee, as applicable, unless otherwise specified here:

 (ii) *"Valuation Date"* has the meaning specified in Paragraph 10, unless otherwise specified here: ....

For purposes of determining the Valuation Date and clause (iii) of the definition of "Local Business Day" in Paragraph 10, *"Valuation Date Location"*^9 means, with respect to each party, each city, region or country specified below:

Party A: ....

Party B: ....

 (iii) *"Valuation Time"* has the meaning specified in Paragraph 10, unless otherwise specified here: ....

 (iv) *"Notification Time"* means 12 noon, London time, on a Local Business Day, unless otherwise specified here: ....

(e) ***Exchange Date.*** *"Exchange Date"* has the meaning specified in Paragraph 3(c)(ii), unless otherwise specified here:

(f) ***Dispute Resolution.***

 (i) *"Resolution Time"* means 1:00 p.m., London time, on the Local Business Day following the date on which the notice is given that gives rise to a dispute under Paragraph 4, unless otherwise specified here:

---

^8 Parties may revise the bracketed language and the related definitions, as applicable.

^9 If applicable, a party can specify more than one Valuation Date Location.

....

(ii) *Value.* For the purpose of Paragraphs 4(a)(4)(i)(C) and 4(a)(4)(ii), the Value of the outstanding Credit Support Balance (VM) or of any transfer of Eligible Credit Support (VM) or Equivalent Credit Support (VM), as the case may be, will be calculated as follows:

....

(iii) *Alternative.* The provisions of Paragraph 4 will apply, unless an alternative dispute resolution procedure is specified here:

(g)   *Distributions and Interest Amount (VM).*

(i)   *Interest Rate (VM).* The *"Interest Rate (VM)"* in relation to each Eligible Currency specified below will be:

Eligible Currency	*Interest Rate (VM)*	*A/365 Currency*
....	....	....
....	....	....
....	....	....

(ii)   *Transfer of Interest Payment (VM) or application of Interest Amount (VM).*

Interest Transfer: [Applicable/Not Applicable]

Interest Payment Netting: [Applicable/Not Applicable]

[The transfer of an Interest Payment (VM) by the Interest Payer (VM) will be made on [the last Local Business Day of each calendar month] [and on any Local Business Day that a Return Amount (VM) consisting wholly or partly of cash is transferred to the Transferor pursuant to Paragraph 2(b)]. The transfer of an Interest Payment (VM) by the Interest Payer (VM) will be made on [the last Local Business Day of each calendar month] [and on any Local Business Day that a Delivery Amount (VM) consisting wholly or partly of cash is transferred to the Transferee pursuant to Paragraph 2(a)].]

Interest Adjustment: [Applicable/Not Applicable]

[The accrued Interest Amount (VM) will be added to the Credit Support Balance (VM) on [the last Local Business Day of each calendar month][each day].]

(iii) *Other Interest Elections.*

Negative Interest: [Applicable/Not Applicable]

Daily Interest Compounding: [Applicable/Not Applicable]

(iv) *Alternative to Interest Amount (VM).* The provisions of Paragraph 5(c)(ii) will apply, unless otherwise specified here: ………………………………………………………

(h)   *Credit Support Offsets.*

If specified here as applicable, then the "Credit Support Offsets" provisions in Paragraph 9(h) of this Annex will apply: [Applicable/Not Applicable].

(i)   *Addresses for Transfers.*

Party
A:

....

Party
B:

....

(j)   *Other CSA.* *"Other CSA"* has the meaning specified in Paragraph 10, unless otherwise specified here:

....
...

(k)   *Other Provisions.*

Appendix 3

2016 ISDA® Credit Support Annex For Variation Margin under New York Law

(Bilateral Form)   (ISDA Agreements Subject to New York Law Only)

International Swaps and Derivatives Association, Inc.

2016 CREDIT SUPPORT ANNEX FOR VARIATION MARGIN (VM)

dated as of …………………………

to the Schedule to the

……………………………………………………………………………………………

dated as of …………………………

between

…………………………………………………   and   ………………………………………………………

("Party A")   ("Party B")

This Annex supplements, forms part of, and is subject to, the above-referenced Agreement, is part of its Schedule and is a Credit Support Document under this Agreement with respect to each party.

Accordingly, the parties agree as follows:—

Paragraph 1. Interpretation

(a)   *Definitions and Inconsistency.* Capitalized terms not otherwise defined herein or elsewhere in this Agreement have the meanings specified pursuant to Paragraph 12, and all references in this Annex to Paragraphs are to Paragraphs of this Annex. In the event of any inconsistency between this Annex and the other provisions of this Schedule, this Annex will prevail, and in the event of any inconsistency between Paragraph 13 and the other provisions of this Annex, Paragraph 13 will prevail.

(b)   *Secured Party and Pledgor.* All references in this Annex to the "Secured Party" will be to either party when acting in that capacity and all corresponding references to the "Pledgor" will be to the other party when acting in that capacity; *provided, however,* that if Other Posted Support (VM) is held by a party to this Annex, all references herein to that party as the Secured Party with respect to that Other Posted Support (VM) will be to that party as the beneficiary thereof and will not subject that support or that party as the beneficiary thereof to provisions of law generally relating to security interests and secured parties.

(c)   *Scope of this Annex and the Other CSA.* The only Transactions which will be relevant for the purposes of determining "Exposure" under this Annex will be the Covered Transactions specified in Paragraph 13. Each Other CSA, if any, is hereby amended such that the Transactions that will be relevant for purposes of determining "Exposure" thereunder, if any, will exclude the Covered Transactions. Except as provided in Paragraphs 8(a), 8(b) and 11(j), nothing in this Annex will affect the rights and obligations, if any, of either party with respect to "independent amounts" or initial margin under each Other CSA, if any, with respect to Transactions that are Covered Transactions.

Paragraph 2. Security Interest

Each party, as the Pledgor, hereby pledges to the other party, as the Secured Party, as security for its Obligations, and grants to the Secured Party a first priority continuing security interest in, lien on and right of Set-off against all Posted Collateral (VM) Transferred to or received by the Secured Party hereunder. Upon the Transfer by the Secured Party to the Pledgor of Posted Collateral (VM), the security interest and lien granted hereunder on that Posted Collateral (VM) will be released immediately and, to the extent possible, without any further action by either party.

Paragraph 3. Credit Support Obligations

(a)   ***Delivery Amount (VM).*** Subject to Paragraphs 4 and 5, upon a demand made by the Secured Party on or promptly following a Valuation Date, if the Delivery Amount (VM) for that Valuation Date equals or exceeds the Pledgor's Minimum Transfer Amount, then the Pledgor will Transfer to the Secured Party Eligible Credit Support (VM) having a Value as of the date of Transfer at least equal to the applicable Delivery Amount (VM) (rounded pursuant to Paragraph 13). Unless otherwise specified in Paragraph 13, the "***Delivery Amount (VM)***" applicable to the Pledgor for any Valuation Date will equal the amount by which:

(i) the Secured Party's Exposure

exceeds

(ii) the Value as of that Valuation Date of all Posted Credit Support (VM) held by the Secured Party.

(b)   ***Return Amount (VM).*** Subject to Paragraphs 4 and 5, upon a demand made by the Pledgor on or promptly following a Valuation Date, if the Return Amount (VM) for that Valuation Date equals or exceeds the Secured Party's Minimum Transfer Amount, then the Secured Party will Transfer to the Pledgor Posted Credit Support (VM) specified by the Pledgor in that demand having a Value as of the date of Transfer as close as practicable to the applicable Return Amount (VM) (rounded pursuant to Paragraph 13). Unless otherwise specified in Paragraph 13, the "***Return Amount***" applicable to the Secured Party for any Valuation Date will equal the amount by which:

(i) the Value as of that Valuation Date of all Posted Credit Support (VM) held by the Secured Party

exceeds

(ii) the Secured Party's Exposure.

Paragraph 4. Conditions Precedent, Transfer Timing, Calculations and Substitutions

(a)   ***Conditions Precedent.*** Unless otherwise specified in Paragraph 13, each Transfer obligation of the Pledgor under Paragraphs 3, 5 and 6(d) and of the Secured Party under Paragraphs 3, 4(d)(ii), 5, 6(d) and 11(h) is subject to the conditions precedent that:

(i) no Event of Default, Potential Event of Default or Specified Condition has occurred and is continuing with respect to the other party; and

(ii) no Early Termination Date for which any unsatisfied payment obligations exist has occurred or been designated as the result of an Event of Default or Specified Condition with respect to the other party.

(b)   ***Transfer Timing.*** Subject to Paragraphs 4(a) and 5 and unless otherwise specified in Paragraph 13, if a demand for the Transfer of Eligible Credit Support (VM) or Posted Credit Support (VM) is made by the Notification Time, then the relevant Transfer will be made not later than the close of business on the Regular Settlement Day; if a demand is made after the Notification Time, then the relevant Transfer will be made not later than the close of business on the next Local Business Day following the Regular Settlement Day.

(c)   ***Calculations.*** All calculations of Value and Exposure for purposes of Paragraphs 3 and 6(d) will be made by the Valuation Agent as of the Valuation Time; *provided* that the Valuation Agent may use, in the case of any calculation of (i) Value, Values most recently reasonably available for close of business in the relevant market for the relevant Eligible Credit Support (VM) as of the Valuation Time and (ii) Exposure, relevant information or data most recently reasonably available for close of business in the relevant market(s) as of the Valuation Time. The Valuation Agent will notify each party (or the other party, if the Valuation Agent is a party) of its calculations not later than the Notification Time on the Local Business Day following the applicable Valuation Date (or in the case of Paragraph 6(d), following the date of calculation).

(d) **Substitutions.**

(i) Unless otherwise specified in Paragraph 13, upon notice to the Secured Party specifying the items of Posted Credit Support (VM) to be exchanged, the Pledgor may, on any Local Business Day, Transfer to the Secured Party substitute Eligible Credit Support (VM) (the "***Substitute Credit Support (VM)***"); and

(ii) subject to Paragraph 4(a), the Secured Party will Transfer to the Pledgor the items of Posted Credit Support (VM) specified by the Pledgor in its notice not later than the Local Business Day following the date on which the Secured Party receives the Substitute Credit Support (VM), unless otherwise specified in Paragraph 13 (the "***Substitution Date***"); *provided* that the Secured Party will only be obligated to Transfer Posted Credit Support (VM) with a Value as of the date of Transfer of that Posted Credit Support (VM) equal to the Value as of that date of the Substitute Credit Support (VM).

Paragraph 5. Dispute Resolution

If a party (a "***Disputing Party***") disputes (I) the Valuation Agent's calculation of a Delivery Amount (VM) or a Return Amount (VM) or (II) the Value of any Transfer of Eligible Credit Support (VM) or Posted Credit Support (VM), then:

(i) the Disputing Party will notify the other party and the Valuation Agent (if the Valuation Agent is not the other party) not later than the close of business on (X) the date that the Transfer is due in respect of such Delivery Amount (VM) or Return Amount (VM) in the case of (I) above, or (Y) the Local Business Day following the date of Transfer in the case of (II) above,

(ii) subject to Paragraph 4(a), the appropriate party will Transfer the undisputed amount to the other party not later than the close of business on (X) the date that the Transfer is due in respect of such Delivery Amount (VM) or Return Amount (VM) in the case of (I) above, or (Y) the Local Business Day following the date of Transfer in the case of (II) above,

(iii) the parties will consult with each other in an attempt to resolve the dispute, and

(iv) if they fail to resolve the dispute by the Resolution Time, then:

(A) In the case of a dispute involving a Delivery Amount (VM) or Return Amount (VM), unless otherwise specified in Paragraph 13, the Valuation Agent will recalculate the Exposure and the Value as of the Recalculation Date by:

(1) utilizing any calculations of Exposure for the Covered Transactions that the parties have agreed are not in dispute;

(2) (I) if this Agreement is a 1992 ISDA Master Agreement, calculating the Exposure for the Covered Transactions in dispute by seeking four actual quotations at mid-market from Reference Market-makers for purposes of calculating Market Quotation, and taking the arithmetic average of those obtained, or (II) if this Agreement is an ISDA 2002 Master Agreement or a 1992 ISDA Master Agreement in which the definition of Loss and/or Market Quotation has been amended (including where such amendment has occurred pursuant to the terms of a separate agreement or protocol) to reflect the definition of Close-out Amount from the pre-printed form of the ISDA 2002 Master Agreement as published by ISDA, calculating the Exposure for the Covered Transactions in dispute by seeking four actual quotations at mid-market from third parties for purposes of calculating the relevant Close-out Amount, and taking the arithmetic average of those obtained; *provided* that, in

either case, if four quotations are not available for a particular Covered Transaction, then fewer than four quotations may be used for that Covered Transaction, and if no quotations are available for a particular Covered Transaction, then the Valuation Agent's original calculations will be used for that Covered Transaction; and

(3) utilizing the procedures specified in Paragraph 13 for calculating the Value, if disputed, of Posted Credit Support (VM).

(B) In the case of a dispute involving the Value of any Transfer of Eligible Credit Support (VM) or Posted Credit Support (VM), the Valuation Agent will recalculate the Value as of the date of Transfer pursuant to Paragraph 13.

Following a recalculation pursuant to this Paragraph, the Valuation Agent will notify each party (or the other party, if the Valuation Agent is a party) not later than the Notification Time on the Local Business Day following the Resolution Time. The appropriate party will, upon demand following that notice by the Valuation Agent or a resolution pursuant to (iii) above and subject to Paragraphs 4(a) and 4(b), make the appropriate Transfer.

Paragraph 6. Holding and Using Posted Collateral (VM)

(a)   *Care of Posted Collateral (VM).* Without limiting the Secured Party's rights under Paragraph 6(c), the Secured Party will exercise reasonable care to assure the safe custody of all Posted Collateral (VM) to the extent required by applicable law, and in any event the Secured Party will be deemed to have exercised reasonable care if it exercises at least the same degree of care as it would exercise with respect to its own property. Except as specified in the preceding sentence, the Secured Party will have no duty with respect to Posted Collateral (VM), including, without limitation, any duty to collect any Distributions, or enforce or preserve any rights pertaining thereto.

(b)   *Eligibility to Hold Posted Collateral (VM); Custodians (VM).*

(i) *General.* Subject to the satisfaction of any conditions specified in Paragraph 13 for holding Posted Collateral (VM), the Secured Party will be entitled to hold Posted Collateral (VM) or to appoint an agent (a "*Custodian (VM)*") to hold Posted Collateral (VM) for the Secured Party. Upon notice by the Secured Party to the Pledgor of the appointment of a Custodian (VM), the Pledgor's obligations to make any Transfer will be discharged by making the Transfer to that Custodian (VM). The holding of Posted Collateral (VM) by a Custodian (VM) will be deemed to be the holding of that Posted Collateral (VM) by the Secured Party for which the Custodian (VM) is acting.

(ii) *Failure to Satisfy Conditions.* If the Secured Party or its Custodian (VM) fails to satisfy any conditions for holding Posted Collateral (VM), then upon a demand made by the Pledgor, the Secured Party will, not later than five Local Business Days after the demand, Transfer or cause its Custodian (VM) to Transfer all Posted Collateral (VM) held by it to a Custodian (VM) that satisfies those conditions or to the Secured Party if it satisfies those conditions.

(iii) *Liability.* The Secured Party will be liable for the acts or omissions of its Custodian (VM) to the same extent that the Secured Party would be liable hereunder for its own acts or omissions.

(c)   *Use of Posted Collateral (VM).* Unless otherwise specified in Paragraph 13 and without limiting the rights and obligations of the parties under Paragraphs 3, 4(d)(ii), 5, 6(d) and 8, if the Secured Party is not a Defaulting Party or an Affected Party with respect to a Specified Condition and no Early Termination Date has occurred or been designated as the result of an Event of Default or Specified Condition with respect to the Secured Party, then the Secured Party will, notwithstanding Section 9-207 of the New York Uniform Commercial Code, have the right to:

(i) sell, pledge, rehypothecate, assign, invest, use, commingle or otherwise dispose of, or otherwise use in its business any Posted Collateral (VM) it holds, free from any claim or right of any nature whatsoever of the Pledgor, including any equity or right of redemption by the Pledgor; and

(ii) register any Posted Collateral (VM) in the name of the Secured Party, its Custodian (VM) or a nominee for either.

For purposes of the obligation to Transfer Eligible Credit Support (VM) or Posted Credit Support (VM) pursuant to Paragraphs 3 and 5 and any rights or remedies authorized under this Agreement, the Secured Party will be deemed to continue to hold all Posted Collateral (VM) and to receive Distributions made thereon, regardless of whether the Secured Party has exercised any rights with respect to any Posted Collateral (VM) pursuant to (i) or (ii) above.

(d) *Distributions, Interest Amount (VM) and Interest Payment (VM).*

    (i) *Distributions.* Subject to Paragraph 4(a), if the Secured Party receives or is deemed to receive Distributions on a Local Business Day, it will Transfer to the Pledgor not later than the following Local Business Day any Distributions it receives or is deemed to receive to the extent that a Delivery Amount (VM) would not be created or increased by that Transfer, as calculated by the Valuation Agent (and the date of calculation will be deemed to be a Valuation Date for this purpose).

    (ii) *Interest Amount (VM) and Interest Payment (VM).* Unless otherwise specified in Paragraph 13 and subject to Paragraph 4(a), in lieu of any interest, dividends or other amounts paid or deemed to have been paid with respect to Posted Collateral (VM) in the form of Cash (all of which may be retained by the Secured Party),

        (A) if "Interest Transfer" is specified as applicable in Paragraph 13, the Interest Payer (VM) will Transfer to the Interest Payee (VM), at the times specified in Paragraph 13, the relevant Interest Payment (VM); *provided* that if "Interest Payment Netting" is specified as applicable in Paragraph 13:

            (I) if the Interest Payer (VM) is entitled to demand a Delivery Amount (VM) or Return Amount (VM), in respect of the date such Interest Payment (VM) is required to be Transferred:

                (a) such Delivery Amount (VM) or Return Amount (VM) will be reduced (but not below zero) by such Interest Payment (VM); *provided* that, in case of such Return Amount (VM), if the amount of Posted Collateral (VM) which is comprised of Cash in the Base Currency is less than such Interest Payment (VM), such reduction will only be to the extent of the amount of such Cash which is Posted Collateral (VM) (the "*Eligible Return Amount (VM)*"); and

                (b) the Interest Payer (VM) will Transfer to the Interest Payee (VM) the amount of the excess, if any, of such Interest Payment (VM) over such Delivery Amount (VM) or Eligible Return Amount (VM), as applicable; and

            (II) if under Paragraph 6(d)(ii)(A)(I)(a) a Delivery Amount (VM) is reduced (the amount of such reduction, the "*Delivery Amount Reduction (VM)*") or a Return Amount (VM) is reduced (the amount of such reduction, the "*Return Amount Reduction (VM)*"), then for purposes of determining Posted Collateral (VM), the Secured Party (a) will be deemed to have received an amount in Cash in the Base Currency equal to any Delivery Amount Reduction (VM), and such amount will constitute Posted Collateral (VM) in such Cash and will be subject to the security interest granted under Paragraph 2 or (b) will be deemed to have Transferred an amount in Cash in the Base Currency equal to any Return Amount Reduction (VM), as applicable, in each case on the day on which the relevant Interest Payment (VM) was due to be Transferred, as applicable; and

        (B) if "Interest Adjustment" is specified as applicable in Paragraph 13, the Posted Collateral (VM) will be adjusted by the Secured Party, at the times specified in Paragraph 13, as follows:

            (I) if the Interest Amount (VM) for an Interest Period is a positive number, the Interest Amount (VM) will constitute Posted Collateral (VM) in the form of Cash in the Base Currency and will be subject to the security interest granted under Paragraph 2; and

(II) if the Interest Amount (VM) for an Interest Period is a negative number and any Posted Collateral (VM) is in the form of Cash in the Base Currency, the Interest Amount (VM) will constitute a reduction of Posted Collateral (VM) in the form of such Cash in an amount (such amount, the "***Interest Adjustment Reduction Amount (VM)***") equal to the absolute value of the Interest Amount (VM); *provided* that if the amount of Posted Collateral (VM) which is comprised of such Cash is less than the Interest Adjustment Reduction Amount (VM), such reduction will only be to the extent of the amount of such Cash which is Posted Collateral (VM) and the Pledgor will be obligated to Transfer the remainder of the Interest Adjustment Reduction Amount (VM) to the Secured Party on the day that such reduction occurred.

Paragraph 7.   Events of Default

For purposes of Section 5(a)(iii)(1) of this Agreement, an Event of Default will exist with respect to a party if:

(i) that party fails (or fails to cause its Custodian (VM)) to make, when due, any Transfer of Eligible Collateral (VM), Posted Collateral (VM) or the Interest Payment (VM), as applicable, required to be made by it and that failure continues for two Local Business Days after notice of that failure is given to that party;

(ii) that party fails to comply with any restriction or prohibition specified in this Annex with respect to any of the rights specified in Paragraph 6(c) and that failure continues for five Local Business Days after notice of that failure is given to that party; or

(iii) that party fails to comply with or perform any agreement or obligation other than those specified in Paragraphs 7(i) and 7(ii) and that failure continues for 30 days after notice of that failure is given to that party.

Paragraph 8.   Certain Rights and Remedies

(a)   ***Secured Party's Rights and Remedies.***   If at any time (1) an Event of Default or Specified Condition with respect to the Pledgor has occurred and is continuing or (2) an Early Termination Date has occurred or been designated as the result of an Event of Default or Specified Condition with respect to the Pledgor, then, unless the Pledgor has paid in full all of its Obligations that are then due, the Secured Party may exercise one or more of the following rights and remedies:

(i) all rights and remedies available to a secured party under applicable law with respect to Posted Collateral (VM) held by the Secured Party;

(ii) any other rights and remedies available to the Secured Party under the terms of Other Posted Support (VM), if any;

(iii) the right to Set-off (A) any amounts payable by the Pledgor with respect to any Obligations and (B) any Cash amounts and the Cash equivalent of any non-Cash items posted to the Pledgor by the Secured Party as margin under any Other CSA (other than any Other CSA Excluded Credit Support) the return of which is due to the Secured Party against any Posted Collateral (VM) or the Cash equivalent of any Posted Collateral (VM) held by the Secured Party (or any obligation of the Secured Party to Transfer that Posted Collateral (VM)); and

(iv) the right to liquidate any Posted Collateral (VM) held by the Secured Party through one or more public or private sales or other dispositions with such notice, if any, as may be required under applicable law, free from any claim or right of any nature whatsoever of the Pledgor, including any equity or right of redemption by the Pledgor (with the Secured Party having the right to purchase any or all of the Posted Collateral (VM) to be sold) and to apply the proceeds (or the Cash equivalent thereof) from the liquidation of the Posted Collateral (VM) to (A) any amounts payable by the Pledgor with respect to any Obligations and (B) any Cash amounts and the Cash equivalent of any non-Cash items posted to the Pledgor by the Secured Party as margin under any Other CSA (other than any Other CSA Excluded Credit Support) the return of which is due to the Secured Party in that order as the Secured Party may elect.

Each party acknowledges and agrees that Posted Collateral (VM) in the form of securities may decline speedily in value and is of a type customarily sold on a recognized market, and, accordingly, the Pledgor is not entitled to prior notice of any sale of that Posted Collateral (VM) by the Secured Party, except any notice that is required under applicable law and cannot be waived.

(b) **Pledgor's Rights and Remedies.** If at any time an Early Termination Date has occurred or been designated as the result of an Event of Default or Specified Condition with respect to the Secured Party, then (except in the case of an Early Termination Date relating to fewer than all Transactions where the Secured Party has paid in full all of its obligations that are then due under Section 6(e) of this Agreement):

(i) the Pledgor may exercise all rights and remedies available to a pledgor under applicable law with respect to Posted Collateral (VM) held by the Secured Party;

(ii) the Pledgor may exercise any other rights and remedies available to the Pledgor under the terms of Other Posted Support (VM), if any;

(iii) the Secured Party will be obligated immediately to Transfer all Posted Collateral (VM) and, if the Secured Party is an Interest Payer (VM), the Interest Payment (VM) to the Pledgor; and

(iv) to the extent that Posted Collateral (VM) or the Interest Payment (VM) is not so Transferred pursuant to (iii) above, the Pledgor may:

(A) Set-off any amounts payable by the Pledgor with respect to any Obligations against any Posted Collateral (VM) or the Cash equivalent of any Posted Collateral (VM) held by the Secured Party (or any obligation of the Secured Party to Transfer that Posted Collateral (VM));

(B) Set-off, net, or apply credit support received under any Other CSA or the proceeds thereof against any Posted Collateral (VM) or the Cash equivalent of any Posted Collateral (VM) held by the Secured Party (or any obligation of the Secured Party to Transfer that Posted Collateral (VM)); and

(C) to the extent that the Pledgor does not Set-off under (iv)(A) or (iv)(B) above, withhold payment of any remaining amounts payable by the Pledgor with respect to any Obligations, up to the Value of any remaining Posted Collateral (VM) held by the Secured Party, until that Posted Collateral (VM) is Transferred to the Pledgor.

(c) **Deficiencies and Excess Proceeds.** The Secured Party will Transfer to the Pledgor any proceeds and Posted Credit Support (VM) remaining after liquidation, Set-off and/or application under Paragraphs 8(a) and 8(b) after satisfaction in full of all amounts payable by the Pledgor with respect to any Obligations; and the Pledgor in all events will remain liable for any amounts remaining unpaid after any liquidation, Set-off and/or application under Paragraphs 8(a) and 8(b).

(d) **Final Returns.** When no amounts are or thereafter may become payable by the Pledgor with respect to any Obligations (except for any potential liability under Section 2(d) of this Agreement, any obligation to Transfer any Interest Payment (VM) under this Paragraph 8(d) or any obligation to transfer any interest payment under any Other CSA), (i) the Secured Party will Transfer to the Pledgor all Posted Credit Support (VM), and (ii) the Interest Payer (VM) will Transfer to the Interest Payee (VM) any Interest Payment (VM).

Paragraph 9. Representations

Each party represents to the other party (which representations will be deemed to be repeated as of each date on which it, as the Pledgor, Transfers Eligible Collateral (VM)) that:

(i) it has the power to grant a security interest in and lien on any Eligible Collateral (VM) it Transfers as the Pledgor and has taken all necessary actions to authorize the granting of that security interest and lien;

(ii) it is the sole owner of or otherwise has the right to Transfer all Eligible Collateral (VM) it Transfers to the Secured Party hereunder, free and clear of any security interest, lien, encumbrance or other restrictions other than the security interest and lien granted under Paragraph 2;

(iii) upon the Transfer of any Eligible Collateral (VM) to the Secured Party under the terms of this Annex, the Secured Party will have a valid and perfected first priority security interest therein (assuming that any central clearing corporation or any third-party financial intermediary or other entity not within the control of the Pledgor involved in the Transfer of that Eligible Collateral (VM) gives the notices and takes the action required of it under applicable law for perfection of that interest); and

(iv) the performance by it of its obligations under this Annex will not result in the creation of any security interest, lien or other encumbrance on any Posted Collateral (VM) other than the security interest and lien granted under Paragraph 2.

Paragraph 10. Expenses

(a) *General.* Except as otherwise provided in Paragraphs 10(b) and 10(c), each party will pay its own costs and expenses in connection with performing its obligations under this Annex and neither party will be liable for any costs and expenses incurred by the other party in connection herewith.

(b) *Posted Credit Support (VM).* The Pledgor will promptly pay when due all taxes, assessments or charges of any nature that are imposed with respect to Posted Credit Support (VM) held by the Secured Party upon becoming aware of the same, regardless of whether any portion of that Posted Credit Support (VM) is subsequently disposed of under Paragraph 6(c), except for those taxes, assessments and charges that result from the exercise of the Secured Party's rights under Paragraph 6(c).

(c) *Liquidation/Application of Posted Credit Support (VM).* All reasonable costs and expenses incurred by or on behalf of the Secured Party or the Pledgor in connection with the liquidation and/or application of any Posted Credit Support (VM) under Paragraph 8 will be payable, on demand and pursuant to the Expenses Section of this Agreement, by the Defaulting Party or, if there is no Defaulting Party, equally by the parties.

Paragraph 11. Miscellaneous

(a) *Default Interest.* A Secured Party that fails to make, when due, any Transfer of Posted Collateral (VM) will be obligated to pay the Pledgor (to the extent permitted under applicable law) an amount equal to interest at the Default Rate multiplied by the Value of the items of property that were required to be Transferred, from (and including) the date that Posted Collateral (VM) was required to be Transferred to (but excluding) the date of Transfer of that Posted Collateral (VM). This interest will be calculated on the basis of daily compounding and the actual number of days elapsed. An Interest Payer (VM) that fails to make, when due, any Transfer of an Interest Payment (VM) will be obligated to pay the Interest Payee (VM) (to the extent permitted under applicable law) an amount equal to interest at the Default Rate (and for such purposes, if the Default Rate is less than zero, it will be deemed to be zero) multiplied by that Interest Payment (VM), from (and including) the date that Interest Payment (VM) was required to be Transferred to (but excluding) the date of Transfer of that Interest Payment (VM). This interest will be calculated on the basis of daily compounding and the actual number of days elapsed.

(b) *Further Assurances.* Promptly following a demand made by a party, the other party will execute, deliver, file and record any financing statement, specific assignment or other document and take any other action that may be necessary or desirable and reasonably requested by that party to create, preserve, perfect or validate any security interest or lien granted under Paragraph 2, to enable that party to exercise or enforce its rights under this Annex with respect to Posted Credit Support (VM) or an Interest Payment (VM) or to effect or document a release of a security interest on Posted Collateral (VM) or an Interest Payment (VM).

(c) *Further Protection.* The Pledgor will promptly give notice to the Secured Party of, and defend against, any suit, action, proceeding or lien that involves Posted Credit Support (VM) Transferred by the Pledgor or that could adversely affect the security interest and lien granted by it under Paragraph 2, unless that suit, action, proceeding or lien results from the exercise of the Secured Party's rights under Paragraph 6(c).

(d) *Good Faith and Commercially Reasonable Manner.* Performance of all obligations under this Annex, including, but not limited to, all calculations, valuations and determinations made by either party, will be made in good faith and in a commercially reasonable manner.

(e) *Demands and Notices.* All demands and notices made by a party under this Annex will be made as specified in the Notices Section of this Agreement, except as otherwise provided in Paragraph 13.

(f) *Specifications of Certain Matters.* Anything referred to in this Annex as being specified in Paragraph 13 also may be specified in one or more Confirmations or other documents and this Annex will be construed accordingly.

(g) *Legally Ineligible Credit Support (VM).* Unless otherwise specified in Paragraph 13, upon delivery of a Legal Ineligibility Notice by a party, each item of Eligible Credit Support (VM) (or a specified amount of such item) identified in such notice (i) will cease to be Eligible Credit Support (VM) for purposes of Transfers to such party as the Secured Party hereunder as of the applicable Transfer Ineligibility Date, (ii) will cease to be Eligible Credit Support (VM) for the other party as the Pledgor for all purposes hereunder as of the Total Ineligibility Date and (iii) will have a Value of zero on and from the Total Ineligibility Date.

"*Legal Ineligibility Notice*" means a written notice from the Secured Party to the Pledgor in which the Secured Party (i) represents that the Secured Party has determined that one or more items of Eligible Credit Support (VM) (or a specified amount of any such item) either has ceased to satisfy, or as of a specified date will cease to satisfy, collateral eligibility requirements under law applicable to the Secured Party requiring the collection of variation margin (the "*Legal Eligibility Requirements*"), (ii) lists the item(s) of Eligible Credit Support (VM) (and, if applicable, the specified amount) that have ceased to satisfy, or as of a specified date will cease to satisfy, the Legal Eligibility Requirements, (iii) describes the reason(s) why such item(s) of Eligible Credit Support (VM) (or the specified amount thereof) have ceased to satisfy, or will cease to satisfy, the Legal Eligibility Requirements and (iv) specifies the Total Ineligibility Date and, if different, the Transfer Ineligibility Date.

"*Total Ineligibility Date*" means the date on which the relevant item of Eligible Credit Support (VM) (or a specified amount of such item) has ceased to satisfy, or will cease to satisfy, the Legal Eligibility Requirements applicable to the Secured Party for all purposes hereunder; *provided* that, unless otherwise specified in Paragraph 13, if such date is earlier than the fifth Local Business Day following the date on which the Legal Ineligibility Notice is delivered, the Total Ineligibility Date will be the fifth Local Business Day following the date of such delivery.

"*Transfer Ineligibility Date*" means the date on which the relevant item of Eligible Credit Support (VM) (or a specified amount of such item) has ceased to satisfy, or will cease to satisfy, the Legal Eligibility Requirements for purposes of Transfers to the Secured Party hereunder; *provided* that, unless otherwise specified in Paragraph 13, if such date is earlier than the fifth Local Business Day following the date on which the Legal Ineligibility Notice is delivered, the Transfer Ineligibility Date will be the fifth Local Business Day following the date of such delivery.

(h) *Return of Posted Credit Support (VM) with a Value of Zero.* Subject to Paragraph 4(a), the Secured Party will, promptly upon demand (but in no event later than the time at which a Transfer would be due under Paragraph 4(b) with respect to a demand for the Transfer of Eligible Credit Support (VM) or Posted Credit Support (VM)), Transfer to the Pledgor any item of Posted Credit Support (VM) (or the specified amount of such item) that as of the date of such demand has a Value of zero; *provided* that the Secured Party will only be obligated to Transfer any Posted Credit Support (VM) in accordance with this Paragraph 11(h), if, as of the date of Transfer of such item, the Pledgor has satisfied all of its Transfer obligations under this Annex, if any.

(i) *Reinstatement of Credit Support Eligibility.* Upon a reasonable request by the Pledgor, the Secured Party will determine whether an item (or a specified amount of such item) of Eligible Credit Support (VM) that was the subject of a prior Legal Ineligibility Notice would currently satisfy the Legal Eligibility Requirements applicable to the Secured Party. If the Secured Party determines that as of such date of determination such item (or specified amount of such item) satisfies the Legal Eligibility Requirements applicable to the Secured Party, the Secured Party will promptly following such determination rescind the relevant Legal Ineligibility Notice with respect to such item (or specified amount of such item) by written notice to the Pledgor. Upon the delivery of such notice, the relevant item (or specified amount of such item) will constitute Eligible Credit Support (VM) hereunder.

(j) **Credit Support Offsets.** If the parties specify that "Credit Support Offsets" is applicable in Paragraph 13, and on any date:

(i) a Transfer of Eligible Credit Support (VM) is due under this Annex to satisfy a Delivery Amount (VM) or a Return Amount (VM) obligation, and a transfer of credit support (other than any Other CSA Excluded Credit Support) is also due under any Other CSA;

(ii) the parties have notified each other of the credit support that they intend to Transfer under this Annex and transfer under such Other CSA (other than any Other CSA Excluded Credit Support) to satisfy their respective obligations; and

(iii) in respect of Paragraph 11(j)(ii), each party intends to transfer one or more types of credit support that is fully fungible with one or more types of credit support the other party intends to transfer (each such credit support, a "**Fungible Credit Support Type**"),

then, on such date and in respect of each such Fungible Credit Support Type, each party's obligation to make a transfer of any such Fungible Credit Support Type hereunder or under such Other CSA will be automatically satisfied and discharged and, if the aggregate amount that would have otherwise been transferred by one party exceeds the aggregate amount that would have otherwise been transferred by the other party, replaced by an obligation hereunder or under such Other CSA, as applicable, upon the party by which the larger aggregate amount would have been transferred to transfer to the other party the excess of the larger aggregate amount over the smaller aggregate amount. If a party's obligation to make a transfer of credit support under this Annex or an Other CSA is automatically satisfied and discharged pursuant to this Paragraph 11(j), then, for purposes of this Annex or the Other CSA, as applicable, the other party will be deemed to have received credit support of the applicable Fungible Credit Support Type in the amount that would otherwise have been required to be transferred, in each case on the day on which the relevant transfer was due.

Paragraph 12. Definitions

As used in this Annex:—

"**Base Currency**" means the currency specified as such in Paragraph 13.

"**Base Currency Equivalent**" means, with respect to an amount on a Valuation Date, in the case of an amount denominated in the Base Currency, such Base Currency amount and, in the case of an amount denominated in a currency other than the Base Currency (the "**Other Currency**"), the amount of Base Currency required to purchase such amount of the Other Currency at the spot exchange rate on such Valuation Date as determined by the Valuation Agent.

"**Cash**" means, respectively, the Base Currency and each other Eligible Currency.

"**Covered Transaction**" has the meaning specified in Paragraph 13.

"**Credit Support Eligibility Condition (VM)**" means, with respect to any item specified for a party as Eligible Collateral (VM) in Paragraph 13, any condition specified for that item in Paragraph 13.

"**Custodian (VM)**" has the meaning specified in Paragraphs 6(b)(i) and 13.

"**Delivery Amount (VM)**" has the meaning specified in Paragraph 3(a).

"**Delivery Amount Reduction (VM)**" has the meaning specified in Paragraph 6(d)(ii)(A)(II).

"**Disputing Party**" has the meaning specified in Paragraph 5.

"***Distributions***" means with respect to Posted Collateral (VM) other than Cash, all principal, interest and other payments and distributions of cash or other property with respect thereto, regardless of whether the Secured Party has disposed of that Posted Collateral (VM) under Paragraph 6(c). Distributions will not include any item of property acquired by the Secured Party upon any disposition or liquidation of Posted Collateral (VM) or, with respect to any Posted Collateral (VM) in the form of Cash, any distributions on that collateral, unless otherwise specified herein.

"***Eligible Collateral (VM)***" has the meaning specified in Paragraph 13.

"***Eligible Credit Support (VM)***" means Eligible Collateral (VM) and Other Eligible Support (VM).

"***Eligible Currency***" means each currency specified as such in Paragraph 13, if such currency is freely available.

"***Eligible Return Amount (VM)***" has the meaning specified in Paragraph 6(d)(ii)(A)(I)(a).

"***Exposure***" means, unless otherwise specified in Paragraph 13, for any Valuation Date or other date for which Exposure is calculated and subject to Paragraph 5 in the case of a dispute:

(i) if this Agreement is a 1992 ISDA Master Agreement, the amount, if any, that would be payable to a party that is the Secured Party by the other party (expressed as a positive number) or by a party that is the Secured Party to the other party (expressed as a negative number) pursuant to Section 6(e)(ii)(2)(A) of this Agreement as if all Covered Transactions were being terminated as of the relevant Valuation Time on the basis that the Base Currency is the Termination Currency; *provided* that Market Quotation will be determined by the Valuation Agent on behalf of that party using its estimates at mid-market of the amounts that would be paid for Replacement Transactions (as that term is defined in the definition of "Market Quotation"); and

(ii) if this Agreement is an ISDA 2002 Master Agreement or a 1992 ISDA Master Agreement in which the definition of Loss and/or Market Quotation has been amended (including where such amendment has occurred pursuant to the terms of a separate agreement or protocol) to reflect the definition of Close-out Amount from the pre-printed form of the ISDA 2002 Master Agreement as published by ISDA, the amount, if any, that would be payable to a party that is the Secured Party by the other party (expressed as a positive number) or by a party that is the Secured Party to the other party (expressed as a negative number) pursuant to Section 6(e)(ii)(1) (but without reference to clause (3) of Section 6(e)(ii)) of this Agreement as if all Covered Transactions were being terminated as of the relevant Valuation Time on the basis that the Base Currency is the Termination Currency; *provided* that the Close-out Amount will be determined by the Valuation Agent on behalf of that party using its estimates at mid-market of the amounts that would be paid for transactions providing the economic equivalent of (X) the material terms of the Covered Transactions, including the payments and deliveries by the parties under Section 2(a)(i) in respect of the Covered Transactions that would, but for the occurrence of the relevant Early Termination Date, have been required after that date (assuming satisfaction of the conditions precedent in Section 2(a)(iii)), and (Y) the option rights of the parties in respect of the Covered Transactions.

"***Fungible Credit Support Type***" has the meaning specified in Paragraph 11(j)(iii).

"***FX Haircut Percentage***" means, for any item of Eligible Collateral (VM), the percentage specified as such in Paragraph 13.

"***Interest Adjustment Reduction Amount (VM)***" has the meaning specified in Paragraph 6(d)(ii)(B)(II).

"***Interest Amount (VM)***" means, with respect to an Interest Period, the aggregate sum of the Base Currency Equivalents of the amounts of interest determined for each relevant currency and calculated for each day in that Interest Period on any Posted Collateral (VM) in the form of Cash in such currency held by the Secured Party on that day, determined by the Secured Party for each such day as follows:

(i) the amount of Cash in such currency on that day plus, only if "Daily Interest Compounding" is specified as applicable in Paragraph 13, the aggregate of each Interest Amount (VM) in respect of such currency determined for each preceding day, if any, in that Interest Period; multiplied by

(ii) the Interest Rate (VM) in effect for that day; divided by

(iii) 360 (or, in the case of pounds sterling or any other currency specified as an "A/365 Currency" in Paragraph 13, 365);

provided that, unless "Negative Interest" is specified as applicable in Paragraph 13, if the Interest Amount (VM) for an Interest Period would be a negative amount, it will be deemed to be zero.

"***Interest Payee (VM)***" means, in relation to an Interest Payer (VM), the other party.

"***Interest Payer (VM)***" means the Secured Party; *provided* that if "Negative Interest" is specified as applicable in Paragraph 13 and an Interest Payment (VM) is determined in respect of a negative Interest Amount (VM), the Interest Payer (VM) in respect of such Interest Payment (VM) will be the Pledgor.

"***Interest Payment (VM)***" means, with respect to an Interest Period, the Interest Amount (VM) determined in respect of such Interest Period; *provided* that in respect of any negative Interest Amount (VM), the Interest Payment (VM) will be the absolute value of such negative Interest Amount (VM).

"***Interest Period***" means the period from (and including) the last day on which (i) a party became obligated to Transfer an Interest Payment (VM) or (ii) an Interest Amount (VM) was included or otherwise became constituted as part of Posted Collateral (VM) (or, if no Interest Payment (VM) or Interest Amount (VM) has yet fallen due or been included or otherwise became constituted as a part of Posted Collateral (VM), respectively, the day on which Eligible Credit Support (VM) in the form of Cash was Transferred to or received by the Secured Party) to (but excluding) the day on which (i) a party is obligated to Transfer the current Interest Payment (VM) or (ii) the current Interest Amount (VM) is included or otherwise becomes constituted as a part of Posted Collateral (VM).

"***Interest Rate (VM)***" means, with respect to an Eligible Currency, the rate specified in Paragraph 13 for that currency.

"***Legal Eligibility Requirements***" has the meaning specified in Paragraph 11(g).

"***Legal Ineligibility Notice***" has the meaning specified in Paragraph 11(g).

"***Local Business Day***", unless otherwise specified in Paragraph 13, means:

(i) in relation to a Transfer of cash or other property (other than securities) under this Annex, a day on which commercial banks are open for business (including dealings in foreign exchange and foreign currency deposits) in the place where the relevant account is located and, if different, in the principal financial center, if any, of the currency of such payment;

(ii) in relation to a Transfer of securities under this Annex, a day on which the clearance system agreed between the parties for delivery of the securities is open for the acceptance and execution of settlement instructions or, if delivery of the securities is contemplated by other means, a day on which commercial banks are open for business (including dealings in foreign exchange and foreign currency deposits) in the place(s) agreed between the parties for this purpose;

(iii) in relation to the Resolution Time, a day on which commercial banks are open for business (including dealings in foreign exchange and foreign currency deposits) in at least one Valuation Date Location for Party A and at least one Valuation Date Location for Party B; and

(iv) in relation to any notice or other communication under this Annex, a day on which commercial banks are open for business (including dealings in foreign exchange and foreign currency deposits) in the place specified in the address for notice most recently provided by the recipient.

"*Minimum Transfer Amount*" means, with respect to a party, the amount specified as such for that party in Paragraph 13; if no amount is specified, zero.

"*Notification Time*" has the meaning specified in Paragraph 13.

"*Obligations*" means, with respect to a party, all present and future obligations of that party under this Agreement and any additional obligations specified for that party in Paragraph 13.

"*Other CSA*" means, unless otherwise specified in Paragraph 13, any other credit support annex or credit support deed that is in relation to, or that is a Credit Support Document in relation to, this Agreement.

"*Other CSA Excluded Credit Support*" means, with respect to an Other CSA, any amounts and items posted as margin under such Other CSA, which, pursuant to the terms of such Other CSA, Party A and Party B have agreed must be segregated in an account maintained by a third-party custodian or for which offsets are prohibited.

"*Other Eligible Support (VM)*" means, with respect to a party, the items, if any, specified as such for that party in Paragraph 13.

"*Other Posted Support (VM)*" means all Other Eligible Support (VM) Transferred to the Secured Party that remains in effect for the benefit of that Secured Party.

"*Pledgor*" means either party, when that party (i) receives a demand for or is required to Transfer Eligible Credit Support (VM) under Paragraph 3(a) or (ii) has Transferred Eligible Credit Support (VM) under Paragraph 3(a).

"*Posted Collateral (VM)*" means all Eligible Collateral (VM), other property, Distributions, and all proceeds thereof that have been Transferred to or received by the Secured Party under this Annex and not Transferred to the Pledgor pursuant to Paragraph 3(b), 4(d)(ii), 6(d)(i) or 11(h) or released by the Secured Party under Paragraph 8. With respect to any Interest Amount (VM) in respect of any Interest Payment (VM) or relevant part thereof not Transferred pursuant to Paragraph 6(d)(ii)(A) or Paragraph 6(d)(ii)(B), as applicable, if such Interest Amount (VM) is a positive number, such Interest Amount (VM) will constitute Posted Collateral (VM) in the form of Cash in the Base Currency.

"*Posted Credit Support (VM)*" means Posted Collateral (VM) and Other Posted Support (VM).

"*Recalculation Date*" means the Valuation Date that gives rise to the dispute under Paragraph 5; *provided, however,* that if a subsequent Valuation Date occurs under Paragraph 3 prior to the resolution of the dispute, then the "Recalculation Date" means the most recent Valuation Date under Paragraph 3.

"*Regular Settlement Day,*" means, unless otherwise specified in Paragraph 13, the same Local Business Day on which a demand for the Transfer of Eligible Credit Support (VM) or Posted Credit Support (VM) is made.

"*Resolution Time*" has the meaning specified in Paragraph 13.

"*Return Amount (VM)*" has the meaning specified in Paragraph 3(b).

"*Return Amount Reduction (VM)*" has the meaning specified in Paragraph 6(d)(ii)(A)(II).

"*Secured Party*" means either party, when that party (i) makes a demand for or is entitled to receive Eligible Credit Support (VM) under Paragraph 3(a) or (ii) holds or is deemed to hold Posted Credit Support (VM).

"*Set-off*" means set-off, offset, combination of accounts, right of retention or withholding or similar right or requirement (whether arising under this Agreement, another contract, applicable law or otherwise) and, when used as a verb, the exercise of any such right or the imposition of any such requirement.

"*Specified Condition*" means, with respect to a party, any event specified as such for that party in Paragraph 13.

"*Substitute Credit Support (VM)*" has the meaning specified in Paragraph 4(d)(i).

"*Substitution Date*" has the meaning specified in Paragraph 4(d)(ii).

"*Total Ineligibility Date*" has the meaning specified in Paragraph 11(g) unless otherwise specified in Paragraph 13.

"*Transfer*" means, with respect to any Eligible Credit Support (VM), Posted Credit Support (VM) or Interest Payment (VM), and in accordance with the instructions of the Secured Party, Pledgor or Custodian (VM), as applicable:

(i) in the case of Cash, payment or delivery by wire transfer into one or more bank accounts specified by the recipient;

(ii) in the case of certificated securities that cannot be paid or delivered by book-entry, payment or delivery in appropriate physical form to the recipient or its account accompanied by any duly executed instruments of transfer, assignments in blank, transfer tax stamps and any other documents necessary to constitute a legally valid transfer to the recipient;

(iii) in the case of securities that can be paid or delivered by book-entry, causing the relevant depository institution(s) or other securities intermediaries to make changes to their books and records sufficient to result in a legally effective transfer of the relevant interest to the recipient or its agent; and

(iv) in the case of Other Eligible Support (VM) or Other Posted Support (VM), as specified in Paragraph 13.

"*Transfer Ineligibility Date*" has the meaning specified in Paragraph 11(g) unless otherwise specified in Paragraph 13.

"*Valuation Agent*" has the meaning specified in Paragraph 13.

"*Valuation Date*" means, unless otherwise specified in Paragraph 13, each day from, and including, the date of this Annex, that is a day on which commercial banks are open for business (including dealings in foreign exchange and foreign currency deposits) in at least one Valuation Date Location for Party A and at least one Valuation Date Location for Party B.

"*Valuation Date Location*" has the meaning specified in Paragraph 13.

"*Valuation Percentage*" means, for any item of Eligible Collateral (VM), the percentage specified as such in Paragraph 13.

"*Valuation Time*" means, unless otherwise specified in Paragraph 13, the time as of which the Valuation Agent computes its end of day valuations of derivatives transactions in the ordinary course of its business (or such other commercially reasonable convenient time on the relevant day as the Valuation Agent may determine).

"*Value*" means for any Valuation Date or other date for which Value is calculated and subject to Paragraph 5 in the case of a dispute, with respect to:

(i) Eligible Collateral (VM) or Posted Collateral (VM) that is:

(A) an amount of Cash, the Base Currency Equivalent of such amount multiplied by $(VP - H_{FX})$; and

(B) a security, the Base Currency Equivalent of the bid price obtained by the Valuation Agent multiplied by $(VP - H_{FX})$, where:

VP equals the applicable Valuation Percentage; and

H_{FX} equals the applicable FX Haircut Percentage;

(ii) Posted Collateral (VM) that consists of items that are not Eligible Collateral (VM) (including any item or any portion of any item that fails to satisfy any (A) Credit Support Eligibility Condition (VM) applicable to it or (B) applicable Legal Eligibility Requirements), zero; and

(iii) Other Eligible Support (VM) and Other Posted Support (VM), as specified in Paragraph 13.

Paragraph 13. Elections and Variables

(a) *Base Currency and Eligible Currency.*

(i) "*Base Currency*" means United States Dollars, unless otherwise specified here: ....

....

(ii) "*Eligible Currency*" means the Base Currency and each other currency specified here:...............................

....

(b) *Covered Transactions; Security Interest for Obligations; Exposure.*

(i) The term "*Covered Transactions*" as used in this Annex includes any Transaction specified below that is entered into on or after [...............................]*, except as otherwise provided in the Confirmation of such Transaction:

(A) For purposes of the foregoing, the term "Covered Transactions" includes: [Any Transaction [that is any of the following] [Swap], [Security-Based Swap], [OTC Derivative], [Physically Settled FX Forward] or [Physically Settled FX Swap]] [and is not any of the following: [Swap], [Security-Based Swap], [OTC Derivative], [Physically Settled FX Forward], or [Physically Settled FX Swap].................................]**

As used above:

["*OTC Derivative*" means an "OTC derivative" or "OTC derivative contract" as defined in Article 2(7) of Regulation (EU) No 648/2012 of the European Parliament and of the Council of 4 July 2012 on OTC derivatives, central counterparties and trade repositories ("*EMIR*") other than one which constitutes (i) a "foreign exchange forward" as defined in Article 7(1)(a) of the final draft regulatory technical standards on risk-mitigation techniques for OTC-derivative contracts not cleared by a CCP under Article 11(15) of EMIR dated March 8, 2016 (the "*EMIR RTS*") for so long as such transactions are subject to the transitional exemption from the variation margin requirements under Article 39(6) of the EMIR RTS and (ii) a single stock equity option or index option transaction as referred to in Article 39(7) of the EMIR RTS for so long as such transactions are subject to the transitional exemption from the variation margin requirements under Article 39(7) of the EMIR RTS.]

["*Physically Settled FX Forward*" means [...............................]]

["*Physically Settled FX Swap*" means [...............................]]

["*Security-Based Swap*" means a "security-based swap" as defined in Section 3(a)(68) of the U.S. Securities Exchange Act of 1934, as amended ("*SEA*"), and the rules adopted thereunder. For the avoidance of doubt, the term "Security-Based Swap" does not include a security-based swap that has been cleared by a "clearing agency," as such term is defined in Section 3(a)(23) of the SEA and the rules adopted thereunder.]

["*Swap*" means a "swap" as defined in Section 1a(47) of the U.S. Commodity Exchange Act, as amended ("*CEA*"), and the regulations adopted thereunder. For the avoidance of doubt, the term "Swap" does not include a swap that has been cleared by a "derivatives clearing organization," as such term is defined in Section 1a(15) of the CEA and the regulations adopted thereunder.]

[For the purposes of the foregoing, a Transaction will be deemed to be entered into on or after the date specified in this Paragraph 13(b)(i) if an amendment, novation or other lifecycle event with respect to such

---

*   Insert the relevant date.

**   Parties may retain, delete, or revise any of these definitions or add any additional definitions, as applicable.

Transaction would cause such Transaction to be entered into after such date under law applicable to either party requiring the collection or delivery of variation margin.]*

(ii) The term "*Obligations*" as used in this Annex includes the following additional obligations:

With respect to Party A: ....

With respect to Party B: ....

(iii) "*Exposure*" has the meaning specified in Paragraph 12, unless otherwise specified here: ....

(c)   *Credit Support Obligations.*

(i) *Delivery Amount (VM) and Return Amount (VM).*

(A) "*Delivery Amount (VM)*" has the meaning specified in Paragraph 3(a), unless otherwise specified here: ....

(B) "*Return Amount (VM)*" has the meaning specified in Paragraph 3(b), unless otherwise specified here: ....

(ii) *Eligible Collateral (VM)*. Subject to Paragraph 11(g), if applicable, and each Credit Support Eligibility Condition (VM) applicable to it specified in Paragraph 13, if any, the following items will qualify as "*Eligible Collateral (VM)*" for the party specified (as the Pledgor):

		Party A	Valuation Percentage	Party B	Valuation Percentage
(A)	cash in an Eligible Currency	[ ]	[ ]%	[ ]	[ ]%
(B)	other:	[ ]	[ ]%	[ ]	[ ]%

(iii) *Legally Ineligible Credit Support (VM)*. The provisions of Paragraph 11(g) will not apply to the [party/parties] specified here (as the Secured Party):**

[ ] Party A

[ ] Party B

(A) "*Total Ineligibility Date*" has the meaning specified in Paragraph 11(g), unless otherwise specified here ....

(B) "*Transfer Ineligibility Date*" has the meaning specified in Paragraph 11(g), unless otherwise specified here: ....

(iv) *Credit Support Eligibility Conditions (VM).* The following conditions will each be a "Credit Support Eligibility Condition (VM)" for the party specified. Any item will not qualify as Eligible Collateral (VM) for a party (as the Pledgor) if such item does not satisfy each Credit Support Eligibility Condition (VM) applicable to it.

[..]

[..]

(v) "*Valuation Percentage*"; "*FX Haircut Percentage*"

(A) "*Valuation Percentage*" means, with respect to each party (as the Pledgor) and item of Eligible Collateral (VM), the percentage (expressed as a decimal) specified in Paragraph 13(c)(ii); *provided* that if

---

*   Parties may retain, delete or revise the bracketed language, as applicable.

**   Parties should leave the relevant box below unmarked unless they agree to disapply Paragraph 11(g) with respect to a party as the Secured Party.

nothing is specified in Paragraph 13(c)(ii), the Valuation Percentage will be 100% unless otherwise specified below. The Valuation Percentage for either party and any item of Eligible Collateral (VM) will further be subject to the terms and conditions, if any, specified below as applicable to such party and item:

....

[If at any time the Valuation Percentage assigned to an item of Eligible Collateral (VM) with respect to a party (as the Pledgor) under this Annex is greater than the maximum permitted valuation percentage (prescribed or implied) for such item of collateral under any law requiring the collection of variation margin applicable to the other party (as the Secured Party), then the Valuation Percentage with respect to such item of Eligible Collateral (VM) and such party will be such maximum permitted valuation percentage.]*

(B) "*FX Haircut Percentage*" means, with respect to each party (as the Pledgor) and item of Eligible Collateral (VM), [[8]%, unless the Eligible Collateral (VM) or Posted Collateral (VM) is in the form of cash [in a Major Currency] or is denominated in a currency that matches [an Eligible Currency], in which case the FX Haircut Percentage will be 0%.]

[As used above, "*Major Currency*" means any of: (1) United States Dollar; (2) Canadian Dollar; (3) Euro; (4) United Kingdom Pound; (5) Japanese Yen; (6) Swiss Franc; (7) New Zealand Dollar; (8) Australian Dollar; (9) Swedish Kronor; (10) Danish Kroner; (11) Norwegian Krone or any other currency specified below:

[....]]**

(vi) *Other Eligible Support (VM).* The following items will qualify as "*Other Eligible Support (VM)*" for the party specified (as the Pledgor):

		Party A	Party B
(A)	....	[ ]	[ ]
(B)	....	[ ]	[ ]

(vii) *Minimum Transfer Amount.*

(A) "*Minimum Transfer Amount*" means with respect to Party A: $ ....

"*Minimum Transfer Amount*" means with respect to Party B: $ ....

(B) *Rounding.* The Delivery Amount (VM) and the Return Amount (VM) will be rounded up and down respectively to the nearest integral multiple of $ ....

(viii) *Transfer Timing.* "*Regular Settlement Day*" has the meaning specified in Paragraph 12, unless otherwise specified here: ....

(d) *Valuation and Timing.*

(i) "*Valuation Agent*" means, for purposes of Paragraphs 3 and 5, the party making the demand under Paragraph 3, and, for purposes of Paragraph 6(d), the Secured Party, as applicable, unless otherwise specified here: ....

(ii) "*Valuation Date*" has the meaning specified in Paragraph 12, unless otherwise specified here: ....

....

---

*   Parties may retain, delete or revise the bracketed language, as applicable.

**   Parties may revise the bracketed language and the related definitions, as applicable.

       ISDA®2016

For purposes of determining the Valuation Date and clause (iii) of the definition of "Local Business Day" in Paragraph 12, "*Valuation Date Location*"* means, with respect to each party, each city, region, or country specified below:

Party A: ....

Party B: ....

(iii) "*Valuation Time*" has the meaning specified in Paragraph 12, unless otherwise specified here: ....

....

(iv) "*Notification Time*" means 10:00 a.m., New York time, on a Local Business Day, unless otherwise specified here: ....

....

(e) **Conditions Precedent and Secured Party's Rights and Remedies.**

(i) The provisions of Paragraph 4(a) will apply, unless otherwise specified here: ....

....

(ii) If the provisions of Paragraph 4(a) are applicable, the following Termination Event(s) will be a "*Specified Condition*" for the party specified (that party being the Affected Party if the Termination Event occurs with respect to that party):

	Party A	Party B
Illegality	[ ]	[ ]
Force Majeure Event**	[ ]	[ ]
Tax Event	[ ]	[ ]
Tax Event Upon Merger	[ ]	[ ]
Credit Event Upon Merger	[ ]	[ ]
Additional Termination Event(s):	[ ]	[ ]

(f) **Substitution.**

(i) "*Substitution Date*" has the meaning specified in Paragraph 4(d)(ii), unless otherwise specified here: ....

(ii) **Consent**. If specified here as applicable, then the Pledgor must obtain the Secured Party's consent for any substitution pursuant to Paragraph 4(d): [applicable/inapplicable]***

(g) **Dispute Resolution.**

(i) "*Resolution Time*" means 1:00 p.m., New York time, on the Local Business Day following the date on which the notice is given that gives rise to a dispute under Paragraph 5, unless otherwise specified here: ....

(ii) **Value.** For the purpose of Paragraphs 5(iv)(A)(3) and 5(iv)(B), the Value of Posted Credit Support (VM) will be calculated as follows: ....

(iii) **Alternative.** The provisions of Paragraph 5 will apply, unless an alternative dispute resolution procedure is specified here: ....

---

*   If applicable, a party can specify more than one Valuation Date Location.

**   Include if the relevant ISDA Master Agreement is an ISDA 2002 Master Agreement.

***   Parties should consider selecting "applicable" where substitution without consent could give rise to a registration requirement to perfect properly the security interest in Posted Collateral (*e.g.*, where a party to the Annex is the New York branch of an English bank).

(h) *Holding and Using Posted Collateral (VM).*

(i) *Eligibility to Hold Posted Collateral (VM); Custodians (VM).* Party A and its Custodian (VM) will be entitled to hold Posted Collateral (VM) pursuant to Paragraph 6(b); *provided* that the following conditions applicable to it are satisfied:

(1) Party A is not a Defaulting Party.

(2) ....

Initially, the **Custodian (VM)** for Party A is ....

....

Party B and its Custodian (VM) will be entitled to hold Posted Collateral (VM) pursuant to Paragraph 6(b); *provided* that the following conditions applicable to it are satisfied:

(1) Party B is not a Defaulting Party.

(2) ....

Initially, the **Custodian (VM)** for Party B is ....

....

(ii) *Use of Posted Collateral (VM).* The provisions of Paragraph 6(c) will not apply to the [party/parties*] specified here:

[ ] Party A

[ ] Party B

and [that party/those parties*] will not be permitted to: ....

(i) *Distributions and Interest Payment (VM).*

(i) *Interest Rate (VM).* The "*Interest Rate (VM)*" in relation to each Eligible Currency specified below will be:

Eligible Currency	*Interest Rate (VM)*	*A/365 Currency*
....	....	....
....	....	....
....	....	....

(ii) *Transfer of Interest Payment (VM) or application of Interest Amount (VM).*

Interest Transfer: [Applicable/Not Applicable]

Interest Payment Netting: [Applicable/Not Applicable]

[The Transfer of an Interest Payment (VM) by the Interest Payer (VM) will be made on [the last Local Business Day of each calendar month] [and on any Local Business Day that a Return Amount (VM) consisting wholly or partly of cash is Transferred to the Pledgor pursuant to Paragraph 3(b)]. The Transfer of an Interest Payment (VM) by the Interest Payer (VM) will be made on [the last Local Business Day of each calendar month] [and on any Local Business Day that a Delivery Amount (VM) consisting wholly or partly of cash is Transferred to the Secured Party pursuant to Paragraph 3(a)].]

Interest Adjustment: [Applicable/Not Applicable]

---

*   Delete as applicable.

ISDA®2016

[The Posted Collateral (VM) will be adjusted by the Secured Party on [the last Local Business Day of each calendar month][each day].]

(iii) *Other Interest Elections.*

Negative Interest: [Applicable/Not Applicable]

Daily Interest Compounding: [Applicable/Not Applicable]

(iv) *Alternative to Interest Amount (VM) and Interest Payment (VM).* The provisions of Paragraph 6(d)(ii) will apply, unless otherwise specified here: ....

....

(j)   *Credit Support Offsets.*

If specified here as applicable, then the "*Credit Support Offsets*" provisions in Paragraph 11(j) of this Annex will apply: [applicable/inapplicable].

(k)   *Additional Representation(s).*

[Party A/Party B] represents to the other party (which representation(s) will be deemed to be repeated as of each date on which it, as the Pledgor, Transfers Eligible Collateral (VM)) that:

(i) ....

(ii) ....

(l)   *Other Eligible Support (VM) and Other Posted Support (VM).*

(i) "*Value*" with respect to Other Eligible Support (VM) and Other Posted Support (VM) means: ....

....

(ii) "*Transfer*" with respect to Other Eligible Support (VM) and Other Posted Support (VM) means: ....

....

(m)   *Demands and Notices.*

All demands, specifications and notices under this Annex will be made pursuant to the Notices Section of this Agreement, unless otherwise specified here:

Party A: ....

....

Party B: ....

....

(n)   *Addresses for Transfers.*

Party A: ....

....

Party B: ....

....

(o)   "*Other CSA*" has the meaning specified in Paragraph 12, unless otherwise specified here: ....

....

(p)   *Other Provisions.*